Cultural Sociology

Series Editors
Jeffrey C. Alexander
Center for Cultural Sociology
Yale University
New Haven, CT, USA

Ron Eyerman
Center for Cultural Sociology
Yale University
New Haven, CT, USA

David Inglis
Department of Sociology Philosophy and Anthropology
University of Aberdeen
Exeter, Aberdeenshire, UK

Philip Smith
Department of Sociology
Yale University
Branford, CT, USA

Cultural sociology is widely acknowledged as one of the most vibrant areas of inquiry in the social sciences across the world today. The Palgrave Macmillan Series in Cultural Sociology is dedicated to the proposition that deep meanings make a profound difference in social life. Culture is not simply the glue that holds society together, a crutch for the weak, or a mystifying ideology that conceals power. Nor is it just practical knowledge, dry schemas, or know how. The series demonstrates how shared and circulating patterns of meaning actively and inescapably penetrate the social. Through codes and myths, narratives and icons, rituals and representations, these culture structures drive human action, inspire social movements, direct and build institutions, and so come to shape history. The series takes its lead from the cultural turn in the humanities, but insists on rigorous social science methods and aims at empirical explanations. Contributions engage in thick interpretations but also account for behavioral outcomes. They develop cultural theory but also deploy middle-range tools to challenge reductionist understandings of how the world actually works. In so doing, the books in this series embody the spirit of cultural sociology as an intellectual enterprise.

More information about this series at
http://www.palgrave.com/gp/series/14945

Danny Kaplan

The Nation and the Promise of Friendship

Building Solidarity through Sociability

Danny Kaplan
Department of Sociology
  and Anthropology and Gender
  Studies Program
Bar-Ilan University
Ramat-Gan, Israel

Cultural Sociology
ISBN 978-3-030-08693-0   ISBN 978-3-319-78402-1 (eBook)
https://doi.org/10.1007/978-3-319-78402-1

© The Editor(s) (if applicable) and The Author(s) 2018
Softcover re-print of the Hardcover 1st edition 2018
This work is subject to copyright. All rights are solely and exclusively licensed by the Publisher, whether the whole or part of the material is concerned, specifically the rights of translation, reprinting, reuse of illustrations, recitation, broadcasting, reproduction on microfilms or in any other physical way, and transmission or information storage and retrieval, electronic adaptation, computer software, or by similar or dissimilar methodology now known or hereafter developed.
The use of general descriptive names, registered names, trademarks, service marks, etc. in this publication does not imply, even in the absence of a specific statement, that such names are exempt from the relevant protective laws and regulations and therefore free for general use.
The publisher, the authors and the editors are safe to assume that the advice and information in this book are believed to be true and accurate at the date of publication. Neither the publisher nor the authors or the editors give a warranty, express or implied, with respect to the material contained herein or for any errors or omissions that may have been made. The publisher remains neutral with regard to jurisdictional claims in published maps and institutional affiliations.

Cover image: © Astral/Alamy Stock

Printed on acid-free paper

This Palgrave Macmillan imprint is published by the registered company Springer International Publishing AG part of Springer Nature
The registered company address is: Gewerbestrasse 11, 6330 Cham, Switzerland

In loving memory of my father Noam Kaplan

Series Editor's Preface

A fault in sociology as a discipline is that we get hooked on certain topics. We research things that seem important to us for normative or theoretical reasons, because they clearly changed the world, or simply because they are intriguing research puzzles. Sometimes, a self-sustaining autocatalytic system is formed in which discourse breeds discourse. The Muslim headscarf, housework, the French Revolution, and the footballer David Beckham all come to mind. Each of these is worth researching, each could be considered a real paradigm case, and each generates thousands of pages every year. Yet there is a cost. The returns to effort decline after the major findings and perspectives are mopped up by those opening a field. We are left with publications indicating a two-minute revision to common estimates on the household division of labor; or an analysis of the latest Beckham photograph spread that indicates—like all other the work—that he challenges, reshapes, and yet also reinforces concepts of masculinity... only this time slightly differently from the last time.

Far more important than diminishing returns are opportunity costs. A well-known experiment in social psychology asked people to watch a television and count the number of times a basketball was passed before a player scored. Nobody noticed that a large man in a gorilla suit walked across the court. Similarly, in the world of sociology we can become victims of our own tightly focused attention, our own niche discourses and obsessions, and those hot-button public interest topics where we feel we should also have our say. As a corollary, so many aspects of social life are left relatively unexplored. Sometimes, these are important in the lifeworld, at other times they have a significant role to play in the social order, others might provide new avenues for theoretical innovation. In the case of friendship, all three of the above apply.

For years, sociology has relentlessly studied race, class, gender, and family. In the lifeworld, these are really important. For most people, in their daily lives friendship is equally so. Yet for sociologists, friendship is like that gorilla. We were so busy doing something else we missed seeing something blindingly obvious as a central element of social life. Philosophy has done somewhat better, approaching friendship from a normative angle, seeing it as a model for ethics and civic membership or obligation. Kaplan uses the tools of cultural sociology to explore the meanings, practices, and consequences of friendship in the real world. He brilliantly demonstrates just how the translation of the stranger into a friend sits at the core of ideas about collective identity and how varied forms of institutional life offer diverse structures of opportunity. They provide spaces for ties to develop and be imagined. From these, in turn we form general ideas about club, community, nation and construct the large-scale and abstract solidarities that connect us with moral ties to those we will never know.

Drawing on Durkheim, Simmel, and others, Kaplan connects micro- to macro- in a way that has rarely been achieved before. At the same time, he brings this classic theory up to date, showing its flexibility and contemporary relevance. Decisively moving on from the initial notion that face-to-face contact, say in cafe society, is essential as a ground zero for friendship, Kaplan shows how the mass media, imagined friendship, distant friendship, and a background belief in friendship as fundamentally sacred all play a role in constituting the social. In our globalized world of Internet communication technology and online social networks, friendship looks to be here to stay. Kaplan's book is a timely reminder that academic sociology had better catch up with what everyone else already knows: Friendships are important.

New Haven, CT, USA   Philip Smith

Preface and Acknowledgements

This book brings to fruition ideas that I have been playing with for more than a decade. After completing my previous book on male friendship and nationalism in Israeli culture (Kaplan 2006), I came to realize that a basic question remained unanswered in my work as well as in others: How to connect between social bonding at the micro-level and feelings of solidarity at the macro-level? I decided to embark on a systematic ethnographic study of intermediate social institutions that model for cooperation between citizens and to examine how they fuse personal and collective attachments, building on my preliminary interactionist analysis of "public intimacy" in the small male group (Kaplan 2005). The accumulated insights from this long-term research program are synthesized into a new theoretical framework presented here along with selected case studies.

Although it is virtually impossible to acknowledge all the people who assisted me on this journey, I would like to extend my thanks to a number of people who supported me in various ways at different stages of this project.

I am grateful to numerous colleagues for their advice and encouragement in pursuing the initial ideas that helped me develop the theoretical framework of this book and to others for offering feedback and support at later stages: Craig Calhoun, Dan Lainer-Vos, Don Handelman, Elihu Katz, Gary Alan Fine, Haim Hazan, Heather Devere, Joane Nagel, Kathleen Gerson, Nadav Gabay, Natan Sznaider, Nicholas (Nik) John, Niza Yanay, Oren Myers, Ronald Asch, Shira Offer, Sibyl

Schwarzenbach, Sinisa Malešević, Steven Fraiberg, Thomas Eriksen, Thomas Kuehne, Tsipy Ivry, Yossi Harpaz, and the late Allan Silver.

In particular, I would like to thank Dmitry Kurakin, Hizky Shoham, Iddo Tavory, Ido Yoav, Ilana Silber, Ori Schwarz, Peter Mallory, Graham Smith, and Robin Wagner-Pacifici for lively conversations and for their careful and thoughtful reading and insightful comments on various earlier drafts of this manuscript.

I wrote several sections of this book during my sabbatical leave at Yale University, where I benefited from the stimulating atmosphere of the Center for Cultural Sociology (CCS) and enjoyed the generous hospitality of Jeffrey Alexander, Philip Smith, CCS Fellows and Program Coordinator Nadine Amalfi, and the faculty of the Sociology Department.

I am grateful to my colleagues and research students in the Department of Sociology and Anthropology and the Program for Gender Studies at Bar-Ilan University for their ongoing support and stimulating conversations and for providing the kind of social club that truly feels like home. I thank my former research student Yoni Kupper for his significant contribution to this project. I am also indebted to the undergraduate students who participated in my research seminars on fraternal societies and the graduate students who attended my courses on virtual social networks and national attachment as a social club and engaged in enthusiastic discussions on these topics.

I presented preliminary thoughts on the phenomenology of friendship and nationalism at the conference Friends, Patrons, Followers held in Freiburg in July 2009 and the interdisciplinary workshop Friendship and the Nation held in Luxembourg in March 2010. I thank participants for their helpful remarks and reflections.

A more developed discussion of my theoretical framework was presented in 2016 at Yale's CCS workshop, at the annual meeting of the Eastern Sociological Society in Boston, and at the Puck Seminar of New York University's Department of Sociology. I am grateful to all the participants for their helpful feedback and rewarding discussions.

My analysis of the *Big Brother* reality show benefited from valuable suggestions made during earlier stages of this research by Oren Livio, Oren Soffer, Paul Frosh, and Yaacov Yadgar. The research was supported by the Hammer Scholarship of the Second Authority for Television and Radio.

The ideas presented in the study of missing soldiers and rituals of commemoration were assisted by helpful discussions and comments made by Eyal Chowers, Gil Eyal, Irit Dekel, John Comaroff, Nissim Mizrachi, Ron Zweig, and Uri Ram.

Special thanks go to Jeffrey Alexander and Philip Smith editors of the Cultural Sociology Series for believing in this project and for the opportunity to be a part of the ongoing conversations in this intellectual community. Their comprehensive review and thoughtful suggestions at different stages of this work greatly improved the overall argument and focus. I also thank the anonymous reviewers for finding merit in the original book proposal and making constructive comments. I am indebted to my editors at Palgrave Macmillan, Mary Al-Sayed, Alexis Nelson, and Kyra Saniewski, for their constant assistance, advice, and practical wisdom and to the skilled production team who saw the book through to publication. Throughout this process, I had the privilege of working with Nikki Littman who has done a fantastic job as language and style editor. I thank my brother Gal Shaked for his assistance in some of the translations.

Several passages in Chapters 3, 5, and 6 first appeared in "Social Club Sociability as a Model for National Solidarity," *American Journal of Cultural Sociology* 6 (1): 1–36. Parts of Chapter 7 previously appeared in "Freemasonry as a Playground for Civic Nationalism," *Nations and Nationalism* 20 (3): 415–435 and in "The Architecture of Collective Intimacy: Masonic Friendships as a Model for Collective Attachments," *American Anthropologist* 116 (1): 81–93. Parts of Chapter 8 previously appeared in "Toward an Interaction-Centered Approach to Media Events: Mediated Public Intimacy on the Reality TV Show *Big Brother*," *Journal of Communication* 67 (5): 758–780. I thank the publishers for granting permission to reprint this material.

Writing a book can be a demanding experience which takes a heavy toll on one's personal life. I want to thank my close friends Hagit Bachar, Elly Teman, Amir Rosenmann, and Yohay Hakak for standing by me during this time and am grateful to my mother and brother for their constant love and support. Thank you to the three little princesses who fill my life with sunshine, Tamar, Shelly, and Naama, for their understanding that Daddy is busy writing a book (even if it has no pictures!). Finally, my deepest gratitude goes to my beloved partner, Itzik. Without his understanding, cooperation, companionship, and love this adventure would not have been possible.

REFERENCES

Kaplan, Danny. 2005. "Public Intimacy: Dynamics of Seduction in Male Homosocial Interactions." *Symbolic Interaction* 28 (4): 571–595.

Kaplan, Danny. 2006. *The Men We Loved: Male Friendship and Nationalism in Israeli Culture*. New York: Berghahn Books.

Contents

1 **Introduction**   1
   Identity and Solidarity   5
   Theoretical Points of Departure   7
   Book Outline and Methodology   11
   References   17

Part I The Theoretical Framework

2 **Friendship and Solidarity: The Road Not Taken in the Study of National Attachment**   23
   Studies Going Beyond Identity Have Not Gone Far Enough   25
   Why Study Solidarity?   28
   National Solidarity as an Abstract Tie Between Strangers   30
   Bringing Friendship Back In   34
   References   38

3 **Social Club Sociability**   43
   The Quest for Community in Intermediate Institutions   43
   Why Social Clubs?   46
   Historical Examples of Social Club Sociability   53
   Online Social Clubs   57
   References   64

4	**Public and Collective Intimacy**	71
	Intimacy Beyond the Private Sphere	71
	Introducing Public Intimacy	75
	Sociability as Social Performance	77
	Collective Intimacy in Public Events: Bringing Sociability Back In	80
	References	88
5	**The Meta-Narrative of Strangers-Turned-Friends**	93
	The Friendship and Family Tropes in National Solidarity Discourse	95
	Friendship as an Imagined Social Construct	98
	The Cultural Codes of Strangers-Turned-Friends	100
	References	105
6	**Can We Really Distinguish Between Civic and National Solidarity?**	109
	Phenomenological Considerations	110
	Empirical Considerations	112
	The Debate Over Civic Nationalism	114
	The Critic of Methodological Nationalism	115
	Normative Considerations	116
	References	119

Part II The Case Studies

7	**Sacred Brotherhood: Freemasonry and Civic-National Sociability**	123
	Institutionalizing Fraternity: The Order of Freemasons	124
	The Case of Israeli Freemasonry	126
	Personal Ties: Strangers Turned into Virtuous Friends	129
	Public Intimacy: Secrecy and Masonic-Coded Communication	133
	Collective Intimacy: Staging and Collapsing the Personal and the Collective	135
	A Playground for Forging Civic-National Attachment	140
	The Nation as a Club of Chosen Friends	143
	References	146

8	Big Brother: Viewers Turned Accomplices on Reality TV	149
	Global Format, National Meaning	150
	Televised Media Event as a Social Club	154
	Big Brother *as a Media Event*	157
	Interactions Between Strangers Under the Gaze of Other Strangers	159
	The Confession Room	161
	Participants Who Were Formerly Viewers	163
	Family Members as Symbolically Present	164
	Social Interactions at Home and at Work	165
	Interactions on Social Media	168
	A Nation of Accomplices	171
	References	177
9	Absent Brother: Military Friendship and Commemoration	183
	The Institutionalization of Military Friendships	184
	The Public Staging of Personal Bonds Between Soldiers	185
	From Public to Collective Intimacy: Expanding Circles of Solidarity with Missing Soldiers	188
	The Living and the Dead: Between Simultaneous and Mythic Time	193
	A Meta-Narrative of Strangers-Turned-Friends-Turned-Brothers	197
	References	200

Part III Concluding Thoughts

10	Toward a Research Program for Studying National Solidarity	207
	The Nation and the Promise of Friendship	207
	Structural Considerations in the Empirical Study of Social Clubs	212
	References	218

Index 221

CHAPTER 1

Introduction

What is national solidarity and how do compatriots bond with one another? The first question is relatively straightforward: Although the definitions are multiple, national solidarity is generally understood as a form of attachment between compatriots that is considered beneficial for mutual cooperation and for legitimizing state power.[1] The second question, however, is far more elusive; in fact, it is rarely even considered in the social science literature. At its core is a basic phenomenological paradox: How do compatriots imagine the nation as a close-knit community of friends even as they know that it is, in reality, an abstract collectivity of strangers?[2]

Focusing on this latter question—on the "how" rather than the "what"—this book claims that at the heart of the national imagination lies a pervasive belief in the magic of transforming strangers into friends; an overarching meta-narrative that brings together the institutional logic of the state—that which prescribes cooperation between anonymous citizens—and the mythic logic of the nation—that which considers interaction between citizens as a modern incarnation of tribal fraternal ties. The result is a deep cultural structure of "strangers-turned-friends" (and ultimately friends-turned-siblings) that gives meaning to institutional social life and places it within the contours of the national state.

This symbolic structure can be unveiled by studying from bottom-up social interactions in modern institutions where participants become increasingly competent in turning particular strangers into friends. People in modern societies live the greater part of their lives in a range

© The Author(s) 2018
D. Kaplan, *The Nation and the Promise of Friendship*, Cultural Sociology, https://doi.org/10.1007/978-3-319-78402-1_1

of institutions which, regardless of their instrumental purpose, engender informal social ties. When strangers interact in clubs and cafés, sing in choirs, listen simultaneously to a live radio broadcast, participate as an active audience in a reality television show, or make friends through social media, they engage in mundane performances of sociability. When acts of sociability are staged in public, certain interactions distinguish themselves as intimate by excluding, teasing, and alienating others. At the same time, such public gestures of intimacy may tempt others to join in. Having participated in similar social clubs in the course of their lives and sharing partly overlapping social networks, compatriots acquire a sense of competence in making friends and gain reassurance in the ability of like-minded "clubbers"—but not others—to do the same.

The growing segmentation and differentiation of institutional life place increasing demands on individuals to negotiate sociability among strangers. Far beyond state-run institutions such as the military and public schools which are noted for their reinforcement of social cohesion, many, if not most, of our modern-day institutions operate as a social club of sorts in which a select group of strangers are expected to cooperate and—whether intentionally or inadvertently—become friends in the process. Since the industrial era, these institutionally mediated interactions have contributed to the social glue of modern mass society, not because they promote civic engagement or democracy, but because they encode and enact the promise of sacred friendship.

The expectation of turning strangers into friends is by no means limited to national settings. But with much of institutional and public life circumscribed (even when not directly controlled) by nation-states, these accumulated acts of friendship are likely to correspond to national boundaries and ultimately acquire national meanings through symbolic cultural processes. Thus, although sociologists have warned against the conflation of society with the nation-state known as the bias of methodological nationalism (Smith 1983; Wimmer and Schiller 2002), historically it is precisely this juxtaposition of modern social institutions and a global order of nation-states that renders the experience of sociability central to people's sense of national attachment.

In this book, I present an empirical, interaction-centered research program for studying national solidarity through the lens of "social club sociability." Sociability in social clubs consists of interactions between participants and spectators-turned-participants that span three levels of analysis: the *interpersonal* ties between individual members of the institution, the *public* staging of these ties in front of other members or non-members, and the *collective* ties between members of the organization as a whole. This translates into a particular research strategy for studying sociability both in everyday life and in public events through the interactionist mechanisms of "public intimacy" and emergent feelings of "collective intimacy." Public intimacy refers to the ways in which members stage intimate ties in public in order to establish their exclusivity and, at the same time, tease selected spectators (but not others) to become confidants and, subsequently, participants in this relationship. Hence, by employing a complex interplay between exclusion and inclusion and between secrecy and disclosure, public intimacy operates as a bonding mechanism by way of seduction.

This interactionist mechanism operating in mundane institutional life can be examined against the backdrop of Durkheimian approaches to sacred ritualized events, understood as highly orchestrated collective action that departs from everyday life, and deemed central to the affirmation of collective identity (Mast 2006). Viewed as "social performance," such ritualized events can achieve "fusion" and reinforce solidarity when audiences identify with performers and background cultural scripts achieve verisimilitude (Alexander 2004, 527). While previous works have explored how such ritualized public events, as well as media events, arouse collective emotions mainly by orchestrating instances of focused attention (e.g., Collins 2004a; Dayan and Katz 1992), we lack a systematic analysis of the interpersonal interactions taking place between the social actors in the performance (both performers and audiences), and how they assign preexisting cultural codes to these interactions. Thus, I suggest that the simultaneous feelings of collective intimacy that arise in public events build on accumulated experiences of public intimacy and enact an alchemic transformation of all qualified members of the community from strangers into friends. The "strong program" in cultural sociology (Alexander and Smith 2001, 137) underscores how collective action is structured by a relatively autonomous cultural realm operating through underlying symbolic binary codes and narratives. Accordingly, I call attention to the meta-narrative of strangers-turned-friends as a key cultural structure that gives collective-national meaning to feelings of solidarity.

In previous work (Kaplan 2006, 2007; Kaplan and Yanay 2006), I explored some of the conceptual, phenomenological, and cultural associations between the nation and the promise of friendship through the lens of gender, hegemonic masculinity, and male homosocial desire. Bearing in mind the masculinist underpinnings of national movements, ideology, and solidarity (Mosse 1996; Nagel 1998; Pateman 1989), I studied fraternal friendship as a key cultural trope for national attachment. In this work, I opted to tone down this emphasis on gender-based analysis in order to introduce other hitherto unexplored issues in the study of national solidarity.

To conclude, this research program offers a specific understanding of national solidarity as both a bottom-up process of socialization in the form of social club sociability and a top-down process of cultural interpretation that gives meaning to social life. This understanding comprises a three-layered model of national solidarity that includes the following elements.

   a. *Institutional setting.* Nationally bounded modern institutions, from state organizations and civic associations to social media practices, operate as social clubs where unaffiliated individuals negotiate modes of cooperation through informal interactions of sociability and transform in the process into acquaintances and potential friends. Each social institution structures its own patterns and codes of sociability and presents a different manifestation of a symbolic meta-narrative of strangers-turned-friends associated with national solidarity.
   b. *Public and collective intimacy.* The interpersonal ties that form between members of any given institution are inevitably managed, disclosed, and staged in front of a third party. This semi-public performance of intimacy is a dramaturgical mechanism that provides insiders with a sense of exclusivity and can, by the same token, also tease outsiders and tempt them to get involved. In this way, triads of public intimacy operate as rites of belonging: They can potentially turn spectators into participants and form the cornerstone for larger collectivities, resulting in feelings of "collective intimacy." This emergent solidarity corresponds to Emile Durkheim's ([1915] 2003, 110) conception of collective "effervescence" and, more broadly, to the sense of "re-fusion" (Alexander 2004, 529) that is ideally accomplished in ritualized events. However, collective intimacy directs attention to the ways in which the ritualized performance reaffirms the existence of the community not only as a tangible body of individuals but also as a

tangible network of confidants and accomplices who share mutual patterns of sociability learned through past experiences with public intimacy.
c. *Meta-narrative of strangers-turned-friends.* Individual experiences of sociability and friendship acquire cultural meaning through a meta-narrative that links them to a national discourse of solidarity, according to which citizens not only cooperate for common interests but also share their passions and destiny. This meta-narrative operates through a set of binary codes that transform mundane interactions between individual strangers in institutional life into sacred ties of friendship in collective life and, in turn, casts the friend as a rediscovered primordial brother.

This three-layered account of national solidarity as a performance of sociability and cultural structure of friendship goes against the grain of current scholarship which dissociates national attachments from friendship (Calhoun 1991; Malešević 2011) and, more generally, separates solidarity and generalized trust from close-knit personal ties (Torche and Valenzuela 2011). Although compatriots do not know each other personally, at important junctures in their collective life they come to feel and care for each other in concrete ways. These junctures are mediated and shaped by myriad institutions of modern life. On such occasions when generalized trust in strangers transforms into collective feelings of familiarity, exclusivity, and loyalty, sentiments of friendship and of national attachment can be said to converge.

IDENTITY AND SOLIDARITY

Although it is widely acknowledged that the raison d'être of nationalism is to account for and legitimize political cooperation between citizens (e.g., Smith 1991; Gellner 1983), the role of sociability in national attachments seems too often to be either taken for granted or explicitly rejected as a valid avenue of study. Theories of nationalism have focused on questions of identity formation far more than on the question of solidarity. A rich body of research in sociology, anthropology, political science, and social psychology examined the cognitive dimension of identity formation—the ways that individuals establish or modify their sense of identification with an abstract entity known as the nation and set boundaries around a shared categorical commonality through collective symbols, rituals, customs, historical narratives, and everyday practices (e.g., Anderson [1983] 1991; Billig 1995; Brubaker and Cooper 2000; Eriksen 1993; Smith 1991; Theiss-Morse 2009; Yuval-Davis 1993). In contrast, scholars rarely addressed the social ties between members of the national community and the socialization processes, which result not from cognitive perceptions but from the experience of these mutual interactions—the ways in which compatriots connect and acquire shared codes of sociability and subsequently distinguish themselves from outgroups precisely through these very same coded interactions.

In other words, existing scholarship has prioritized questions about the ways actors assume a common identity and overlooked the question of social ties between actors as an equally important category of analysis.[3] As argued by Mustafa Emirbayer (1996, 1997), social ties—including imaginary and fantasized relationships—constitute appropriate units of sociological analysis no less, if not more, than preconstituted entities such as the individual or society.

Hence, throughout this book I espouse an analytic distinction between the crystallization of collective *identity* and the emergence of collective *solidarity*, that is, between instances of cognitive classification enacted through group boundary work and patterns of sociability enacted through social interaction. While the former explains *who* is categorized as belonging to the collective, the latter explains *how* we-feelings develop among members of the collective. Although solidarity is often considered a by-product of group identification, the causality can also run in the opposite direction from interactions and feelings of connectedness to collective identification. Ultimately, we should be able to determine how such interactions and feelings feed into discursive processes of identification and vice versa in a recursive and cyclic fashion.

Distinguishing identity from solidarity is relatively straightforward in many forms of belonging other than national belonging. For instance, we can easily make out the role that collective identification and a sense of common descent play in a highly dispersed *ethnic* community that lacks daily interactions between members. Likewise, we can readily acknowledge the importance of social interactions and patterns of sociability for *civic* cooperation in so-called global cities whose residents are mainly immigrants lacking a common collective identity but managing to build mutual ties of solidarity. From these simplistic examples, ethnicity can be taken as a form of belonging expected to be high on the "identity" dimension even when low on the "solidarity" dimension (understood as a social bond), while civic attachment is expected to be high on solidarity even when low on identity.

It is when we turn to national attachments that this distinction between identity and solidarity becomes more complex and the two often appear in tandem (because, inter alia, nation-ness incorporates the category of both ethnicity and citizenship to varying degrees). Since people tend to live within the bounds of their national communities and inevitably interact with fellow nationals on a regular basis, the underlying sentiments are not particularly salient in their lives and they have little reason to set them apart in terms of shared identity and sociability.[4] In contrast, when fellow nationals meet while travelling abroad, national feelings may surge and become more relevant. They may not only appreciate their shared commonality but also experience a sense of immediate mutual connection, which often comes in stark contrast to their difficulty in establishing social ties in the foreign country. Although here too collective identity and feelings of solidarity appear in tandem, the analytic distinction between the two becomes more apparent.

This sense of immediate connection between fellow nationals meeting abroad can be taken as a prototypical or rather an accelerated scenario of strangers-turned-friends. However, a similar scenario inevitably occurs in mundane circumstances in everyday life: While people do not make new friends every day, they continually participate in institutions where they socialize according to shared patterns of sociability and gain reassurance in their ability as well as the ability of other participants to make friends. Friendship should thus be taken as integral and not opposed to civic and national attachment; it is the social glue of state and nation.

THEORETICAL POINTS OF DEPARTURE

This book's initial point of departure is where Benedict Anderson (1991) left off in *Imagined Communities*. Anderson observed that while all communities are imagined, what distinguishes the modern nation from pre-modern social forms, such as a traditional village, is the style in which it is imagined. He noted that the nation is always conceived as a simultaneous, bounded, and "deep, horizontal comradeship" (7); however, he failed to analyze this close-knit bond as such and instead built his argument on the premise that the national imagination is based on novel abilities for abstraction. Thus, while many critics of Anderson have misunderstood his use of the term "imagination" as an artificially invented illusion rather than simply a social construction, I see his claim to be that the national imagination reflects a move from tangible to less tangible representations of the collectivity. For example, Anderson's emblematic examples of the national imagination are the mass ceremony of reading the daily newspaper and the erection of tombs for the unknown soldier. As I discuss in later chapters, these are examples of ritualized performances in which the mass of individuals forming the modern nation becomes more tangible to the participants. For Anderson, however, they serve paradoxically to emphasize the abstractedness of the national imagination, in other words, to imply that what people actually imagine are abstract entities.

In contrast to Anderson, I understand the term "imagination" as the cognitive and cultural process, whereby the intangible becomes tangible.[5] While the exact definition of the term may seem merely a semantic matter, when it comes to a research program, it is in fact a major point of departure from Anderson's as well as most other scholarly analysis of nationalism. If the nation is a cognitive abstraction, imagining the national community is a consistent act of concretization. Thus, instead of examining how national collectivities have become ever more abstract, we should study how nations are consistently and increasingly experienced in concrete terms—partly as a response to this shift toward greater abstraction in actual social structures. Furthermore, to understand how this tendency for concreteness generates and sustains national solidarity, it should be studied in terms of the imagination of *social ties* between members of the nation rather than the imagination of commonality and shared identity of members—yet another major difference from Anderson's approach. This can be further explicated by considering Paul James' (1996) more systematic approach to abstractedness, which engaged with Anderson's work and started out with a similar paradox to that which opened this book:

> How can the nation be experienced as a concrete gut-felt relation to common souls and a shared landscape, and nevertheless be based upon abstract connections to largely unknown strangers and unvisited places? As part of the "nation of strangers" we live its connectedness much more through the abstracting mediations of mass communications and the commodity market than we do at the level of the face-to-face, but we continue to use the metaphor of the face-to-face to explain its cultural power. (xii)

It therefore appears that for James, face-to-face relations are an unwarranted metaphor for national attachment that scholars should best avoid.

Similar to Anderson, James sees the essence of national imagination in people's growing ability for abstraction; he described how extensions of face-to-face interactions into wider social formations gradually served to reinforce this imagination. Despite his intention to connect between the subjectivities of national consciousness and the objective structures of the nation-state (e.g., James 1996, 7), his work does not explain how fellow nationals interact and experience their connectedness.[6]

My work can be seen to provide a complementary and partly orthogonal approach to the project pursued by Anderson (1991) and James (1996). While they showed how national consciousness developed historically from macro-level structural changes in objective social relations, I ask how the systematic erasure of objective distinctions between mass society and traditional communities is possible. In other words, I focus on how national solidarity is experienced as an extension of interpersonal and group ties. As James (2006) himself noted in passing in a later book on nationalism and globalization: "As the dominant social form became more abstract, we became more and more obsessed by making the content more palpable, more embodied, more 'real'" (89). In the language of social ties, it is this "obsession" with making the abstract familiar that translates into a pervasive cultural code of modern national life, namely the expectation of turning strangers into friends.

In an attempt to bridge between the interpersonal and collective level of analysis, I take Georg Simmel's micro-level perspective as my second point of departure. As the classical scholar "most deeply committed to relational theorizing" in sociology (Emirbayer 1997, 288), Simmel focused on interactions between actors as a primary category of analysis. Similar to other classical theorists, Simmel's work offers little discussion of national attachments. Moreover, unlike writings by Durkheim and Max Weber, his micro-level perspective has not been taken up by subsequent scholars of nationalism (Smith 1983; Thompson and Fevre 2001).[7]

For Simmel, social structure is realized only through interpersonal interactions between individuals: "individuals in their directly perceptible existence [are] the bearers of the processes of association, who are united by these processes into the higher unity which one calls 'society'" (Simmel 1949, 254). In the modern era, national solidarity is one of the dominant forms that this sense of higher unity has taken. In Simmelian terms, the challenge is, therefore, to account for national solidarity through processes of social bonding and interpersonal association. It is partly this challenge that has inspired me to develop my notion of public intimacy, which builds, among other things, on Simmel's (1949) discussion of sociability—[8] a form of social interaction pursued for its own sake irrespective of anything participants have to gain from it. While for Simmel this form of playful sociability entails a temporal suspension of external binding social roles and is separated from concrete forms of "real" associations, I understand public intimacy as having collective implications.

My third and probably most significant point of departure is the Durkheimian tradition that informs my understanding of higher-level collective intimacy. Durkheim's work on the cohesive power of ritual and symbolic meanings in religious life posed questions which are just as relevant for national life (Alexander 2003, 8–9; Smith 1983, 30). In particular, Durkheim (2003) underscored the importance of public events or mass assemblies where individuals can engage in rituals which reassert their common sentiments, including ceremonies of modern society such as "a citizens meeting commemorating the advent of a new moral charter or some other great event of national life" (119).

These ritualized public events give rise to collective "effervescence," a social energy of pure collective sentiment which continues to infuse social relations after the immediate period of ritual interaction and which may have the long-term consequence of fortifying solidarity (Alexander 2003, 173). Durkheim (2003, 141–142) illustrated the moral effect of this solidarity both in exceptional historical circumstances, such as the French Revolution, and in everyday relations between neighbors. Building in part on this tradition, researchers have offered various analytical constructs for thinking about solidarity in terms of micro-level interactions, among them primary groups (Cooley 1962), horizontal associations (Putnam et al. 1993), and media events (Dayan and Katz 1992). Randall Collins' (2004a, b) theory of "interaction ritual chains" as a source of collective solidarity provided the most systematic (and radically micro-level) analysis to date for Durkheim's notion of effervescence.

Finally, an understanding of how the interactional aspects of sociability can give rise to meanings associated with society at large requires us to consider how social practice is linked to cultural structures. In this, my fourth theoretical anchor is the strong program in cultural sociology developed by Jeffrey Alexander and Philip Smith (2001), a revitalizing force within the Durkheimian tradition which, among other things, locates Durkheimian interest in ritual and public events in the wider theoretical framework of cultural pragmatics and social performance that is informed by a structural-hermeneutic approach (Alexander 2004). This approach views individual and collective action as embedded in a specific horizon of affect and meaning. The relatively autonomous cultural realm should be studied as a "social text" operating through codes and narratives that both enable and constrain social action (Alexander and Smith 2001, 136–137). While trying to balance between the agency and pragmatic creativity of meaning-making actors, and the autonomy of the underlying cultural structures, this approach contends that in modern societies "cultural practice must continue to be capable of capturing sacrality and of displaying it in successful symbolic performance" (Alexander and Mast 2006, 15).

Book Outline and Methodology

Part one of the book presents the theoretical argument for studying national solidarity through sociability. Chapter 2 makes the case for studying friendship and solidarity, a "road not taken" in the study of national attachment. I describe how recent reappraisals of national identity discourse have ignored the question of social ties. The limited discussions centering on national solidarity either take for granted or explicitly reject the imagining of close-knit bonds between compatriots and instead conceive of mass solidarity as a type of productive relationship between strangers. I review various analytic justifications for bringing friendship back into the study of public and political life. However, these have remained largely at the discursive level and demand a more empirically grounded research program for studying the continuum between interpersonal and collective ties and its role in the national imagination. To this end, the next three chapters unfold my three-layered model of national solidarity.

Chapter 3 argues that in order to understand how "intermediate" social institutions transform strangers into acquaintances and friends, we need to consider how they occasion a non-instrumental social club sociability along the lines of the expressive sociability highlighted by Simmel (1949). Each social club presents its own informal norms of conduct, and members need to acquire the "right" exclusive idioms and codes of intimate communication. With the growing differentiation of modern institutional life, compatriots increasingly participate in a sequence of social clubs and are more likely to attend various social clubs simultaneously. Facing increasing demands to negotiate sociability among strangers, compatriots do not simply pursue a standardized form of communication but sustain feelings of familiarity, exclusivity, and mutual loyalty carried over from one institutional setting to the next. It is this emotional competence which enables a mass society to be imagined as a nation. This chapter presents brief historical examples of a variety of social clubs and their implications for civic or national life, culminating with the case of "phatic exchange" on online social media sites, particularly Facebook.

Chapter 4 spells out the second element in the proposed model, namely the research strategy of public and collective intimacy. First, it revisits the concept of intimacy and its use in public and national life, problematizing the "identitarian" focus in much of the current scholarship, which understands intimacy as a form of communication. Second, it describes how, instead, one can study intimacy as a form social relationship. Public intimacy mediates between interpersonal and collective ties through a dynamic of seduction—staging personal relationships under the gaze of spectators in ways that tease and invite others to become participants. Third, in order to understand how public intimacy affects collective level solidarity, the chapter considers the broader theoretical framework of social performance and draws correspondences between the move from occurrences to events and from sociability and friendship to solidarity.

On this latter point, the chapter goes on to address feelings of collective intimacy that underlie ritualized public events and media events. Other neo-Durkheimian accounts of public events have centered on how this performative reaffirmation of the national community is formed in terms of shared knowledge, values, and group boundaries, in other words, in terms of the group's collective identity. In contrast, building on past experiences of public intimacy, collective intimacy points to the emergence of shared feelings of group complicity, an imagining of the community as a cohesive network of friends.

Chapter 5 unravels the third element in the model of national solidarity, namely how the meta-narrative of strangers-turned-friends operates at the symbolic cultural level. National rhetoric reconciles two distinct tropes for close-knit ties, family and friendship, by invoking the figure of the "brother." The magic of the national imagination lies not only in the transformation of strangers into friends but also in imagining these new friends as rediscovered brothers (and, only obliquely, sisters) of the same primordial tribe. Epitomizing the continuing demand for salvation in modern social life, this meta-narrative gives sacred meaning to mundane performances of sociability, operating as a set of binary codes that transform abstract, anonymous, inclusive, indifferent, and interest-based relations between strangers into concrete, familiar, intimately exclusive, loyal, and passionate relations between friends.

Finally, while this book centers on national rather than civic attachments, Chapter 6 calls attention to the fact that when it comes to the question of solidarity (as opposed to identity), the two are not easily distinguishable beyond the symbolic cultural level. Reviewing other prominent bottom-up approaches to mass solidarity, it is shown how from a phenomenological and empirical point of view the analytic distinction between civic and national solidarity is too often overstated. This begs a reconsideration of the civic model of nationalism too easily dismissed by recent scholars.

Part two illustrates the proposed research program in three very different cases of social club sociability: Masonic lodges, the reality TV show *Big Brother*, and military bonding. Each of these social institutions exemplifies a particular form of sociability originating at a different historical juncture in the development of modern nation-states and was purposely chosen so as to showcase different elements in the three-layered theoretical model of national solidarity.

Each case study is examined both globally and locally. The global-level analysis includes a brief overview of the historical development and global diffusion of the organizational model in question and explains how the model has been adopted and translated into local, national settings. The local-level analysis draws on extended ethnographic fieldwork on specific practices of sociability and solidarity in a range of social clubs conducted in Israel at different periods between 2004 and 2014. Data were gathered through semi-structured interviews with local participants or audiences, focus groups, participant observations in selected arenas of sociability, content analysis of selected television broadcasts, and analysis of public discourse in print media, Web sites, and social media. In line with a bottom-up grounded theory analysis (Strauss and Corbin 1990), recurrent themes were identified through a cyclic reading and rereading of the data derived from all the sources.[9] In order to advance an interpretive argument, the current presentation is limited to selected pieces of data as representative exemplars of the larger phenomenon and followed by a critical analysis (Lindlof and Taylor 2011). Quotes from the interviews and other data sources were translated from Hebrew by the author. Names of interviewees have been replaced with pseudonyms.

Only by employing a grounded approach that situates global social clubs within a localized national setting can we begin to unravel the workings of national solidarity. My intention, however, is not to focus on the Israeli context as such but to use it to decipher how each of these global institutions presents distinctive patterns of sociability that manifest underlying symbolic structures.

Israel is an overwhelmingly immigrant society. Israeli culture places strong emphasis on national integration, expressed in metaphors like the melting pot and in the cultural trope of fraternal friendship (Kaplan 2006). This provides fertile ground for exploring the paradox of a collectivity of strangers imagined as a community of friends. At the same time, and unlike classic "Western" nation-states, as a self-declared Jewish state Israel subscribes primarily to an ethno-cultural rather than a civic model of nationalism (Rouhana and Ghanem 1998). The former presupposes tribal ancestry and kinship ties, whereas the latter underscores a voluntary contract and is therefore more readily associated with friendship. Consequently, when members of local Israeli clubs demonstrate practices and values of civic nationalism, this is less likely to result from pre-established ideological indoctrination to this national model (as might be the case when studying their American counterparts, for example) and can be far more easily attributed to the effect of social club sociability.

Along these lines, Chapter 7 explores how members of Masonic lodges in Israel extend the logic of friendship to a broader organizational and civic context. The study follows the intersections of interpersonal, public, and collective intimacy in members' ritual activities and everyday life. Lodge members take on the roles of citizen, bureaucrat, priest, and president concurrently, partly collapsing the distinctions between personal and collective ties, between the familiar and the revered. Their understanding of fraternity carries over to questions of citizenship and patriotism and straddles particularist and universalist interpretations of national solidarity, a tension best captured in the model of civic nationalism.

Chapter 8 presents the case of the highly popular reality television show *Big Brother*. Drawing on semiotic analysis and extended audience research in Israel, the chapter demonstrates various practices of "mediated public intimacy" taking place between two or more contestants with the audience serving as an absent third party. Certain features built into the Big Brother format create atypical "folds" in the veil that separates insiders from outsiders. These serve to mobilize viewers' sense of participation, moving them from the position of spectator to privileged confidants of the contestants. Interactions between viewers in everyday life and on social media locate them as accomplices and reinforce emergent feelings of collective intimacy. This analysis emphasizes the importance of social ties for understanding how media events generate national solidarity.

The final case study in Chapter 9 deals with a form of sociability more readily associated with national solidarity: military friendships and commemoration rituals. The chapter explores the manifestation of the meta-narrative of strangers-turned-friends in the public staging of personal bonds between soldiers and in grassroots campaigns for Israeli soldiers missing in action. Moral values of military friendship extend to expanding circles of solidarity in Israeli society, such as schoolchildren and commercial entrepreneurs who expressed feelings of familiarity and loyalty to soldiers they have never met. Identification with missing soldiers merges two temporal dimensions of national solidarity, simultaneous time and mythic time, and highlights a symbolic shift from ties of friendship to bonds of brotherhood.

Lastly, in Chapter 10, which forms the third and final part of the book, I sum up the proposed research program for studying national solidarity through social club sociability and the promise of friendship and lay out the main structural issues to be considered in the empirical investigation of social clubs.

Notes

1. The exact definitions and operationalizations of national solidarity vary and are entangled with related terms such as social cohesion, social (or generalized) trust, and social capital. Some formulations emphasize collective integration, whereas others focus on elements of social support. The implications of national solidarity for civic engagement or democratic participation are also continually debated. Studies in political psychology provide some useful and succinct discussions of these various issues, although they rarely employ the actual term national solidarity (for some recent overviews and empirical analyses, see Chan et al. 2006; Ariely 2014; Li and Brewer 2004; Reeskens and Wright 2013).

2. Contrary to scholarly efforts to distinguish between civic and national attachments in its common usage, the term "compatriot" does not distinguish between the two. As I discuss in Chapter 6, this ambiguity highlights the centrality of the civic component in formulations of national solidarity, particularly when studied from bottom-up.
3. For lack of space, I shall give just one example of the ways scholars of nationalism tend to take for granted the study of solidarity as a residue or by-product of collective identity formation. Elizabeth Theiss-Morse (2009), a social psychologist actually interested in questions of solidarity, emphasized that national identity "is inherently social and is centered on people's strong bond and sense of community with their fellow group members." She further proposed that it is the boundaries of national identity that explain the feelings of solidarity, or, in her terminology, whoever counts as American can explain "how Americans treat one another and help each other in times of trouble" (3). However, she provided no explanation as to why identifying someone as fellow American should lead to mutual feelings of solidarity and cooperation or how these feelings are generated.
4. Indeed, the analytic distinction between shared identity and shared sociability or solidarity has gone unacknowledged even by scholars aiming to unearth the banal expressions of national attachment in everyday life (following Billig 1995), such as Tim Edensor (2002) and John Fox and Cynthia Miller-Idriss (2008). While they often described practices revolving around social relations, their discussion is framed solely in terms of collective identity.
5. This corresponds to Cornelius Castoriadis' (1987) formulation of the social imaginary as a form of imagination not in the sense of being a mere reflection or distortion of the "real" but of mediating the real in the first place: "it is the unceasing and essentially undetermined creation of figures/forms/images, on the basis of which alone there can even be a question of 'something'" (as quoted in James 1996, 7 referring to Castoriadis 1987, 3).
6. James (1996) provided a comprehensive sociohistorical formulation of nationalism based on "agency extension" (25) that resulted in "disembodied integration" (45). His notion of "abstraction" pertained "both to ideas and material relations" and related "forms of subjectivity" to particular social formations "without reducing the former to the latter" (188). Interestingly, however, he addressed social relations (as in face-to-face interactions, kinship ties, or larger formations) only in conjunction with objective social conditions, in other words, as forms and social structures rather than as a subjective experience.
7. One exception is Simmel's (1964, 100) allusion to violent, antagonistic interactions between ethnic groups as a source of in-group national solidarity, which informs recent work on interactional aspects of national solidarity by Collins (2004b).

8. I switch to Kurt Wolff's translation of the same essay (Simmel 1950) in places where it is more helpful in getting across specific points in Simmel's argument that I wish to emphasize.
9. Sources with rich narrative content were further analyzed according to Amedeo Giorgi's (1975) proposal for phenomenological research adapted into a five-stage procedure: (1) a free reading of each source; (2) dividing the source into separate sequences according to natural "meaning units"; (3) rereading each unit with the research questions in mind, namely focusing on the social interactions between actors (participants and spectators) and how they reflect public and collective intimacy; (4) collecting non-redundant themes from each source; and (5) gleaning dominant themes from the entire selection in order to derive a theory of nomothetic value.

References

Alexander, Jeffrey C. 2003. *The Meanings of Social Life: A Cultural Sociology.* New York: Oxford University Press.
Alexander, Jeffrey C. 2004. "Cultural Pragmatics: Social Performance Between Ritual and Strategy." *Sociological Theory* 22 (4): 527–573.
Alexander, Jeffrey, and Philip Smith. 2001. "The Strong Program in Cultural Theory: Elements of a Structural Hermeneutics." In *Handbook of Sociological Theory*, edited by Jonathan H. Turner, 135–150. New York: Springer.
Anderson, Benedict. [1983] 1991. *Imagined Communities: Reflections on the Origins and Spread of Nationalism.* London: Verso.
Ariely, Gal. 2014. "Does Diversity Erode Social Cohesion? Conceptual and Methodological Issues." *Political Studies* 62 (3): 573–595.
Billig, Michael. 1995. *Banal Nationalism.* London: Sage.
Brubaker, Rogers, and Frederick Cooper. 2000. "Beyond 'Identity'." *Theory and Society* 29 (1): 1–47.
Calhoun, Craig. 1991. "Nationalism, Political Community and the Representation of Society: Or, Why Feeling at Home is Not a Substitute for Public Space." *European Journal of Social Theory* 2: 217–231.
Castoriadis, Cornelius. 1987. *The Imaginary Institution of Society.* Cambridge: MIT Press.
Chan, Joseph, Ho-Pong To, and Elaine Chan. 2006. "Reconsidering Social Cohesion: Developing a Definition and Analytical Framework for Empirical Research." *Social Indicators Research* 75 (2): 273–302.
Collins, Randall. 2004a. *Interaction Ritual Chains.* Princeton: Princeton University Press.
Collins, Randall. 2004b. "Rituals of Solidarity and Security in the Wake of Terrorist Attack." *Sociological Theory* 22 (1): 53–87.

Cooley, Charles H. [1909] 1962. *Social Organization*. New York: Schocken.
Dayan, Daniel, and Elihu Katz. 1992. *Media Events: The Live Broadcasting of History*. Cambridge, MA: Harvard University Press.
Durkheim, Emile. [1915] 2003. "The Elementary Forms of Religious Life," translated by Karen E. Fields. In *Emile Durkheim: Sociologist of Modernity*, edited by Mustafa Emirbayer, 109–121, 140–141. Malden, MA: Blackwell.
Edensor, Tim. 2002. *National Identity, Popular Culture and Everyday Life*. Oxford: Berg.
Emirbayer, Mustafa. 1996. "Useful Durkheim." *Sociological Theory* 14 (2): 109–130.
Emirbayer, Mustafa. 1997. "Manifesto for a Relational Sociology." *American Journal of Sociology* 103 (2): 281–317.
Eriksen, Thomas Hylland. 1993. *Ethnicity and Nationalism: Anthropological Perspectives*. London: Pluto.
Fox, Jon E., and Cynthia Miller-Idriss. 2008. "Everyday Nationhood." *Ethnicities* 8 (4): 536–563.
Gellner, Ernst. 1983. *Nations and Nationalism*. Oxford: Blackwell.
Giorgi, Amedeo. 1975. "An Application of Phenomenological Method in Psychology." In *Duquesne Studies in Phenomenological Psychology*, edited by Amedeo Giorgi, Constance T. Fisher, and Edward L. Murray, vol. 2, 82–103. Pittsburgh, PA: Duquesne University Press.
James, Paul. 1996. *Nation Formation: Towards a Theory of Abstract Community*. London: Sage.
James, Paul. 2006. *Globalism, Nationalism, Tribalism: Bringing Theory Back In*. London: Sage.
Kaplan, Danny. 2006. *The Men We Loved: Male Friendship and Nationalism in Israeli Culture*. New York: Berghahn Books.
Kaplan, Danny. 2007. "What Can the Concept of Friendship Contribute to the Study of National Identity?" *Nations and Nationalism* 13 (2): 225–244.
Kaplan, Danny, and Niza Yanay. 2006. "Fraternal Friendship and Commemorative Desire." *Social Analysis* 50 (1): 127–146.
Li, Qiong, and Marilynn B. Brewer. 2004. "What Does It Mean to be an American? Patriotism, Nationalism, and American Identity After 9/11." *Political Psychology* 25 (5): 727–739.
Lindlof, Thomas R., and Bryan C. Taylor. 2011. *Qualitative Communication Research Methods*. Thousand Oaks, CA: Sage.
Malešević, Siniša. 2011. "The Chimera of National Identity." *Nations and Nationalism* 17 (2): 272–290.
Mast, Jason. 2006. "The Cultural Pragmatics of Event-ness: The Clinton/Lewinsky Affair." In *Social Performance: Symbolic Action, Cultural Pragmatics, and Ritual*, edited by Jeffrey C. Alexander, Bernhard Giesen, and Jason Mast, 115–145. Cambridge: Cambridge University Press.
Mosse, George L. 1996. *The Image of Man: The Creation of Modern Masculinity*. New York: Oxford University Press.

Nagel, Joan. 1998. "Masculinity and Nationalism: Gender and Sexuality in the Making of Nations." *Ethnic and Racial Studies* 21 (2): 242–269.
Pateman, Carole. 1989. *The Disorder of Women: Democracy, Feminism and Political Theory.* Stanford: Stanford University Press
Putnam, Robert, Robert Leonardi, and Raffaella Y. Nanetti. 1993. *Making Democracy Work: Civic Traditions in Modern Italy.* Princeton, NJ: Princeton University Press.
Reeskens, Tim, and Matthew Wright. 2013. "Nationalism and the Cohesive Society: A Multilevel Analysis of the Interplay among Diversity, National Identity, and Social Capital Across 27 European Societies." *Comparative Political Studies* 46 (2): 153–181.
Rouhana, Nadim, and Asad Ghanem. 1998. "The Crisis of Minorities in Ethnic States: The Case of Palestinian Citizens in Israel." *International Journal of Middle East Studies* 30: 321–346.
Simmel, Georg. 1949. "The Sociology of Sociability," translated by Everett C. Hughes. *American Journal of Sociology* 55 (3): 254–261.
Simmel, Georg. [1915] 1950. *The Sociology of Georg Simmel.* translated by Kurt H. Wolff. Glencoe, IL: Free Press.
Simmel, Georg. 1964. *Conflict and the Web of Group-Affiliations.* New York: The Free Press.
Smith, Anthony D. 1983. "Nationalism and Classical Social Theory." *British Journal of Sociology* 34 (1): 19–38.
Smith, Anthony D. 1991. *National Identity.* Reno: University of Nevada Press.
Strauss, Anselm C., and Juliet M. Corbin. 1990. *Basics of Qualitative Research: Grounded Theory Procedures and Techniques.* Newbury Park, CA: Sage.
Theiss-Morse, Elizabeth. 2009. *Who Counts as an American? The Boundaries of National Identity.* Cambridge: Cambridge University Press.
Thompson, Andrew, and Ralph Fevre. 2001. "The National Question: Sociological Reflections on Nation and Nationalism." *Nations and Nationalism* 7 (3): 297–315.
Torche, Florencia, and Eduardo Valenzuela. 2011. "Trust and Reciprocity: A Theoretical Distinction of the Sources of Social Capital." *European Journal of Social Theory* 14 (2): 181–198.
Wimmer, Andreas, and Nina Glick Schiller. 2002. "Methodological Nationalism and Beyond: Nation-State Building, Migration and the Social Sciences." *Global Networks* 2 (4): 301–334.
Yuval-Davis, Nira. 1993. "Gender and Nation." *Ethnic and Racial Studies* 16 (4): 621–632.

PART I

The Theoretical Framework

CHAPTER 2

Friendship and Solidarity: The Road Not Taken in the Study of National Attachment

Scholars of nationalism and national attachment have focused on questions of collective identity far more than on questions of collective solidarity. Their attention has been given to the ways in which individuals establish, maintain, or modify their sense of commonality as they identify with the abstract entity known as the nation rather than to the ways in which they interact with compatriots and socialize according to shared patterns of sociability.[1]

Prominent modernist scholars of nationalism, such as Ernest Gellner (1983), Anderson (1991), and Eric Hobsbawm (1991), charted long-term political, economic, and cultural preconditions for the emergence of national attachment, typically addressing one of three different, though often related, processes (Wimmer and Feinstein 2010): nationalism as a political movement, a shift in institutional state structures, and a gradual spread of national consciousness among a local population. Others rejected this kind of macro-level developmentalist approach in favor of a micro-level lens. Roger Brubaker (1996) called for an "eventful" perspective that considers epistemological shifts in the meaning of nationness to be determined by "contingent, conjuncturally fluctuating" yet potentially "transformative" events (19).[2] Philip Gorski (2000) opted for a postmodern genealogical perspective that focuses on surface characteristics, localized narratives, and a specific set of categories around which the coherence of a particular nationalist discourse is determined. Both the macro- and micro-historical approaches concentrate primarily on the "what," namely on transformations in *conceptual* meanings

© The Author(s) 2018
D. Kaplan, *The Nation and the Promise of Friendship*, Cultural Sociology, https://doi.org/10.1007/978-3-319-78402-1_2

associated with national consciousness. However, as noted by Anthony Smith (2009, 42–43), they leave lingering questions about the emotional experience of nationalism unanswered. In particular, they have not addressed the "how," namely how national consciousness conveys a sense of a close-knit community.

Anderson (1991) famously noted that conceiving the nation as a "deep, horizontal comradeship" (7) is what has ultimately led millions of people to willingly sacrifice themselves for the sake of fellow nationals. And yet, precisely on this point, the limited discussions that explicitly address national attachments in terms of solidarity have described it as a form of disinterested, impersonal relationship between strangers (e.g., Anderson 1991; Calhoun 1991; Gellner 1983). They thus presuppose a dichotomous distinction between personal friendship and collective solidarity and fall short of answering how the community of strangers is experienced as a deep comradeship.

The focus in current scholarship on questions of commonality privileges actors (whether individuals or groups) as the primary unit of analysis and overlooks the role of interactions between actors as an equally important category of analysis. While national attachments crucially depend on cognitive perceptions of group commonality that shape the boundaries of the national community, these perceptions cannot account for how compatriots develop mutual feelings of trust and solidarity.

I purposefully employ the term national "attachment" as an umbrella term encompassing issues of both identity and solidarity. Although seldom used in the literature beyond studies in political psychology, Dan Lainer-Vos (2012) clarified how the term "attachment" circumvents the theoretical and analytic closure that emerges from the current scholarly focus on identity discourse and identity work. That is, it does not presuppose that the formation of national groupings rests wholly on the emergence of collective representations which generate perceived commonalities between members; rather, it invites researchers to identify both agents and processes involved in the formation of groups and directs attention to an entire range of practices (including cultural activities and social events) used to generate national associations based on concrete contact between national actors. Among other things, attachment brings to mind the imagery of a "network" and directs researchers to examine the practical challenge of incorporating groups in national networks within which members can engage in productive cooperation.

As an overarching concept, national attachment is also more effective than other umbrella terms, such as "national belonging," in clearly evoking the emotional component crucial to both national identity and solidarity. At the same time, precisely because of its all-encompassing scope, it does not specifically assume interactions or ties between actors and does not replace the analytic importance of addressing and underlining the question of solidarity and social ties per se as a distinct aspect of national attachment.

STUDIES GOING BEYOND IDENTITY HAVE NOT GONE FAR ENOUGH

In recent years, a growing body of literature has questioned the uncritical acceptance and reification of national attachments as a fixed collective identity and drawn attention to the processes of institutionalization involved in producing and transforming popular imaginations of national identity. However, despite its promise, this literature has not expanded the prism of analysis to the institutional process involved in imagining other aspects of the national beyond identity, such as social relations between co-nationals. I delineate several arguments in this critical reappraisal of national identity discourse and related discussions of national solidarity and explain what I view as missed opportunities in this line of research.

In their influential work, Rogers Brubaker and Frederick Cooper (2000) argued that the salience of identity as a category of practice in national discourse does not require its use as a category of analysis. The uncritical use of identity when theorizing about nationalism may reify conceptions of the nation as an unchanged, fixed entity and replicate nationalist preconceptions of nations as "real communities" (5). As further elaborated by Siniša Malešević (2011), national identity has become a sweeping conceptual chimera used to describe assumed social reality or to offer a shortcut explanation for particular forms of collective behavior. Malešević noted how despite conceptual differences between modernist approaches (e.g., Gellner 1983) and ethno-symbolist approaches (e.g., Smith 1986) to nationalism, both consider collective identity as a key epistemological category, whether it is studied as an offshoot of pre-modern ethnic and religious attachments or as a product of structural transformations in modern societies.

Instead, Brubaker (1996) proposed an understanding of the nation as an institutionalized category of practice and directed attention to contingent historical events that helped shape these very processes of reification. In other words, analysts should seek to explain the processes through which the concept of the nation "crystallize[d], at certain moments, as a powerful, compelling reality" (Brubaker and Cooper 2000, 5). This "cognitive" perspective shifted attention from group identities such as race, ethnicity, and nationality to group-making activities of classification, categorization, and identification: "Groupings are not things *in* the world, but perspectives *on* the world—not ontological but epistemological realities" (Brubaker et al. 2004, 45). This approach emphasized the productive and transformative power of institutional processes as they engineer cognitive frames that engender nationality. A telling example is the Soviet classification system that, despite a repression of national ideology, institutionalized territorial and ethnic nationality as enduring social categories and as a legacy that later shaped post-Soviet nationalist politics (Brubaker 1996).[3] Malešević (2011) likewise suggested shifting attention to the historical and ideological processes that generate and reproduce such a widespread belief in national identity.

Similar attempts to problematize and destabilize essentialist conceptions of national identity have been made by several scholars within the ethnographic tradition who focused on processes of collective identification in everyday life. Richard Handler (1994) provided a pointed critique against studies of culture which employ the concept of identity in ways that underpin nationalist ideology. He argued that collective groupings should be taken as symbolic and communicative processes rather than bounded objects, for even "to talk about identity is to change or construct it" (30). Following Fredrik Barth's (1969) pioneering work on how ethnic identity is constituted through boundary-making interactions, Thomas Hylland Eriksen (1993) called for a more elaborated understanding of identities as situated and relational, distinguishing between "us-hood" and "we-hood" as distinct external and internal viewpoints in national identification (67).

In addition, building on Michael Billig's (1995) influential paradigm of "banal nationalism," researchers have considered the role of "ordinary people" as social agents actively producing representations of the nation during mundane, everyday activities and in the consumption of popular culture (Edensor 2002; Foster 2002). In particular, Jon Fox and Cynthia

Miller-Idriss (2008) explored how collective practices and cultural artifacts acquire national significance not because of their intrinsic properties but because of the ways meaning is attached to them by everyday users as a result of institutionally mediated choices.

However, the call to reject essentialist accounts of national identity and to avoid reification of nations does not in and of itself replace the *subject matter* of analysis and fails to provide the crucial shift away from the scholarly focus on identity. Brubaker (1996) recast national identity as a contingent form of classification that is a product of institutionalized collective action rather than its stable underlying cause (20). In replacing the notion of national identity as cause with national identity as product, this suggestion neither abandons group identity as the subject of study nor expands the prism of analysis to altogether different institutionalized aspects of imagining the national beyond identity.

Taken together, these various anti-essentialist and cognitive approaches to nationalism significantly advance our understanding of collective systems of identification and classification, foregrounding ethnographic perspectives and analytical tools that are highly valuable for studying how social actors attribute meaning to nationalism or ethnicity, such as boundary maintenance, transformative events, institutional practices, or us-hood versus we-hood. Yet, in the end, by proposing alternative terms to identity that nonetheless do "the theoretical work 'identity' is supposed to do" (Brubaker and Cooper 2000, 14), this critique remains within the bounds of national identity discourse.

The problem with the focus on identity in studies of nationalism is not only the reification of identity. It is, in addition, the privileging of actors (whether individuals or groups) as the primary unit of analysis and the overlooking or rejection of the role of the ties between actors as an equally important epistemological category. Brubaker and Cooper (2000) argued explicitly that for large-scale collectivities such as nations, "a strongly bounded sense of groupness…is likely to depend not on relational connectedness, but rather on a powerfully imagined and strongly felt commonality" (19–21). In this regard, privileging actors over interactions between actors is just as pervasive in constructionist approaches to nationalism as in traditional scholarship. Eriksen (2004) affirmed that interpersonal networks are rarely considered by sociologists writing about nationalism and noted in passing that solidarity grows out not only of shared commonalities but also out of trust and commitment that can only emerge through "enduring interaction" and acts of reciprocity

(56). Ultimately, rejecting connectedness in favor of commonality brings us right back to the study of identity.

Why Study Solidarity?

Although the distinction between mechanisms of cooperation and processes of identification is not clear-cut, such a distinction is analytically useful in bringing attention to the full range of practices involved in nation building and in maintaining national consciousness (Lainer-Vos 2012, 75). In most circumstances, we can expect feelings of solidarity among compatriots to converge with a deep sense of national identity. The engagement in exclusive cooperation and development of familiarity and mutual loyalty make it easier for participants to believe that they belong to the same nation. At the same time, acknowledgment of group commonalities is what defines the boundaries of this cooperation in the first place.

But the two processes may also diverge. For example, individuals who find it hard to identify with certain attributes of their ascribed national identity may still feel deeply connected to their fellow nationals by virtue of the multiple (nonsectarian) social institutions that they are embedded in and the shared sociability that they have experienced. In contrast, other individuals may find pride in their national identity despite having limited opportunities to engage in shared social institutions, minimal experiences of shared sociability, and weak feelings of connectedness to their fellow nationals. Thus, assuming the proposed distinction between identification and solidarity is indeed viable, if we were to make a comparison between individuals within a given country, we could expect that: (a) Those who have participated significantly in (nonsectarian) social institutions in the course of their lives will report higher levels of connectedness and feelings of national solidarity than individuals with limited participation in shared social clubs; and (b) while predictive of national solidarity, such high participation in social institutions may be somewhat less predictive of reported levels of national identification.

We could also make a related comparison across countries. According to the theoretical model presented here, citizens are likely to report higher levels of national solidarity in countries with greater access to and participation in nonsectarian social institutions than in countries with limited opportunities to participate in institutional life. Thus, in a cross-country comparison the extent of participation in social institutions is likely to be more predictive of national solidarity than of national identification. While an empirical examination of these predictions is beyond the present scope, such an inquiry could enrich our understanding of nationness beyond the prism of identity.

Shifting the focus of study to solidarity and framing solidarity in terms of sociability could also prove beneficial in the continuing debate on the historical periodization of the nation-state. A growing body of work challenges the empirical and conceptual validity of the modernist approach, which considers nationalism a distinctly modern phenomenon. Gorski (2000) reviewed historical evidence for the existence of various national movements and ideologies in medieval and early modern European polities and contended that contrary to the modernists' search for universal, essentialist accounts of nationalism and its causality, periodization, and scope, what is needed "is not a deep definition, but a superficial one...one might define nationalism as any set of discourses or practices that invoke 'the nation' or equivalent categories" (1461). Although I agree that we should forego deep definitions of national ideology given the diversity and heterogeneity of nationalist discourses and practices, we should not abandon the quest to understand the deep meanings underlying people's general sense of national attachment.

And while I also concur with Gorski (2000, 1461) that the modernist attempt to provide universal answers to key wh-questions such as "what is nationalism?," "when did it happen?," and "why does it happen?"—and, one could add, "who does it include?"—is bound to fail, I suggest instead that we raise a fifth question that can be framed in universal terms. In keeping with the age-old Durkhemian query "how do societies cohere?," this question asks, "how do national communities cohere?" and, more specifically, "how do compatriots bond with one another?" Once the national question is construed in terms of mechanisms that are relatively context-free rather than in terms of historical effects and once these general mechanisms are then explored in specific institutional and cultural contexts, it might be easier to place and relocate the answers within an historical framework.

This is the explanatory logic that guides the present work. While most of this book is devoted to theorizing general mechanisms of public intimacy and to elaborating how they engender feelings of solidarity in specific case studies of social club sociability, I also offer tentative suggestions as to why, on the whole, the historic spread of national consciousness (but not the rise of specific national movements and discourses) can be linked to the modern era. Specifically, in Chapter 3, I connect the rise of national consciousness with growing participation in (nonsectarian) social clubs and, consequently, with the ever-growing demands to turn strangers into friends; demands which can be situated in the historical processes of modernization and institutional differentiation. Without diminishing the importance of studying specific discourses and cognitive processes of categorization that lead to the crystallization of national identity at certain historical moments (Brubaker 1996; Gorski 2000), a study of social ties between compatriots that centers on the meso-level of social institutions and applies historically informed ethnographic research can provide a complementary avenue for exploring national attachments.[4]

National Solidarity as an Abstract Tie Between Strangers

Despite widespread recognition among theorists of nationalism that compatriots experience strong ties of "comradeship" or "fraternity," there is little systematic exploration of how such ties between distant others are imagined as a close-knit bond. As underscored by Malešević (2011), neither modernist nor ethno-symbolist perspectives have sufficiently addressed the processes that mobilized people to extend their loyalties from the small, kinship-based groupings toward large-scale collectivities. Indeed, this question seems too often to be overlooked, taken for granted, or explicitly rejected as a valid direction of analysis. For example, Anderson's (1991) ground-breaking phenomenological approach highlighted how gradual changes in technology and communication enabled people to perceive the abstract idea of the nation as directly relevant to their daily lives and as lending meaning to the arbitrariness of death. But even as he noted that this new consciousness is imagined as a horizontal comradeship, Anderson stopped short of examining precisely that, namely, the mechanisms that render national solidarity a transparent, close-knit social bond. In a similar fashion, as noted by Malešević (2004), Anthony Smith's (1986) ethno-symbolist approach follows a Durkheimian distinction between traditional solidarity premised on resemblance of kin and modern national solidarity premised on functional interdependence. While noting that national societies are conceived as a collectivity of autonomous yet quasi-egalitarian individuals linked by "impersonal but fraternal" ties (1986, 170), Smith offered little analysis of this tension between the impersonal and the fraternal.

Several scholars of nationalism have explicitly rejected the comparison between collective solidarity and close-knit bonds of friendship, instead bringing up the notion of strangership (Brunkhorst 2005; Calhoun 1991). Following Simmel's (1950) writing on the role of strangers in modern society (1950, 402–408, 409–424), sociologists and cultural theorists began to employ the term strangership to denote a form of impersonal yet socially and politically significant form of interaction between individuals in modern society (Karakayali 2006; Mallory 2012). Strangers were taken to be social actors embodied in mutual acts of recognition (Ahmed 2000) who could, therefore, also engage in a productive form of solidarity, such as in a civil society of strangers (e.g., Vernon 2014). As discussed by Mervyn Horgan (2012), building on Erving Goffman's (1963, 84) notion of "civil inattention," relations between strangers require physical co-presence and mutual agreement about forming a space of non-hostile recognition and indifference. Since encounters between strangers often increase as a result of social mobility, strangership may act as an equalizing force (Horgan 2012), as, for example, in eighteenth-century European coffee houses where people of different social classes engaged in shared practices of sociability (Davetian 2009).

A similar claim about the equalizing force of strangership and its productive role in society has been made in connection with non-present mass audiences. John Hartley (1999) discussed how television brings together individuals who "may otherwise display few connections among themselves and positions them as its audience 'indifferently,' according to all viewers the same 'rights' and promoting among them a sense of common identity as television audiences" (158). In a discussion of audience "witnessing" during media events, Paul Frosh (2006) further maintained that, similar to civil inattention, contemporary mediated relations between strangers habituate individuals to the otherness of others and create a productive and morally enabling form of indifferent civil equivalence among strangers. Such relations sustain "the thin threads by which the most distant and different can be bound together" and share similar (albeit the most general) features "only because they connect a great many people" (280, and quoting Simmel 1950, 406).

Following Paddy Scannell (2000), Frosh noted how television addresses its audiences by intertwining the impersonal and the personal:

It is directed to anyone who happens to be watching (or listening) and not tailor-made for a particular individual, yet it nonetheless addresses the individual viewer directly, quite often informally and with apparent intimacy. This "for-anyone-as-someone" structure of contemporary broadcasting (Scannell 2000, 5) can be linked to the care structure of modern society, for it enables us to care about the lives of others without knowing them personally. While avoiding the exclusiveness of intimacy, Frosh (2006) argued that these depersonalized relations enable viewers to feel sufficiently similar to other viewers to be able to imagine what it might be like to be in their shoes and to empathize with them. As he concluded, media witnessing reveals how "the care structure of modern society is that to be someone you must first be anyone. Its unrealized ideal is that anyone can be someone" (281).

It is precisely on this latter note that discussions of strangership as a form of solidarity appear to miss a crucial point. By noting in passing that the "unrealized ideal" of modern society is that "anyone can be someone," Frosh (2006) inadvertently invoked—not the structural constraints of mass society, which he charted compellingly throughout his analysis—but the fundamental cultural structure of a national community; to put it in relational terms, it is the ideal that strangers can be friends. In contrast to Frosh, I would therefore argue that from a phenomenological and cultural sociological perspective the ideal of being someone—or, rather, of being someone's friend—is, in fact, part and parcel of the care structure of society; it is proclaimed and partly realized on a daily basis in social institutions and expresses itself in the paradox at the heart of this book, namely that compatriots constantly imagine the nation as a community of friends, even as they know that in reality it is an abstract collectivity of strangers.

The widespread understanding of contemporary mass solidarity as a relationship between strangers can be traced back to classic liberal thought and is couched in the modern distinction between friendship as a strictly personal bond and solidarity as a political bond (Kaplan 2006; Mallory 2012). Allan Silver (1990) explained that liberal Enlightenment theorists envisioned modern civil society as based on cooperation between sympathetic but disinterested strangers described as "authentically indifferent co-citizens" (1482). Replacing the dichotomy of "friend" versus "enemy" in premodern tribal politics, this emotionally regulated civil solidarity allowed for a new kind of intimate and interpersonal friendship that was to inhabit a distinctive domain of private life, detached from impersonal public interactions (Silver 1990).

It is possibly this prevailing distinction between personal friendship and collective solidarity as well as the novel conceptualization of strangership as a productive form of co-present or mediated interaction that predisposed some contemporary theorists to look upon national solidarity as an abstract relationship and to dissociate it from interpersonal ties. Craig Calhoun (1991, 1997) presented the most articulate argument in this vein. First, he drew an analytic distinction between the "relational" and "categorical" modes of identification (foreshadowing Brubaker and Cooper's (2000) aforementioned reappraisal of national identity discourse). He argued that in large-scale collectivities individuals are linked through their membership in a set of abstract categorical attributes rather than through their participation in webs of concrete interpersonal relationships (Calhoun 1997, 46).

Second, Calhoun (1991) made a related claim with regard to solidarity, rejecting the use of equivalent terms to "refer simultaneously to face-to-face networks and whole nations" because "on a larger scale, community in the sense of dense, multiplex networks of interpersonal relationships becomes impossible" (222). Instead, he posited, large-scale solidarity reflects impersonal relationships between strangers. The prototypical stranger relationships take place in public settings or "publics," understood as "arenas in which people speak to each other at least in part as strangers" (223). In such settings, as opposed to personal interactions, it is the merits of the arguments and not the identities of the arguers that are crucial. People in publics, he claimed, are not bound by dense webs of common understandings or shared social ties and have to "establish rather than take for granted where they agree and disagree" (223).

Informed by conceptions of the modern public sphere as an abstract, depersonalized arena for communicating a rational-critical discourse (Habermas 1991), Michael Warner (2002) made a similar association between publics and nations, arguing that an environment of strangerhood and norms of disinterested subjects have become the hallmark of modern life: "The modern social imaginary does not make sense without strangers. A nation, market, or public in which everyone could be known personally would be no nation, market, or public at all" (57).

An understanding of collective solidarity as a form of disinterested sympathy between strangers bound by a commitment to abstract principles is consistent with the internal logic of classic liberal ideology (Silver 1990). But it underestimates the degree of connectedness between fellow citizens in modern states where people live in relatively enduring, multiple interdependent relationships (Honohan 2001). And while there is, by definition, no nation in which everyone could be known personally, the point is that if we want to understand the phenomenology of national attachment, this imagined continuum between personal familiarity and collective solidarity is worthy of study in its own right.

Lastly, among the few scholars to call attention to the centrality of national solidarity, the position taken by Malešević (2011) is most telling. On the one hand, he affirmed the importance of solidarity in lieu of identity as an object of study in order to examine how it is possible "to make a person feel so attached to an abstract entity that he or she allegedly expresses willingness to treat and cherish this entity in the same way one cherishes his or her close family?" (282). On the other hand, instead of taking this question at face value, Malešević seemed to reject the very idea that this imagined continuum between personal and collective attachments should be thus explored. Rather, he suggested that it is epistemologically important to analyze them separately as two different phenomena, arguing that the organizationally produced interactions that characterize large-scale entities such as nations are not a "real" form of solidarity. In particular, Malešević contended contra Durkheim that "genuine, deep-felt emotional solidarity is only possible on the micro, face-to-face level of interactions where individuals are familiar and physically interact with other individuals" (284). By presupposing that some social ties are more genuine and real than others, Malešević did not pay sufficient heed to the phenomenology of solidarity as a social tie and stopped short of providing a substantial alternative to the study of identity.

Bringing Friendship Back In

The rise of modern nationalism is closely related to the partial decline in the role of kinship ties as a central organizing principle of the social order and the rise of friendship as an alternative principle. The increasing importance of friendship, however, has gone largely unacknowledged, mostly due to the aforementioned modern divide between personal ties of friendship and collective ties of solidarity; the former are regarded in liberal thought as detached from the social order, while the latter are seen as central but remain profoundly undertheorized.

A diverse body of literature has challenged the dichotomy of interpersonal friendship and collective solidarity. This can be roughly divided into three main lines of research. The first, mainly anthropological, contests the Eurocentric and modern-centric link between friendship and heightened individualism and explores how practices of friendship are embedded in the wider societal context and carry collective significance (Bell and Coleman 1999; Desai and Killick 2010). Male homosocial enclaves, in particular, have received rich ethnographic attention (Gutmann 1997) with studies that have addressed practices of friendship as varied as joking relations among fraternity students (Lyman 1987), café sociability among working-class men (Vale de Almeida 1996), and reciprocal acts of animal theft among villagers (Herzfeld 1985).

In his seminal study of preadolescent boys participating in Little League baseball, Gary Alan Fine (1987) called attention to the localized "idioculture"—the system of shared beliefs, behaviors, and customs—that emerges in small groups and depends on both individual and collective ties of friendship ("chum" and "gang," respectively) (8–9). Fine pointed out that friendship is not simply an affective bond charged with positive feelings. It is "also a staging area for interaction, a cultural institution for the transmission of knowledge and performance techniques," and one which "has implications for interaction within and outside of the friendship bond" (Fine 1988, 225). Fine's later theory of "tiny publics" (Fine 2012a; Fine and Harrington 2004), while less focused on friendship per se, laid out a research agenda for exploring how collective solidarity emerges from interactions in the small group. By providing a structure for affiliation and cohesion, groups offer a model for participation in larger social settings. Some ethnographic work on identity formation in social movements likewise noted the various ways that friendship ties served as a vehicle for communal solidarity (e.g., Polletta 2002; Tavory and Goodman 2009).

A second line of research which has explicitly contested the public–private divide in studies of friendship can be found in historical and gender scholarship that has examined male fraternal friendship as a key cultural trope for mobilizing national identification (Kaplan 2006; Lake 1992; Mosse 1982; Nelson 1998). While these studies highlighted rhetorical and performative practices—such as popular literature and rituals of commemoration—through which hegemonic representations of male homosociality figure in specific national cultures, they did not provide a broader conceptual understanding of how the bonds of friendship are linked to the political sphere.

The third and most extensive discussions of friendship as a collective sentiment can be found in the work of political theorists who investigated friendship as a normative model for civic or national attachments (Allen 2004; Devere and Smith 2010; Honohan 2001; Mallory 2012; Schwarzenbach 1996; Yack 2012). I briefly elaborate on some of this literature, much of which is based on Aristotle's views on civic friendship as discussed in *Nicomachean Ethics*. As delineated by Sibyl Schwarzenbach (1996, 2015), Aristotle's conceptualization of genuine and virtuous friendship entails a reciprocal awareness of the other as a moral equal, goodwill toward the other for the sake of the other and not for oneself, and practical doing for the other. These qualities can extend from personal friendship to the political sphere as the binding force of the community, allowing citizens to experience a form of friendship with each other and do things for their fellow citizens both individually and as a citizen body on the basis of shared values, goals, and a sense of justice. Moreover, in such a just society the values of friendship ideally become indirectly embodied in the basic structure of society, its laws, and its institutions (Schwarzenbach 2015). Within this framework, the fundamental quality of good citizenship is friendship. Individuals who conduct themselves openly as friends to one another will make better citizens, have a capacity for (critical) loyalty, and act as equal agents in the community (Frazer 2008).

Aristotle, however, favored a selective and elitist citizenship regime, much less egalitarian than the democratic vision of modern civil societies (Brunkhorst 2005). Schwarzenbach (2015) thus underscored how Aristotle's vision presupposed an "equal fraternal" model of friendship based a priori on sameness and equal standing (a relation between two self-sufficient, virtuous, and similarly situated male friends) and precluded a model of friendship based on difference and diversity (in terms of age, gender, class, religion, race, or culture) (8).

Danielle Allen (2004) connected this Aristotelian framework to the problem of solidarity among strangers. She described how strangers can negotiate norms of democratic citizenship through practices of political friendship considered a set of hard-won habits used to bridge individual, social, and racial differences. Despite having different lives, friends share common events, environments, and social structures. Political friendship begins from this recognition of a shared horizon of experience and moves to a second recognition "that a core citizenly responsibility is to prove oneself trustworthy to fellow citizens" (Allen 2004, xxii). In order to win this trust, one must interact self-confidently with strangers. Only by engaging in reciprocal interactions and conversations can strangers turn into political friends, drawing each other into networks of mutual responsibility and developing a political bond sustained by equitable rather than rivalrous self-interest.

Lastly, Iseult Honohan (2001) offered some qualifications to Aristotle's notion of civic friendship. While adopting the basic assumption that personal ties can serve as a normative model for collective ties, she argued that relations between citizens are comparable only to a specific kind of personal relations, namely to ties between colleagues and not to personal friendships, familial bonds, or interactions between strangers. People's civic responsibilities are grounded in irregularly extending and overlapping networks. This interdependence entails special obligations without being as radically exclusive and sharply bounded as national attachment but also without being too thin to generate commitment as in the case of cosmopolitan identification. In order to address the particular obligations of citizenship, Honohan opted for a social tie that is less intimate, committed, emotional, and voluntary than friendship and came up with collegial relationships. Unlike personal friends and similar to colleagues, "citizenship does not lose its meaning when 'diluted,' even if direct contact with many fellow-citizens remains latent rather than being realized" (63–64).

I have found this comparison between colleagues, friends, and civic and national ties to be instructive on various levels. Above all, it informs my own formulation of the ties between co-nationals as analogous to membership in social clubs. Relations between social club members can be situated exactly in between relations with colleagues and close friendships. Social club interactions are emotionally more expressive and less instrumental than collegial relationships and, in this respect, are better suited to account for national than for civic attachment. At the same time, such membership does not preclude civic aspects of solidarity, an issue which I address in Chapter 6.

Taken together, these various analytic discussions have provided important justifications for bringing friendship back into the study of public and political life. But the argument they make has remained largely at the discursive level. In line with Fine's (1988, 225) aforementioned depiction of friendship as a "staging area," a social performance that has wider collective significance, what is called for is a more grounded and empirical approach in order to address the question of a continuum between interpersonal ties and macro-level solidarity and to explore how the social bonds of friendship stimulate national attachment.

NOTES

1. A simple search in *Google Scholar* can illustrate this disparity. A search for article titles with the phrase "national identity" and "national identities" conducted on September 24, 2017, resulted in 23,600 hits. The phrase "national solidarity," on the other hand, yielded only 282 references. After combining additional terms related to solidarity, "national integration" (2090 entries), "national unity" (1700 entries), and "national cohesion" (149 entries), these article titles are still outnumbered by titles with the term "national identity" by a ratio of almost 1:6. The search was conducted with option "all in title."
2. More recently, Robin Wagner-Pacifici (2010) laid down a programmatic framework for studying such epistemological shifts in social meaning by proposing a comprehensive eventful approach that attends to the performative, demonstrative-orientational, and mimetic-representational features underlying historical transformations.
3. In this, Brubaker (1996, 24) adopted a new institutionalist perspective that emphasizes the constitutive rather than merely constraining role of institutions. I adopt a similar approach in considering the crucial role of social clubs in constituting sociability and solidarity.
4. See Fine (2012b) for a general argument on the role of meso-level group interactions in establishing social order and contributing to civil society.

REFERENCES

Ahmed, Sara. 2000. *Strange Encounters: Embodied Others in Post-Coloniality*. London: Routledge.

Allen, Danielle. 2004. *Talking to Strangers: Anxieties of Citizenship Since Brown V. Board of Education*. Chicago: University of Chicago Press.

Anderson, Benedict. [1983] 1991. *Imagined Communities: Reflections on the Origins and Spread of Nationalism*. London: Verso.

Barth, Fredrik. 1969. "Introduction." In *Ethnic Groups and Boundaries: The Social Organization of Culture Difference*, edited by Fredrik Barth, 1–38. London: Allen & Unwin.

Bell, Sandra, and Simon Coleman, eds. 1999. *The Anthropology of Friendship*. Oxford: Berg.
Billig, Michael. 1995. *Banal Nationalism*. London: Sage.
Brubaker, Rogers. 1996. *Nationalism Reframed: Nationhood and the National Question in the New Europe*. Cambridge: Cambridge University Press.
Brubaker, Rogers, and Frederick Cooper. 2000. "Beyond 'Identity'." *Theory and Society* 29 (1): 1–47.
Brubaker, Rogers, Mara Loveman, and Peter Stamatov. 2004. "Ethnicity as Cognition." *Theory and Society* 33 (1): 31–64.
Brunkhorst, Hauke. 2005. *Solidarity: From Civic Friendship to a Global Legal Community*. Translated by Jeffrey Flynn. London: Routledge.
Calhoun, Craig. 1991. "Nationalism, Political Community and the Representation of Society: Or, Why Feeling at Home is Not a Substitute for Public Space." *European Journal of Social Theory* 2: 217–231.
Calhoun, Craig. 1997. *Nationalism*. Minneapolis: University of Minnesota Press.
Davetian, Benet. 2009. *Civility: A Cultural History*. Toronto: Toronto University Press.
Desai, Amit, and Evan Killick, eds. 2010. *The Ways of Friendship: Anthropological Perspectives*. New York: Berghahn.
Devere, Heather, and Graham M. Smith. 2010. "Friendship and Politics." *Political Studies Review* 8 (3): 341–356.
Edensor, Tim. 2002. *National Identity, Popular Culture and Everyday Life*. Oxford: Berg.
Eriksen, Thomas Hylland. 1993. *Ethnicity and Nationalism: Anthropological Perspectives*. London: Pluto.
Eriksen, Thomas Hylland. 2004. "Place, Kinship and the Case for Non-Ethnic Nations." *Nations and Nationalism* 10 (1–2): 49–62.
Fine, Gary Alan. 1987. *With the Boys: Little League Baseball and Preadolescent Culture*. Chicago: University of Chicago Press.
Fine, Gary Alan. 1988. "Friends, Impression Management, and Preadolescent Behavior." In *Childhood Socialization*, ed. Gerald Handel, 209–234. New Brunswick, NJ: Transaction.
Fine, Gary Alan. 2012a. *Tiny Publics: A Theory of Group Action and Culture*. New York: Russell Sage Foundation.
Fine, Gary Alan. 2012b. "Group Culture and the Interaction Order: Local Sociology on the Meso-Level." *Annual Review of Sociology* 38: 159–179.
Fine, Gary Alan, and Brooke Harrington. 2004. "Tiny Publics: Small Groups and Civil Society." *Sociological Theory* 22 (3): 341–356.
Foster, Robert J. 2002. *Materializing the Nation: Commodities, Consumption, and Media in Papua New Guinea*. Bloomington, IN: Indiana University Press.
Fox, Jon E., and Cynthia Miller-Idriss. 2008. "Everyday Nationhood." *Ethnicities* 8 (4): 536–563.

Frazer, Elizabeth 2008. "Mary Wollstonecraft on Politics and Friendship." *Political Studies* 56 (1): 237–256.
Frosh, Paul. 2006. "Telling Presences: Witnessing, Mass Media, and the Imagined Lives of Strangers." *Critical Studies in Media Communication* 23 (4): 265–284.
Gellner, Ernst. 1983. *Nations and Nationalism*. Oxford: Blackwell.
Goffman, Ervin. 1963. *Behavior in Public Places: Notes on the Social Organization of Gatherings*. New York: The Free Press.
Gorski, Philip S. 2000. "The Mosaic Moment: An Early Modernist Critique of Modernist Theories of Nationalism." *American Journal of Sociology* 105 (5): 1428–1468.
Gutmann, Matthew C. 1997. "Trafficking in Men: The Anthropology of Masculinity." *Annual Review of Anthropology* 26: 385–409.
Habermas, Jürgen. [1962] 1991. *The Structural Transformation of the Public Sphere: An Inquiry into a Category of Bourgeois Society*. Cambridge, MA: MIT Press.
Handler, Richard. 1994. "Is Identity a Useful Cross-Cultural Concept?" In *Commemorations: The Politics of National Identity*, edited by John Gillis, 27–40. Princeton: Princeton University Press.
Hartley, John. 1999. *Uses of Television*. London: Routledge.
Herzfeld, Michael. 1985. *Poetics of Manhood: Contest and Identity in a Cretan Mountain Village*. Princeton: Princeton University Press.
Hobsbawm, Erik. 1991. *Nations and Nationalism Since 1780: Programme, Myth, Reality*. Cambridge: Cambridge University Press.
Honohan, Iseult. 2001. "Friends, Strangers or Countrymen? The Ties Between Citizens as Colleagues." *Political Studies* 49 (1): 51–69.
Horgan, Mervyn. 2012. "Strangers and Strangership." *Journal of Intercultural Studies* 33 (6): 607–622.
Kaplan, Danny. 2006. *The Men We Loved: Male Friendship and Nationalism in Israeli Culture*. New York: Berghahn Books.
Karakayali, Nedim. 2006. "The Uses of the Stranger: Circulation, Arbitration, Secrecy, and Dirt." *Sociological Theory* 24 (4): 312–330.
Lainer-Vos, Dan. 2012. "Manufacturing National Attachments: Gift-Giving, Market Exchange and the Construction of Irish and Zionist Diaspora Bonds." *Theory and Society* 41 (1): 73–106.
Lake, Marilyn. 1992. "Mission Impossible: How Men Gave Birth to the Australian Nation: Nationalism, Gender and Other Seminal Acts." *Gender & History* 4 (3): 305–322.
Lyman, Peter. 1987. "The Fraternal Bond as a Joking Relationship: A Case Study of the Role of Sexist Jokes in Male Group Bonding." In *Changing Men: New Directions in Research on Men and Masculinity*, edited by Michael Kimmel, 148–163. Newbury Park: Sage.
Malešević, Siniša. 2004. "'Divine Ethnies' and 'Sacred Nations': Anthony D. Smith and the Neo-Durkhemian Theory of Nationalism." *Nationalism and Ethnic Politics* 10 (4): 561–593.

Malešević, Siniša. 2011. "The Chimera of National Identity." *Nations and Nationalism* 17 (2): 272–290.
Mallory, Peter. 2012. "Friendship and Strangership: Rethinking Political Friendship Through the Work of Adam Smith." *Journal of Intercultural Studies* 33 (6): 591–605.
Mosse, George L. 1982. "Friendship and Nationhood: About the Promise and Failure of German Nationalism." *Journal of Contemporary History* 17: 351–367.
Nelson, Dana D. 1998. *National Manhood: Capitalist Citizenship and the Imagined Fraternity of White Men*. Durham, NC: Duke University Press.
Polletta, Francesca. 2002. *Freedom Is an Endless Meeting: Democracy in American Social Movements*. Chicago: Chicago University Press.
Scannell, Paddy. 2000. "For-anyone-as-someone structures." *Media, Culture & Society* 22(1): 5–24.
Schwarzenbach, Sibyl. 1996. "On Civic Friendship." *Ethics* 107: 97–128.
Schwarzenbach, Sibyl. 2015. "Fraternity, Solidarity and Civic Friendship." *AMITY: The Journal of Friendship Studies* 3 (1): 3–18.
Silver, Allan. 1990. "Friendship in Commercial Society: Eighteenth-Century Social Theory and Modern Sociology." *American Journal of Sociology* 95 (6): 1474–1504.
Simmel, Georg. [1915] 1950. *The Sociology of Georg Simmel*. Translated by Kurt H. Wolff. Glencoe, IL: Free Press.
Smith, Anthony D. 1986. *The Ethnic Origins of Nations*. Oxford: Blackwell.
Smith, Anthony D. 2009. *Ethno-Symbolism and Nationalism: A Cultural Approach*. London: Routledge.
Tavory, Iddo, and Yehuda C. Goodman. 2009. "'A Collective of Individuals': Between Self and Solidarity in a Rainbow Gathering." *Sociology of Religion* 70 (3): 262–284.
Vale de Almeida, Miguel. 1996. *The Hegemonic Male: Masculinity in a Portuguese Town*. Providence: Berghahn.
Vernon, James. 2014. *Distant Strangers: How Britain Became Modern*. Berkeley: University of California Press.
Wagner-Pacifici, Robin. 2010. "Theorizing the Restlessness of Events." *American Journal of Sociology* 115 (5): 1351–1386.
Warner, Michael. 2002. "Publics and Counterpublics." *Public Culture* 14 (1): 49–90.
Wimmer, Andreas, and Yuval Feinstein. 2010. "The Rise of the Nation-State Across the World, 1816 to 2001." *American Sociological Review* 75 (5): 764–790.
Yack, Bernard. 2012. *Nationalism and the Moral Psychology of Community*. Chicago: University of Chicago Press.

CHAPTER 3

Social Club Sociability

THE QUEST FOR COMMUNITY IN INTERMEDIATE INSTITUTIONS

Ever since Max Weber characterized the nation as "a community of sentiment which would adequately manifest itself in a state of its own" (Gerth and Wright Mills 1998, 176), theories of nationalism have sought to understand the rise and spread of nation-states as a sense of and quest for community in modern societies. In this, students of nationalism draw on the Great Divide within sociological thought between "community" and "society" (James 1996), which goes back to Ferdinand Tönnies' (1955) distinction between Gemeinschaft and Gesellschaft. Theorists fall back on this divide either to identify national ideology as an attempt to re-enchant modern structures with primordial meanings, or, on the contrary, to associate the nation-state with the transformative structures of modern polity. Homi Bhabha (2013) called attention to the systematic ambiguity in narrating and theorizing about the nation as a realm of both the social and the political: "The nation's 'coming into being' as a system of cultural signification, as the representation of social life rather than the discipline of social polity, emphasizes this instability of knowledge" (2).

The focus on the nation as a form of community is a central theme in the neo-Durkheimian school. Although Durkheim wrote very little on nationalism explicitly (Smith 1983, 30), one could argue that in theorizing about society he was actually looking at the problem of nation formation and national revival (Dingley 2008). And while his insights into collective solidarity projected back to premodern, tribal societies, his account of religious social life has been increasingly called upon to explain ideological reactions to dilemmas of modern political life (Thompson 1993; Alexander 1988), for instance, seeing political revolutions as an attempt to revive the sacredness of the nation over the profanations of the state (Tiryakian 1988). Similarly, Anderson's (1991) work on the national imagination can be understood as simply asking how mass society is imagined as a community. However, as I noted earlier in the introduction, most of Anderson's analysis centered on the transformations of modern polities and how these lead people to imagine an abstract collectivity rather than a close-knit entity.

Peter Simonson (1996) saw one tradition of thought in this long-standing sociological concern with community as following what he termed the "Gemeinschaft pole" in community talk, which has been preoccupied with the question of close-knit social relations (325).[1] Against the backdrop of an atomistic modern society, in which social ties are mainly utilitarian and rationalized and bounded by political contract, this school of thought understands community as a sense of social ties based on close-knit and affect-laden interactions, high social integration, and strong conformity to localized customs, norms, and values (e.g., Fernback 2007; Etzioni 1996). An enduring historical narrative within this tradition considers group solidarity as a precious commodity (Malešević 2011) connected to nostalgia for past or eclipsed ways of life (Simonson 1996). This translates into a programmatic inquiry into how a sense of integrated and cohesive community remains possible in modern societies or should be restored and reproduced (Thomson 2005). This question has, subsequently, been approached empirically using diverse analytic constructs ranging from collective effervescence (Durkheim 2003), primary groups (Cooley 1962), and to social capital (Putnam 2000), social networks (Wellman 2002), and interaction ritual chains (Collins 2004), many of which I discuss below.

Within this context, Durkheimian scholarship has often turned to intermediate institutions between private and public life as a means to overcome the Great Divide between community and society and to address the question of mass solidarity, often with little direct allusion to national attachment but rather to issues of civic solidarity and democracy. This doctrine, often referred to as "associationalism," was famously advanced by Alexis de Tocqueville (2003) who considered the institutionally organized realm of sociability taking place in civic associations as beneficial for wider societal integration. Civic associations allowed people to engage in differentiated, interpersonal interactions based on horizontal bonds of friendship through which they could negotiate the nature of their common life (Mallory 2012). Durkheim's (1960) view was even more explicit:

> A nation can be maintained only if between the State and the individual, there is intercalated a whole series of secondary groups near enough to the individuals to attract them strongly in their sphere of action and drag them, in this way, into the general torrent of social life. (28)

Accordingly, secondary associations not only assist in overcoming alienation but also promote positive forms of individualism by enabling members to develop collective loyalties independent of state rule or familial allegiances.

The doctrine of associationalism remained influential in twentieth-century social thought. As part of his interest in the emergence of public opinion, Jürgen Habermas (1991) connected specific forms of localized civic associations with democratic culture, noting especially the rise of bourgeois café culture and salons in eighteenth-century Europe, which provided a differentiated public sphere freely accessed by citizens. Ideally, this authentic public sphere established by private people suspended the power and authority of state institutions. It enabled citizens to exchange ideas and deliberate about common affairs by engaging in face-to-face, yet depersonalized, rational, and critical debate.

In the USA, associationalism first appeared in the form of mass society theory (Kornhauser 2013) and, more recently, in social capital theory (Putnam 2000; Putnam et al. 1993), both of which were concerned with mass alienation or decreased interpersonal trust and emphasized the importance of tying individuals to localized, horizontal associations (Thomson 2005). Robert Putnam considered mutual, face-to-face interactions in localized voluntary groups as a social good conducive to wider societal welfare and cohesion and argued that the interpersonal networks and norms of reciprocity that develop in civic associations—including leisure activity organizations such as choral societies and bowling leagues—are important for democracy and civic solidarity irrespective of the content of the association or its ideological purpose.

These various associational views of civil society have been criticized extensively. As reviewed by Theiss-Morse Theiss-Morse and Hibbing (2005), the empirical support for the assumption that joining civic associations increases democratic values and fosters political participation is rather weak and can be refuted on various grounds: First, that civic groups may hold non-democratic goals and values or be disdainful of the political process; second, that even when democratic procedures are practiced within a group, they don't necessarily generalize beyond the group; and third, that competition between multiple civic groups may lead to fragmentation and distrust in government involvement.[2]

Nina Eliasoph (1996) argued against the assumption that civic associations impact the public sphere and disseminate a wide range of ideas. Following an interaction-centered analysis of American civic activism, she found that activists expressed different beliefs from one context to the next. In particular, whenever they broadened the circulation of their political ideas and made them public, these ideas narrowed and became less open to debate and less connected to the wider world. Eliasoph concluded that simply advocating civic participation is not enough for creating group contexts that enable freewheeling conversations on common concerns and explicit expressions of political engagement. Alexander (2006, 99) further highlighted that it is not the mere existence of rich associational life that is instrumental in democratic life nor the public engagement in rational deliberation (as assumed by Habermas 1991); rather, it is whether associations display an outward civil orientation and are able to publicly communicate and justify their interests. Alexander emphasized that this question cannot be answered through an interactionist account of civic practices alone but also requires an examination of underlying symbolic cultural structures, such as the discourse of civil society which provides a universal source of legitimacy for civic action.

Why Social Clubs?

Despite their differences, the various theories and critics of civil society and solidarity described above—both those endorsing associationalism and those rejecting it—share what is, essentially, a normative approach: They focus on whether, how, and exactly which middle-range associations operate in ways that assist the common good of society, understood primarily in terms of political participation and democracy. As Theiss-Morse and Hibbing (2005) concluded in their review of associationalism, the key of their critic "is letting people know that becoming active in their favorite clubs does not fulfill their citizenship obligations" (245).

My approach departs from this debate by rejecting both the instrumental and normative implications of associational life and adopting instead an *expressive* dimension. There is, I believe, something to be said about the way that myriad forms of intermediate social institutions—from state organizations and civic associations to interactive media practices—share the basic act of making friends and through it project feelings of solidarity to the wider community. I further argue that these feelings are best captured by an undifferentiated civic-national model of solidarity, an issue which I take on in Chapter 6.[3]

While I agree with Putnam that middle-range social institutions matter for collective solidarity regardless of their content or ideological purpose, I claim that this is not because the kind of social organization and cooperation required for singing in choirs or bowling in leagues necessarily contributes to democracy but, instead, because it binds the participants in a shared sociability which carries collective—aka national—significance.[4] By the same token, people who join associations need not publicly justify their civic-moral standing, as suggested by Alexander (2006), in order for them to enact the emotional building blocks of national solidarity.

To highlight this expressive dimension of social institutions, I suggest replacing terms such as "secondary," "voluntary," or "civic associations" and simply considering them as broadly defined "social clubs." Social clubs occasion interpersonal encounters between members that typically revolve around a common activity, interest, or purpose, establish criteria for membership, and prescribe certain rules of conduct. But their moral purpose, effect, and organizational structure notwithstanding, social clubs constitute an arena of sociability through which members are transformed from unaffiliated strangers into acquaintances and friends. Furthermore, club membership carries collective significance. As noted by Barbara Black (2012), who conducted a wide-ranging study of nineteenth-century British male club culture, participation in social clubs satisfies a "fundamental human desire to join like-minded comrades as a way of forging community beyond blood ties" (27).

Simmel (1949) considered sociability an informal social interaction pursued for its own sake irrespective of anything the participants have to gain from it. Whereas sociality denotes the entire matrix of social relations in which individuals are embedded, such informal sociability builds on a desire for mutual interaction devoid of any instrumental end, a social exchange in which the mere expressive dimension of the interaction "becomes its own self-sufficient content" (259). This "play-form of association" (255) is often confined to fleeting moments in a social interaction and can easily drift into an overly objective, purposeful exchange or, on the contrary, a preoccupation with overly personal matters. But whenever pure sociability takes place, it enables a sense of communitas and equality:

> It demands the purest, most transparent, most engaging kind of interaction—that among *equals*. It must, because of its very nature, posit beings who give up so much of their objective content, who are so modified in both their outward and their inner significance, that they are socially equal, and every one of them can win sociability values for himself only under the condition that the others, interacting with him, can also win them. It is a game in which one 'acts' as though all were equal, as though he especially esteemed everyone. (Simmel 1949, 257)

As further discussed by Goffman (1967), when the purpose of socializing becomes talk for its own sake, the social gathering becomes a "little social system with its own boundary-maintaining tendencies; a little patch of commitment and loyalty with its own heroes and its own villains" (113–114). When members of the group take care not to threaten the sense of ease of other members, they can create euphoric moments of harmony that confirm and solidify their sense of shared identity. Precisely because such practices of informal sociability are open-ended and avoid purposeful closure, they provide relief from the demands of utilitarian life (Davetian 2009).

Historically speaking, how is such expressive sociability implicated in nation-building? Erik Ringmar (1998) provided a possible starting point for addressing this question. He proposed an overarching account of the ways that democracy became connected to nationalism in Western Europe in the wake of growing demands for expressivity in public life. This expressivity was partly mediated by the secluded spaces of civic associations. According to his account, eighteenth-century romantic conceptions of the individual as a unique person with a rich interior life gave rise to expectations that interactions in the public sphere be construed in expressive and intimate terms. People increasingly anticipated that not only their political interests but also their unique exclusive qualities would be acknowledged in political decision-making processes.

Thus, expression of the self evolved from both play-acting and formal interactions during negotiations with absolutist authorities to an authentic expression of self in the sanctuary of secluded social clubs and civic associations. This culminated in the national era with the idea that politicians are akin to fellow citizens, ideally sharing the same collective identity as their constituents. In the course of this cultural transformation, clubs and associations formed an alternative public sphere where individuals could open up and reveal their true selves to others, forging informal links with relative disregard for rank and social hierarchy. This new sociability featured not only critical and abstract reasoning, as suggested by Habermas (1991), but also intimacy and emotional trust: "In the club or in the lodge, the new man could be who he really was: an autonomous individual, a creature of scientific reason, but also of emotions and sentiments" (Ringmar 1998). In this way, the political community was remade in the image of civic associations, perceived to have become both more democratic and more authentic. The emerging vocabulary of nationalism guaranteed a public sphere populated with like-minded individuals who could speak to one another on free and intimate terms based on a sense of shared identity or rather, and more in line with the present discussion, based on shared experiences of social club sociability.

In order to unpack this historical trajectory, while paying greater attention to the underlying institutional dimension, we should consider several organizing principles of social clubs and how they may affect collective solidarity. First, despite or perhaps because of the egalitarian ideal of pure sociability, social clubs always necessitate a preselection of those strangers who qualify to become members according to some form of sameness. It is this ethos of sameness that has transformed political identification, leading citizens to expect their rulers to share a similar social background (and not only similar opinions), such that "the public sphere be populated by people like themselves with whom they could speak on free and intimate terms—hence nationalism" (Ringmar 1998, 545).

Consequently, the deepening of the relationships between club members consists of growing familiarity and loyalty alongside a shared sense of exclusivity and privilege. Black (2012) noted that club members earn some sort of status (related to power, respectability, taste, etc.) due to the fact that they are part of a group while others are not: "A club's very existence relies on the imperative of protecting the group from nonmembers. That sense of connectedness—with some but not with all—provides legitimacy, purpose, and comfort to those who are connected" (28).[5]

These qualities are best captured by the term "clubbability," which first appeared in the context of eighteenth-century London club culture. As reviewed by Valérie Capdeville (2016), "clubbability" emerged as a nationally unique cultural code of English male sociability that implied socializing among equals who shared the same esteemed values, upbringing, and rank. More than simply his sociable qualities, conviviality, and manners, clubbability singled out a man's ability to be accepted and well regarded in exclusive circles. It combined "the Englishman's aspiration towards individuality, distinction, eccentricity or excess and his appetite for social cohesion, community experience and normative behaviour" (Capdeville 2016, 77).

Second, although historically most intermediate social institutions were probably male dominated, if not male exclusive, the term "club," as evident from the English example, carries with it far more explicit gendered undertones than corresponding terms in the aforementioned discussions of associationalism and community talk such as secondary groups and civic or voluntary associations. In this respect, rather than concealing the masculinist history of civil society and national movements, the concept of the social club attests to this history and serves to evoke the deep cultural connections between the flourishing of male-only social enclaves in Enlightenment Europe (Hoffmann 2001; Jacob 1991), a homosocial fraternal contract that replaced one form of patriarchal rule with another (Pateman 1989), and the accompanying national ideology that was devised by men and for men in response to their experiences of humiliation, their fears, and their fantasies (Mosse 1996; Nagel 1998).

Third, and crucial to the present argument, in order for social club sociability to impact national solidarity, it must have a socializing effect that goes beyond a given institution. Claus Offe (1999) noted the role played by institutions in bridging between strangers and attempting to create generalized trust. Institutions provide a pervasive ethos and normative reference points about the preferred way of conducting social life, leading each member to believe that other members share the same commitments embodied in the norms of the institution. The same logic can potentially extend to collective solidarity:

> we trust our fellow citizens…due to the fact that we share a significant institutional space with a sufficiently strong meaning so as to make the overwhelming majority of "strangers" among my fellow citizens worthy of being trusted because I anticipate them to be appreciative of that meaning. (22)

Thus, having traveled through various social clubs, each with its own differentiated norms of conduct, compatriots learn how to generalize informal codes of sociability and reemploy them in future interactions. This institutionally mediated effect of socialization can be compared to Gellner's (1983) discussion of national socialization in terms of "exo-training" and "exo-socialization." According to Gellner, the nation-state was historically able to train the masses to the demands of industrialization by uprooting them from local communities and mobilizing them through public institutions such as schools and the military. The aim was to facilitate efficient interactions between strangers by advancing standardized and precise communication "involving a sharing of explicit meaning, transmitted in a standard idiom and in writing when required" (34).

I would argue, however, that shared institutional life is constitutive of national solidarity not so much because it facilitates sharing explicit meaning, but because the expressive sociability that it creates is premised on the suspension of explicit meaning and on sharing something that is more implicit, namely the actual bond between the participants. Along these lines, Simmel (1950) emphasized how the purely sociable form of talk is a generative act that establishes and maintains the "common consciousness of the party":

> ...talk is the purest and most sublimated form of two-way-ness. It thus is the fulfillment of a relation that wants to be nothing but relation—in which, that is, what usually is the mere form of interaction becomes its self-sufficient content...the telling and reception of stories, etc., is not an end in itself but only a means for the liveliness, harmony, and common consciousness of the 'party.' (53)

In this way, unaffiliated individuals can come together simply by sharing internal codes of communication, distinctive jargon, and exclusive, intimate humor, which is learned and generalized from one institutional setting to the next. In so doing, they are not just pursuing standardized communication in modern society but are trying to overcome the pressures of differentiation and segmentation through the fulfillment of social bonds.

Fourth, the idea that intermediate institutions facilitated the development of friendship ties is certainly not unique to the modern era. Life in premodern societies can be presumed to have also offered specific forms of social clubs where individuals could meet unrelated kin (e.g., the workplace, place of worship, and village square). But whereas people in traditional communities participated in a limited set of social clubs and their respective social networks tended to converge, life in modern societies consists of a multitude of social clubs with relatively differentiated social networks. With the growing intensity, differentiation, and fragmentation of modern institutional life, people increasingly participate in a series of social clubs and are also more likely to attend various social clubs simultaneously.

Consider, for example, how modern schooling consists of a chain of institutions from nurseries and preschools to three different stages of mandatory schooling and various phases of higher education. In each of these consecutive stages, children and young adults enter a distinct social club that entails the acquisition of new friends and, possibly, new codes of sociability. In most cases, pupils within the same school are likely to share a single class year after year until they graduate; however, in some educational systems, such as in the USA, pupils may participate in several different classes simultaneously depending on their choice of courses (as in the university system). This means that, effectively, they participate in several social clubs concomitantly and partly change clubs every year. In other words, American children, possibly more than children elsewhere, are required to learn over and over again how to transform strangers into friends. This competence, I suggest, is part of what enables a mass society of this size and complexity to be imagined as a nation.

Finally, a general analogy can be drawn between the kind of boundary work that takes place in social clubs and in nation-states. Club membership is, of course, based on choice, trust, and formal or informal rules of inclusion and exclusion, whereas the universe of members in a national community is seemingly "given" and compatriots cannot be admitted or excluded depending on some measure of trustworthiness (Offe 1999). There are, nonetheless, some basic similarities in how membership is construed in both cases. Although most states grant citizenship automatically based on birthright or kinship ties, states are still understood as "associations of free and equal citizens" premised "on the principles of voluntariness" (Habermas 1995, 25) and often provide a second path of admission that involves an oath of allegiance to the state and its founding principles (Pickus 2005). Moreover, just as social clubs build friendship through exclusiveness and privilege, national communities often attach transcendent meaning to its members as belonging to an elect, "chosen people"

(Gorski 2000). In practice, social clubs vary greatly in the kinds of boundaries, selections, and exclusion that they impose, as do nation-states. But all social clubs and all national communities are premised on a purposeful selection of strangers with the intention of transforming those who have been thus distinguished, and only those, into confidants and friends.

To conclude, although it may appear overly broad in scope, the concept of social club sociability may prove valuable for studying how institutionalized forms of group-level interactions contribute to sentiments of solidarity at the broader societal level. As feelings of solidarity per se neither depend on nor imply a democratic culture, we should be attentive to those aspects of associational life that trigger a more generalized form of expressive solidarity, producing practices of exclusive sociability which are staged in public and carried over to others settings. In this regard, choral societies and bowling leagues, to go back to Putnam's (2000) powerful examples, are simply two of many social institutions in which, irrespective of their outward civil orientation, clubbiness can be practiced, learnt, and extended to the wider civic-national community.[6]

HISTORICAL EXAMPLES OF SOCIAL CLUB SOCIABILITY

Having laid out the preliminary rationale for considering social club sociability as a model for civic-national attachments, I briefly point out a variety of historical examples of such social clubs. I do not, as yet, analyze how these examples operate in terms of the interactionist mechanisms of public intimacy nor how they implicate national solidarity (this is my concern in the case studies presented in Part Two), but I merely summarize how existing studies have addressed these institutionalized forms of sociability and linked them, albeit sometimes obliquely, with broader aspects of civic or national life.

Beginning with the epitome of the modern social club, the aforementioned English gentlemen's club, this elite social institution took shape in late eighteenth-century London and became an enduring hallmark of English and, subsequently, British sociability. Capdeville (2016) claimed that these clubs helped to shape the cultural and national identity of English gentlemen. By cultivating a masculinity that emphasized politeness and refined conversations, club membership became a visible sign of success and a key to social prestige and political power. The club's rule-governed social relations reinforced participants' sense of belonging to a selective community whose members were elected by a regime of ballots and black balls and underwent elaborate initiation rites.

Black (2012) described how this model expanded and flourished during the Victorian era with the growing primacy and affluence of the British empire in the aftermath of Napoleon's defeat. The rise in the living standards of the British middle classes created a demand for goods and status previously reserved for the upper classes. The notion of the gentleman changed to accommodate this social mobility: "With social status no longer determined solely by birth, one could become a gentleman by behaving like one and by possessing the tastes and habits, and pursuing the lifestyle practices, of a gentleman" (28–29). Once the privilege of the few, membership in social clubs enabled the new bourgeoisie to acquire this social distinction more easily and, with it, to take on what became a distinct and recognizable national character.

Another illustration of social club sociability can be found in the rich historical accounts of café sociability of nineteenth-century France. Despite their mundane and seemingly spontaneous nature, interpersonal interactions in this relatively unstructured social institution held collective significance for the formation of modern French civility and civic practices. Unlike English middle-class men who tended to close themselves off in private clubs, the public culture of French café sociability offered a mixed-gender and partially mixed-class counter model. The flourishing of café culture accommodated both the working-class and some members of the bourgeoisie and partly tempered the status-bound culture of French aristocratic court society (Capdeville 2016; Davetian 2009; Smith 2011).

Café sociability was mainly expressive. This space of "intimate anonymity" (Haine 1996, 150) provided an opportunity to create relations based on spontaneous solidarity. The fact that social, political, and ideological concerns were being discussed in a public space, rather than being confined to the private spaces of the courtly or intellectual salons, allowed discourse to be more animated, less restrained by formalities, and more emotionally expressive. The habit of collective drinking had its own liberating effect and added to the experience of group solidarity. At the same time, the gathering of people from relatively varied backgrounds in the same public space gave rise to café etiquette and practices of sociability that were designed to contain disagreements and minimize outbursts of violence (Davetian 2009; Haine 1996).

Café sociability also served more instrumental civic and political purposes. Eugen Weber (1976, 261–270) demonstrated how practices of organized sociability in French rural taverns remote from elite national politics gave illiterate peasants and workingmen the chance to mix with local agents of political change (tradesmen, civil servants, etc.). A variety of associations developed around local taverns and cafés, providing the lower classes access to newspapers and offering opportunities to talk politics. French cafés became known, using Balzac's famous words, as the "parliament of the people" (cited in Davetian 2009, 132). In some extreme cases, such as during the revolutionary era, they served as a hotbed for political dissent and for challenging public opinion, but from a broader civic perspective, café sociability simply gave citizens the opportunity to assemble, address current topics, and engage in the discussion of ideas for their own sake (Davetian 2009). Michael Schaich (2008, 128) further noted that café culture was closely tied up with the circulation and production of public media. Upscale venues often supplied local newspapers, magazines, and pamphlets not only for casual reading but also for discussions of current events among fellow patrons. In some instances, coffeehouses even served as the editorial offices for local newsletters and journals.

As is clear from these well-researched cases of British club culture and French café society, social club sociability in and of itself is not directly related to national attachment. But since the emergence and spread of nation-states, most intermediate social institutions have become increasingly circumscribed by national boundaries and, in varying degrees, need to justify their actions and establish their legitimacy within the confines of a national community.[7] Thus, to the extent that the social clubs in question are not limited to a strictly sectarian or otherwise particularistic membership and allow for at least a partial overlap with other social clubs in terms of shared networks, the patterns of sociability acquired through these clubs are likely to affect national-level solidarity. As argued by Alexander (1997), because national states continue to form the most effective boundaries for solidary ties and to determine patterns of inclusion and exclusion, civil society can be currently considered a community roughly isomorphic with the nation.

There are, of course, many historical instances where the connection between social club sociability and national attachment is more explicit, such as during formative phases of a national movement when practices of sociability embraced by national or proto-national activists become incorporated in local national discourse or directly contribute to the social infrastructure of the national movement. It is worthwhile briefly noting a few such examples. In mid-nineteenth-century Germany, the gymnastic movement was a significant agent of socialization used to spread national consciousness. The horizontal network of gymnastic clubs with their pedagogic objectives gave content and meaning to the innovative cause of German nationalism. By advocating physical, social, and spiritual activities, they sanctioned moral behavior characterized by both individual freedom and group spirit, subscribing to a distinctly male code of conduct in line with classical Greek aesthetics of male beauty, health, and virtue (Mosse 1975, 128). The hundreds of gymnastic organizations established in the German-speaking states pursued the political unification of a German nation and believed themselves to be the masculine elite that could fulfill such a vision (Caplan 2003, 177).

Similarly, Gabriella Romani (2007) described the role played by nineteenth-century Italian literary salons in creating the realm of public opinion at the national level which preceded Italy's political unification. These salons provided a space for intellectuals to come together and share original ideas and news, which then immediately circulated among the wider literary community. They served as an actual and imagined social space, representative of the national political body. Their code of polite behavior enhanced the idea that in order to earn access to the new national elite and enjoy its prestige, one had to adhere to the rules of Italian salon sociability.

A different example is the movement of Practical Zionism at the turn of the twentieth century, which materialized in the founding of Jewish agricultural settlements in Palestine. Central to these was the close-knit socialist commune known as the kibbutz, considered a model for the Jewish nation-state and forming the political leadership for its future institutions and military organization. The kibbutz movement was, above all, a geographically dispersed network of elitist and exclusivist social clubs. It entailed official criteria for membership, pervasive rules of conduct, and a rich arena of sociability, which formed the blueprint for wider *sabra* (native-born) Israeli sociability (Almog 2000; Kaplan 2006).

The case of Palestinians held in Israeli prisons provides yet another unexpected case in point of how social networks among political activists consolidate national solidarity. Since the 1970s, large numbers of Palestine Liberation Organization and Hamas militants convicted of terrorism have been held in Israeli prisons. Upon their release, some have assumed leadership positions in the Palestinian national movement and military struggle. The inmates, coming from diverse social backgrounds and geographically dispersed localities, have transformed from loosely affiliated strangers into a committed group of mates and fellow fighters to the cause. This forced social club of sorts has engendered collective attachments through complex channels of formal and informal communication and stimulates political processes of community-building both within and outside the prison walls (Nashif 2008).

In all of these latter cases in which actors are explicitly involved in nation-building or preoccupied with national ideology, the association between sociability and national solidarity is fairly self-evident. The greater challenge and potential insights to be gained lie in exploring how interactions between compatriots in social clubs not directly associated with nation-building can likewise contribute to national attachment. In other words, to borrow from Billig's (1995) conception of "banal nationalism," it is cases of "banal" social clubs that may contribute more to our understanding of the centrality, omnipresence, and endurance of national solidarity.

Online Social Clubs

Possibly the most explicit manifestation of banal social club sociability can be found in the present-day social media (also termed "social networks sites"). These online platforms exhibit similar characteristics to historic social clubs: They facilitate interpersonal interactions, entail criteria for membership, and prescribe certain rules of conduct. Whereas in the classical club members engage in face-to-face interactions within a bounded and finite network structure, a social media platform is essentially an infinite structure of partly overlapping personal networks.[8] Yet despite the mass audience and the different functions offered by various social media sites (e.g., those geared to a specific interest such as the career-oriented LinkedIn or operating as a general-purpose platform such as Facebook), social media sites echo their offline counterparts by constituting an arena of informal, expressive sociability in which participants engage in mostly mundane and seemingly non-instrumental interactions and in the process transform from strangers into acquaintances and friends.

Participation in social media also carries collective significance. In fact, a platform such as Facebook provides perhaps the best example of the dynamic of public intimacy and its role in creating collective solidarity—a solidarity which emerges from actual interactions between individual members and not only through top-down processes of collective identity formation. While a theoretical exposition of public intimacy is the subject of the next chapter, Facebook sociability provides a good glimpse into how the public staging of interpersonal ties in front of other friends and strangers retains the basic feelings of exclusivity, familiarity, and loyalty associated with close friendships, even as they extend to a much larger collective.

Social media researchers danah boyd and Nicole Ellison (2008) reviewed the history of online networks and characterized its distinguishing features. They traced the first recognizable social network site to SixDegrees.com, a site launched in 1997 which allowed users to create profiles, list their friends, and surf their friends lists, integrating certain functions provided by preexisting Web sites based on user-generated content with those of instant messaging services. Boyd and Ellison defined social network sites as "web-based services that allow individuals to: (1) construct a public or semi-public profile within a bounded system; (2) articulate a list of other users with whom they share a connection; and (3) view and traverse their list of connections and those made by others within the system" (211). They noted that the information presented on the personal profile (with descriptors such as name, picture, place of residence, interests, and an "about me" section) is a central aspect of self-presentation that enables profile owners to manage their identity. This function was already salient in earlier dating and community Web sites. The second function, namely the public display of connections (often termed "friends"), means that even more information about users' identities can be inferred by the company they keep (Donath and boyd 2004). By navigating a user's list of friends and traversing the connections of these friends, a person's extended social network becomes accessible and serves as an important identity "signal" that helps validate the information presented on the personal profile (73).

In addition, platforms such as Facebook allow users to reveal and make public the specific interactions taking place with their friends in the form of an ongoing exchange which appears on their "wall," the main feature in the owner's personal Facebook page (or "profile page"). This exchange remains visible overtime in a narrative-like structure which constitutes the owner's personal "timeline." Viewers thus become privy not just to a profile owner's identity, the number of friends on his or her network, and the friends' identities but also, and no less importantly, to the ongoing and past interactions with these friends. On each profile, page owners and their friends can engage in mutual interaction by posting content on the wall (subject to the owner's restrictions), commenting on existing posts, or indicating their interest by pressing the "like" button or specific "reaction" emojis (love, haha, wow, sad, or angry). Friends' actions are reported on their own profile wall, where they can also "share" the full content of the post. For each post, viewers can observe the number of likes, comments, shares, creation time, and time of last interaction, all of which provide further quantitative indication of the post's popularity (Cvijikj and Michahelles 2014).

Given this public staging of interactions with one's friends, to reduce the distinguishing features of social network sites to the claim that such display of connections serves "as identity markers for the profile owner" (boyd and Ellison 2008, 220; Donath and boyd 2004) is to miss an important point about social media that goes beyond self-identity, namely, that they give rise to performances of public intimacy. For what, above all, distinguishes social media from other online interactions is that they entail a dramaturgical display of interpersonal ties in front of a third party, providing insiders with a sense of exclusivity and simultaneously teasing outsiders and tempting them to "join the party" by a click of a button, by simply sending a friend request. In this way, viewers become confidants of the profile owner both in terms of sharing information and as potentially active participants and accomplices in the owner's social club. The magical transformation from strangers to friends—the hallmark of modern-day communities—was never more explicit and immediate.

Similar to other social clubs, social media operates as a theater of social interactions. In social club sociability, it is the expressive dimension of the interaction which "becomes its own self-sufficient content" (Simmel 1949, 259) rather than the exchange of purposeful information. This distinction becomes all the more apparent in the case of online social media. As argued by Vincent Miller (2008), interactions on social network sites are characterized by "phatic exchange," a term initially used by anthropologist Bronisław Malinowski (1923, 315) and by linguist Roman Jakobson (1999) to describe a communicative gesture that does not exchange any meaningful information about the world and whose sole purpose is to signal one's present state, express sociability, and maintain social connections. Along these lines, unlike the appeal of some user-generated content, such as personal blogs which encourage the creation of a substantive text in a diary-like, narrative form, the content generated by social media users is mostly confined to generic status updates, passing comments, anecdotes from everyday life, recommendation on products, and so on. This form of communication is motivated less by "having something in particular to say" as by a desire "to say 'something' to maintain connections or audiences, to let one's network know that one is still 'there'" (Miller 2008, 393).

Phatic exchange thus concerns the process of communication rather than its content; it aims to strengthen social ties and maintain a "connected presence" in an ever-expanding social network (Licoppe and Smoreda 2005). While substantively content-less, Miller (2008) granted that the communication of phatic messages may entail "the recognition, intimacy and sociability in which a strong sense of community is founded" (395) but seems to dismiss the implications, namely, that, similar to my formulation of social club sociability, social media sites are constitutive of solidarity precisely because they suspend a sharing of explicit meaning and share something that is more implicit: the actual bond between participants. As stated by Simmel (1950), "the telling and reception of stories, etc., is not an end in itself but only a means for the liveliness, harmony, and common consciousness of the 'party'" (53).

General-purpose social network sites such as Facebook are characterized by social convergence. They collapse diverse social contexts into one and merge private and public interests (Marwick and boyd 2011). Users must communicate simultaneously with acquaintances from different social circles (professional, friends and family, hobby or interest groups, present or past school friends, etc.) and share the same information with all irrespective of how close they are. Moreover, although each Facebook user sets up a selected list of acquaintances to form his or her very own "public" due to network connectivity, this personalized public sphere readily becomes part of a much wider collective. As noted by Ori Schwarz and Guy Shani (2016), this makes it difficult for users to engage in the kind of strategies available to them in offline social life, such as switching between interaction "group styles" (Eliasoph and Lichterman, 2003), saving face, and engaging in flexible impression management according to the audience (Goffman 1959). Instead, social media users manage their self-presentation by maintaining a delicate balance between personal and public information, avoiding certain topics, and attempting to portray an authentic self (Marwick and boyd 2011). In this way, Facebook sociability provides a sense of presence among divergent circles of friends and acquaintances by facilitating ongoing conversation and glimpses of social play. This sociability resembles everyday small talk among close friends, one that is expanded to a larger co-audience (Jensen and Sørensen 2013).

These qualities have important implications for collective solidarity. Various studies have examined the active role played by networking sites such as Facebook and Twitter in mobilizing public opinion and political action. A well-studied case is the 2011 Egyptian national democratic revolt (Alexander 2012; Papacharissi and de Fatima Oliveira 2012; Zhuo et al. 2011). In the face of government censorship on traditional mass media activists rallied popular support for the revolution by expanding their ability to communicate the events from word of mouth to social media. The use of social media supplanted the strong ties of kinship and personal friendship with more diversified networks within Egyptian society that could bridge between localized groups.

The crux of the matter, however, was not simply the advantage of spreading information across weak ties and thereby exploiting more resources to potentially bring about social change (Zhuo et al. 2011); rather, it is in considering these weak ties as equivalent to strong ties in their affective expression and in their sense of involvement, connection, and solidarity (Papacharissi and de Fatima Oliveira 2012). In other words, Egyptian social media users were able to express their feelings and convictions about current affairs as if they were talking to a selected group of friends. In turn, distant others were encouraged to respond as if they were their friends. Whereas most collective events and media events take the form of a social performance with clear distinctions between the roles of spectators, confidants, and full participants (Alexander 2004), the horizontal structure of a social network site implies that all actors in the performance can effortlessly shift from a position of passive spectator to confidant and to full participant.

Unlike in premodern communities where people participated in a limited set of social clubs and their respective social networks tended to converge, in modern societies individuals engage in a multitude of differentiated social clubs and sustain relatively diverse social networks. Yet since the early modern era, a growing numbers of individuals act under the assumption or fantasy that the institutions and networks in which they are embedded do, in fact, converge in a bounded and homogenous community, an imagined community which they call the nation.

Facebook sociability makes this fantasy of convergence come true but with a price. An illustrative example of the solidifying function of social media resulting from its convergence of audiences can be found in a study of political befriending by Schwarz and Shani (2016). During the 2014 conflict between Israel and the Palestinian Hamas regime in the Gaza strip (termed by the Israeli government operation "Protective Edge"), Facebook became a central arena for boundary work and internal symbolic cleansing among Israeli users. Users who took offense at what people on their personal network had posted employed online and offline sanctions such as defriending, shaming, and workplace persecution. According to Nicholas John and Shira Dvir-Gvirsman (2015), a total of 16% of users are estimated to have unfriended or unfollowed a Facebook friend during the operation.

While this example clearly demonstrates how Facebook may promote political polarization (John and Dvir-Gvirsman 2015), it does not support the understanding of social media connectivity as representing a decline in well-bounded solidary communities in favor of a highly individualized, loosely bounded structure of interpersonal networks (Rainie and Wellman 2012).[9] Schwarz and Shani (2016) suggested that acts of political defriending and shaming reveal how rather than weakening social control on individuals, Facebook networks subject them to scrutiny by the very collectives to which they belong. Due to the inability to compartmentalize and present different activities to different audiences, Facebook users were exposed to war-related political comments and conversations that were often taken out of their original context and received new meanings that rendered them morally flawed and sacrilegious in the eyes of users with opposing political leanings. Particularly "in times of collective effervescence such as war, Facebook's structure of sociation and visibility allows collectives to exert power of coercion and demand loyalty" (413–414). Despite increasing fragmentation of modern social life, people imagine themselves as members of homogeneous solidary groups. Online social interactions actually realize this union of sentiment, as they tend to collapse private and public life and converge multiple intimate spheres into one. As a result, in times of collective crisis users may feel compelled to engage in political defriending in order to translate their "imagined homogeneity" into "actual homogeneity" (408).

Online social clubs thus reveal and epitomize the missing link between friendship and national attachment. Rather than making stark distinctions between face-to-face networks and whole nations and limiting our understanding of the latter to membership in a set of abstract categorical attributes (Brubaker and Cooper 2000; Calhoun 1991), Web sites such as Facebook make us realize how relations between compatriots are far from abstract and anonymous, for a growing number of them now have a name and face.

This explains why despite its clear potential to connect people beyond localized and territorial borders, the use of social media does not undermine national attachments but may possibly reinforce them. Current research has pointed to the ways in which communication preferences among internet users continue to reproduce communities that correspond to national structures and engage in national discourse (Eriksen 2007; Soffer 2013). Social media may bolster national solidarity by morally "summoning" members of the community (Tavory 2016) and forcing them to choose sides and demonstrate their loyalty to fellow nationals (Schwarz and Shani 2016). In this way, social media practices reinforce a widespread understanding of the nation as the ultimate social club.

Notes

1. In addition to the Gemeinschaft pole, Simonson (1996) delineated the *Sittlichkeit* pole according to which the concern with community is conceived in terms of the moral life that emerges from participation in concrete social institutions.
2. For an empirical refutation of specific predictions deriving from three views of associationalism, see Jason Kaufman (1999).
3. Andreas Wimmer's macro-historical model of state formation provides significant empirical support for the suggestion that civic associations contribute to the emergence of an encompassing, trans-ethnic, national community irrespective of the question of democratization (Wimmer 2002, 247; also Kroneberg and Wimmer 2012). This comparative work suggests that when the existence of a dense network of clubs, associations, trade unions, etc. preceded state centralization, local nation-building processes were likely to take an inclusive form, allowing political elites to legitimize their rule and mobilize mass support independent of ethnic cleavages. In the absence of such civic networks, however, political rule and alliances were more likely to rely on ethno-cultural groupings.
4. Civil societies may be rich in associational life without exhibiting key democratic attributes. Noted examples are Nazi Germany and Hamas rule in Gaza where grassroots civic and religious associations bolstered national solidarity but were inimical to democracy (see also Theiss-Morse and Hibbing 2005; Armony 2004).
5. This form of elitist sociability is often stereotypically contrasted with ostensibly non-exclusionary alternatives, such as "cosmopolitan sociability," defined as "forms of competence and communication skills that are based on the human capacity to create social relations of inclusiveness and openness to the world" (Schiller et al. 2011, 402).

6. While lacking the current theoretical lens, several studies have pointed to a historical connection between European choral societies and the assertion of national identities (Lajosi and Stynen 2015).
7. Global social institutions that travel across borders often gain institutional legitimacy in the target country by taking on local, national meanings and adopting a patriotic stance (Kaplan 2012; Kaplan and Hirsch 2012). This holds true even for unequivocally cosmopolitan organizations, as demonstrated in Shai Dromi's (2016) study of the international spread of the Red Cross movement.
8. Each online personal network operates as a bounded "egocentric network," representing the ties between the user (formally called ego) and all of their immediate contacts (or "friends," formally called alters) (Arnaboldi et al. 2011). But because most social media platforms allow users to access the network of each of their own contacts and beyond ("friends of friends" and so on), the overall network is almost infinite in size. This is particularly so in the case of Facebook, which as of June 2017 reported 2.01 billion monthly active users (Facebook 2017), each of whom is connected to other Facebook users by an estimated average of 3.57 steps (Bhagat et al. 2016).
9. According to Barry Wellman's (2002) vision of "networked individualism" and in line with Simmel's (1955) view of affiliations in modern society as based on informational segregation, loosely bounded, egocentric networks of multiple and increasingly voluntary ties are gradually replacing well-bounded solidary groups (see Schwarz and Shani 2016).

References

Alexander, Jeffrey C. 1988. "Culture and Political Crisis: 'Watergate' and Durkheimian Sociology." In *Durkheimian Sociology: Cultural Studies*, edited by Jeffrey. C. Alexander, 187–224. New York: Oxford University Press.
Alexander, Jeffrey C. 1997. "The Paradoxes of Civil Society." *International Sociology* 12 (2): 115–133.
Alexander, Jeffrey C. 2004. "Cultural Pragmatics: Social Performance Between Ritual and Strategy." *Sociological Theory* 22 (4): 527–573.
Alexander, Jeffrey C. 2006. *The Civil Sphere*. New York: Oxford University Press.
Alexander, Jeffrey C. 2012. *Performative Revolution in Egypt: An Essay in Cultural Power*. London: Bloomsbury Academic.
Almog, Oz. 2000. *The Sabra: The Creation of the New Jew*. Berkeley: University of California Press.
Anderson, Benedict. [1983] 1991. *Imagined Communities: Reflections on the Origins and Spread of Nationalism*. London: Verso.
Armony, Ariel. 2004. *The Dubious Link: Civic Engagement and Democratization*. Stanford: Stanford University Press.

Arnaboldi Valerio, Andrea Passarella, Maurizio Tesconi, and Davide Gazzè. 2011. "Towards a Characterization of Egocentric Networks in Online Social Networks." In *On the Move to Meaningful Internet Systems: OTM 2011 Workshops*, edited by Robert Meersman, Tharam Dillon, and Pilar Herrero, 524–533. Berlin: Springer.

Bhabha, Homi K. ed. [1990] 2013. *Nation and Narration*. London: Routledge.

Bhagat, Smriti, Moira Burke, Carlos Diuk, Ismail Onur Filiz, and Sergey Edunov. 2016. "Three and a Half Degrees of Separation." *Facebook Research*, February 4. https://research.fb.com/three-and-a-half-degrees-of-separation/. Accessed September 29, 2017.

Billig, Michael. 1995. *Banal Nationalism*. London: Sage.

Black, Barbara. 2012. *A Room of His Own: A Literary-Cultural Study of Victorian Clubland*. Athens, OH: Ohio University Press.

boyd, danah., and Nicole B. Ellison. 2008. "Social Network Sites: Definition, History, and Scholarship." *Journal of Computer-Mediated Communication* 13 (1): 210–230.

Brubaker, Rogers and Frederick Cooper. 2000. "Beyond 'Identity.'" *Theory and Society* 29 (1): 1–47.

Calhoun, Craig. 1991. "Nationalism, Political Community and the Representation of Society: Or, Why Feeling at Home is Not a Substitute for Public Space." *European Journal of Social Theory* 2: 217–231.

Capdeville, Valérie. 2016. "'Clubbability': A Revolution in London Sociability?" *Lumen: Selected Proceedings from the Canadian Society for Eighteenth-Century Studies* 35: 63–80.

Caplan, Gregory A. 2003. "Militarism and Masculinity as Keys to the 'Jewish Question' in Germany." In *Military Masculinities: Identity and the State*, edited by Paul R. Higate, 175–190. Westport: Praeger.

Collins, Randall. 2004. *Interaction Ritual Chains*. Princeton: Princeton University Press.

Cooley, Charles, H. [1909] 1962. *Social Organization*. New York: Schocken.

Cvijikj, Irena Pletikosa, and Florian Michahelles. 2014. "Online Engagement Factors on Facebook Brand Pages." *Social Network Analysis and Mining* 3 (4): 843–861.

Davetian, Benet. 2009. *Civility: A Cultural History*. Toronto: Toronto University Press.

Dingley, James. 2008. *Nationalism, Social Theory and Durkheim*. Basingstoke: Palgrave Macmillan.

Donath, Judith, and danah boyd. 2004. "Public Displays of Connection." *BT Technology Journal* 22 (4): 71–82.

Dromi, Shai M. 2016. "For Good and Country: Nationalism and the Diffusion of Humanitarianism in the Late-Nineteenth-Century." *The Sociological Review Monographs* 64 (2): 79–97.

Durkheim, Emile. [1902] 1960. *The Division of Labor in Society*. Glencoe, IL: Free Press.
Durkheim, Emile. [1915] 2003. "The Elementary Forms of Religious Life." Translated by Karen E. Fields. In *Emile Durkheim: Sociologist of Modernity*, edited by Mustafa Emirbayer, 109–121, 140–141. Malden, MA: Blackwell.
Eliasoph, Nina. 1996. "Making a Fragile Public: A Talk-Centered Study of Citizenship and Power." *Sociological Theory* 14 (3): 262–289.
Eliasoph, Nina, and Paul Lichterman. 2003. "Culture in Interaction." *American Journal of Sociology* 108 (4): 735–794.
Eriksen, Thomas Hylland. 2007. "Nationalism and the Internet." *Nations and Nationalism* 13 (1): 1–17.
Etzioni, Amitai. 1996. *The New Golden Rule: Community and Morality in a Democratic Society*. New York: Basic Books.
Facebook. 2017. "Stats." https://newsroom.fb.com/company-info. Accessed September 29, 2017.
Fernback, Jan. 2007. "Beyond the Diluted Community Concept: A Symbolic Interactionist Perspective on Online Social Relations." *New Media & Society* 9 (1): 49–69.
Gellner, Ernst. 1983. *Nations and Nationalism*. Oxford: Blackwell.
Gerth, Hans Heinrich, and Charles Wright Mills, eds. [1948] 1998. *From Max Weber: Essays in Sociology*. London: Routledge.
Goffman, Ervin. 1959. *Presentation of Self in Everyday Life*. Garden City, NY: Doubleday.
Goffman, Ervin. 1967. *Interaction Ritual: Essays on Face-To-Face Behavior*. Chicago: Aldine.
Gorski, Philip S. 2000. "The Mosaic Moment: An Early Modernist Critique of Modernist Theories of Nationalism." *American Journal of Sociology* 105 (5): 1428–1468.
Habermas, Jürgen. [1962] 1991. *The Structural Transformation of the Public Sphere: An Inquiry into a Category of Bourgeois Society*. Cambridge, MA: MIT Press.
Habermas, Jürgen. 1995. "Citizenship and National Identity." In *The Condition of Citizenship*, edited by Bart Van Steenbergen, 20–35. London: Sage.
Haine, William Scott. 1996. *The World of the Paris Café: Sociability Among the French Working Class, 1789–1914*. Baltimore: John Hopkins University Press.
Hoffmann, Stefan-Ludwig. 2001. "Civility, Male Friendship and Masonic Sociability in Nineteenth-Century Germany." *Gender and History* 13 (2): 224–248.
Jacob, Margaret C. 1991. "The Enlightenment Redefined: The Formation of Modern Civil Society." *Social Research* 58 (2): 475–495.
Jakobson, Roman. [1960] 1999. "Linguistics and Poetics." In *The Discourse Reader*, edited by Adam Jaworski and Nikolas Coupland, 54–62. London: Routledge.

James, Paul. 1996. *Nation Formation: Towards a Theory of Abstract Community*. London: Sage.
Jensen, Jakob Liñaa, and Anne Scott Sørensen. 2013. "'Nobody Has 257 Friends': Strategies of Friending, Disclosure and Privacy on Facebook." *Nordicom Review* 34 (1): 49–62.
John, Nicholas A., and Shira Dvir-Gvirsman. 2015. "'I Don't Like You Any More': Facebook Unfriending by Israelis During the Israel-Gaza Conflict of 2014." *Journal of Communication* 65 (6): 953–974.
Kaplan, Danny. 2006. *The Men We Loved: Male Friendship and Nationalism in Israeli Culture*. New York: Berghahn Books.
Kaplan, Danny. 2012. "Institutionalized Erasures: How Global Structures Acquire National Meanings in Israeli Popular Music." *Poetics* 40 (3): 217–236.
Kaplan, Danny, and Orit Hirsch. 2012. "Marketing Nationalism in the Absence of State: Radio Haifa During the 2006 Lebanon War." *Journal of Contemporary Ethnography* 41 (5): 495–525.
Kaufman, Jason Andrew. 1999. "Three Views of Associationalism in 19th-Century America: An Empirical Examination." *American Journal of Sociology* 104 (5): 1296–1345.
Kornhauser, William. [1959] 2013. *Politics of Mass Society*. Abingdon: Routledge.
Kroneberg, Clemens, and Andreas Wimmer. 2012. "Struggling Over the Boundaries of Belonging: A Formal Model of Nation Building, Ethnic Closure, and Populism." *American Journal of Sociology* 118 (1): 176–230.
Lajosi, Krisztina, and Andreas Stynen, eds. 2015. *Choral Societies and Nationalism in Europe*. Leiden: Brill.
Licoppe, Christian, and Zbigniew Smoreda. 2005. "'Are Social Networks Technologically Embedded?' *Social Networks* 27 (4): 317–335.
Malešević, Siniša. 2011. "The Chimera of National Identity." *Nations and Nationalism* 17 (2): 272–290.
Malinowski, Bronisław. 1923. "Supplement 1: The Problem of Meaning in Primitive Languages." In *The Meaning of Meaning*, edited by Charles Kay Ogden and Ivor Armstrong Richards, 296–336. London: Routledge & Keegan Paul.
Mallory, Peter. 2012. "Political Friendship in the Era of 'the Social': Theorizing Personal Relations with Alexis de Tocqueville." *Journal of Classical Sociology* 12 (1): 22–42.
Marwick, Alice E., and danah boyd. 2011. "I Tweet Honestly, I Tweet Passionately: Twitter Users, Context Collapse, and the Imagined Audience." *New Media & Society* 13 (1): 114–133.
Miller, Vincent. 2008. "New Media, Networking and Phatic Culture." *Convergence* 14 (4): 387–400.
Mosse, George L. 1975. *Nationalization of the Masses: Political Symbolism and Mass Movements in Germany from the Napoleonic Wars Through the Third Reich*. New York: Meridian.
Mosse, George L. 1996. *The Image of Man: The Creation of Modern Masculinity*. New York: Oxford University Press.

Nagel, Joan. 1998. "Masculinity and Nationalism: Gender and Sexuality in the Making of Nations." *Ethnic and Racial Studies* 21 (2): 242–269.
Nashif, Esmail. 2008. *Palestinian Political Prisoners: Identity and Community.* London: Routledge.
Offe, Claus. 1999. "How Can We Trust Our Fellow Citizens." In *Democracy and Trust*, edited by Mark E. Warren, 42–87. Cambridge: Cambridge University Press.
Papacharissi, Zizi and Maria de Fatima Oliveira. 2012. "Affective News and Networked Publics: The Rhythms of News Storytelling on #Egypt." *Journal of Communication* 62 (2): 266–282.
Pateman, Carole. 1989. *The Disorder of Women: Democracy, Feminism and Political Theory.* Stanford: Stanford University Press.
Pickus, Noah. 2005. *True Faith and Allegiance: Immigration and American Civic Nationalism.* Princeton: Princeton University Press.
Putnam, Robert. 2000. *Bowling Alone.* New York: Simon and Schuster.
Putnam, Robert, Robert Leonardi, and Raffaella Y. Nanetti. 1993. *Making Democracy Work: Civic Traditions in Modern Italy.* Princeton, NJ: Princeton University Press.
Rainie, Lee, and Barry Wellman. 2012. *Networked: The New Social Operating System.* Cambridge, MA: MIT Press.
Ringmar, Erik. 1998. "Nationalism: The Idiocy of Intimacy." *British Journal of Sociology* 49 (4): 534–549.
Romani, Gabriella. 2007. "A Room with a View: Interpreting the Ottocento through the Literary Salon." *Italica* 84 (2–3): 233–246.
Schaich, Michael. 2008. "The Public Sphere." In *A Companion to Eighteenth-Century Europe*, edited by Peter H. Wilson, 125–140. Malden, MA: Blackwell.
Schiller, Nina Glick, Tsypylma Darieva, and Sandra Gruner-Domic. 2011 "Defining Cosmopolitan Sociability in a Transnational Age. An Introduction." *Ethnic and Racial Studies* 34 (3): 399–418.
Schwarz, Ori, and Guy Shani. 2016. "Culture in Mediated Interaction: Political Defriending on Facebook and the Limits of Networked Individualism." *American Journal of Cultural Sociology* 4 (3): 385–421.
Simmel, Georg. 1949. "The Sociology of Sociability." Translated by Everett C. Hughes. *American Journal of Sociology* 55 (3): 254–261.
Simmel, Georg. [1915] 1950. *The Sociology of Georg Simmel.* Translated by Kurt H. Wolff. Glencoe, IL: Free Press.
Simmel, Georg. [1922] 1955. *Conflict and the Web of Group Affiliation.* New York: Free Press.
Simonson, Peter. 1996. "Dreams of Democratic Togetherness: Communication Hope from Cooley to Katz." *Critical Studies in Media Communication* 13 (4): 324–342.

Smith, Anthony D. 1983. "Nationalism and Classical Social Theory." *British Journal of Sociology* 34 (1): 19–38.
Smith, Philip. 2011. "Book Review: 'Civility: A Cultural History.'" *Teaching Sociology* 39 (3): 329–333.
Soffer, Oren. 2013. "The Internet and National Solidarity: A Theoretical Analysis." *Communication Theory* 23 (1): 48–66.
Tavory, Iddo. 2016. *Summoned: Religious Life in an Orthodox Jewish Neighborhood*. Chicago: Chicago University Press.
Theiss-Morse, Elizabeth, and John R. Hibbing. 2005. "Citizenship and Civic Engagement." *Annual Review of Political Science* 8: 227–249.
Thompson, Kenneth. 1993. "Durkheim, Ideology and the Sacred." *Social Compass* 40 (3): 451–461.
Thomson, Irene Taviss. 2005. "The Theory That Won't Die: From Mass Society to the Decline of Social Capital." *Sociological Forum* 20 (3): 241–448.
Tiryakian, Edward. 1988. "From Durkheim to Managua: Revolutions as Religious Revivals." In *Durkheimian Sociology: Cultural Studies*, edited by Jeffrey C. Alexander, 44–65. New York: Oxford University Press.
Tocqueville, Alexis De. [1835/1840] 2003. *Democracy in America*. New York: Penguin.
Tönnies, Ferdinand. [1887] 1955. *Community and Association*. London: Routledge and Kegan Paul.
Weber, Eugen. 1976. *Peasants into Frenchmen: The Modernization of Rural France, 1870–1914*. Stanford: Stanford University Press.
Wellman, Barry. 2002. "Little Boxes, Glocalization, and Networked Individualism." In *Digital Cities II: Second Kyoto Workshop on Digital Cities*, edited by Makoto Tanabe, Peter van den Besselaar, and Toru Ishida, 10–25. Heidelberg: Springer.
Wimmer, Andreas. 2002. *Nationalist Exclusion and Ethnic Conflict: Shadows of Modernity*. New York: Cambridge University Press.
Zhuo, Xiaolin, Barry Wellman, and Justine Yu. 2011. "Egypt: The First Internet Revolt?" *Peace Magazine* 27 (3): 6–10.

CHAPTER 4

Public and Collective Intimacy

Intimacy Beyond the Private Sphere

Building on the preceding theorization of national solidarity as an offshoot of sociability practices, this chapter introduces a research strategy for studying how social club sociability turns individual strangers into collective friends through the mechanisms of public intimacy and emergent feelings of collective intimacy. As noted by Gary Alan Fine and Brooke Harrington (2004), despite the long list of scholars who have addressed the role played by secondary groups in promoting civic engagement, theorists have typically lacked a micro-level social psychology with which to analyze their claims, such as interactionist group dynamics. To give one example, while Putnam's (2000) influential work on civic associations might be empirically driven, it does not offer any concrete mechanisms to explain how group-level interactions affect macro-level solidarity.

And yet, micro-level interactionist analysis alone is similarly insufficient for explaining the predominance of certain macro-level cultural phenomena, such as the sentiments of national solidarity. A case in point is Paul Lichterman and Nina Eliasoph's (2014) recent ethnographic approach for studying the civic outcomes of micro-level group interactions. They have provided a rich and systematic analysis of the distinct "scene styles" that shape activists' civic engagement, such as distinct speech norms and shared perceptions about the group's boundaries and practices of sociability. However, in attempting to pluralize the

© The Author(s) 2018
D. Kaplan, *The Nation and the Promise of Friendship*, Cultural Sociology, https://doi.org/10.1007/978-3-319-78402-1_4

political outcomes of civic action and underscoring how distinct styles of action engender "different kinds of solidarity" (852), this approach does not solve the basic paradox of collective solidarity in modern societies, namely how despite the growing differentiation and fragmentation of social life compatriots may experience a deep comradeship premised on a monolithic order of unity and singularity (Handelman 1990) rather than on heterogeneity and multiple solidarities.

The current study undertakes a more narrowly tailored interactionist approach designed to explain how social club sociability mediates between interpersonal and collective life. To this end, it considers three dimensions of sociability: (1) interpersonal ties between particular social club members; (2) public intimacy, which is the public staging of interpersonal ties in front of other members or nonmembers; and (3) collective intimacy, which refers to emotions of solidarity shared simultaneously by members of the institution or community as a whole.

I make a crucial distinction here between the "public" dimension, namely the ways in which interactions of sociability are disclosed *in* public and the "collective" dimension, which designates a form of sociability shared collectively *by* the public.[1] Since interpersonal interactions taking place in institutions are inevitably performed in a public or semi-public setting, public intimacy is effectively a dramaturgical mechanism for managing personal bonds and establishing their exclusivity under the gaze of different kinds of spectators. But it is also a mechanism of inclusion, as certain spectators are invited to become participants. Recurrent instances of spectators-turned-participants may, ultimately, extend feelings of closeness to wider circles and give rise to emotions of collective intimacy, which can materialize in ritualized performances of solidarity, such as the public events studied extensively by neo-Durkheimian scholars. I spell out these sets of issues in the following pages. By way of introduction, I first present a brief overview of the ways in which cultural sociologists have addressed intimacy beyond the private sphere.

The application of the term "intimacy"—a term mostly associated with emotions or interactions in the private sphere—to describe sociability at the institutional and national level merits some clarification. Even theorists who make a point of addressing friendship as a political bond often do so by attempting to decouple friendship from intimacy, such as Hannah Arendt (1968) who argued that "it is hard for us to understand the political relevance of friendship" because we see friendship "solely as a phenomenon of intimacy, in which the friends open their hearts to each other unmolested by the world and its demands" (24). The automatic association of intimacy with expressive interactions in the private sphere is shaped by the public–private divide in sociological thought and builds on the aforementioned classic liberal distinction between premodern and modern patterns of friendships (Silver 1990). Anthony Giddens (1991) famously contrasted the kinds of instrumental ties that characterized social life in premodern Europe with the growing propensity in democratic Western societies for practicing the more expressive forms of intimate, "pure relationships" associated with individual choice and heightened emotionality.

In recent decades, however, the term intimacy has been increasingly employed in popular and cultural discourse in connection with the public sphere. Interestingly, the meanings of intimacy in this discourse straddle, often inadvertently, two analytically distinct dimensions: intimacy as a confiding style of *communication*, associated with the authentic disclosure of self, and intimacy as a preferential and particularist style of *relationship* connecting two or more individuals in various exclusive bonds. These dimensions echo a distinction made by Jeff Weintraub (1997) between two different logics governing the public–private dichotomy: one associated with "visibility" and the other with "collectivity" (5).[2]

In private life, denotations of intimacy as a form of communication and intimacy as a form of relationship often overlap. Intimacy is employed interchangeably to denote self-disclosure, privileged knowledge, and familiarity as well as close association, strong positive emotions toward significant others, and high levels of trust (Jamieson 2005). In contrast, recent attempts to theorize the growing use of intimacy in the public sphere have focused mainly on intimacy-as-communication, locating it within an "identitarian" framework and neglecting its second meaning as a form of social tie.

Central to this line of work is the critical engagement with what has come to be known as the rise of "therapeutic discourse" in post-industrial societies. As described by Eva Illouz (2007), this dominant cultural structure challenges individuals to become more self-reflective and to create an authentic narrative of personal transformation from suffering to salvation by adopting a confiding style of communication along the lines of therapy conversations. The therapeutic discourse is rooted in the science of psychology, processes of individualization, and the ideals of liberalism (see also Furedi 2004). Robert Bellah et al. (1985) lamented how this form of "expressive individualism" has permeated public culture, and Richard Sennett (1977) criticized the overinvestment in intimate life for causing a falling away from public involvement and undermining the impersonal practices of sociability and civility through which strangers can interact qua strangers. Echoing these earlier observations, a growing body of sociological and media studies has started to examine the ways that this preferred style of intimate communication and heightened self-disclosure has come to dominate the public sphere and to govern the appearances of both celebrities and ordinary people on traditional and social media, encouraging individual actors to publicly "share" their inner feelings and true self (Illouz 2007; John 2013; Livingstone and Lunt 1993).

A similar understanding of intimacy-as-communication is employed in several discussions of nationalism and authenticity. Scholars noted how Romanticist notions of authentic selfhood appear in formulations of national identity (Greenfeld 1992) as a realization of the "true collective 'self'" and "inner voice" of the purified community (Smith 1991, 77). Calhoun (1997) noted that the ideological shifts associated with nationalism made the association of people and state "seem more intimate" (77). Ringmar's (1998) thesis, introduced in Chapter 3, presented a brilliant discussion of this cultural transformation in terms of political identification. Ringmar suggested that the modern, democratic public sphere became associated with nationalism once public interactions were linked with the authentic expression of the self and were expected to become "as intimate and true as the interaction taking place in a company of friends" (542).[3] The growing importance attached to the identity and character of politicians and not just to their interests and policies led to the expectation that rulers and the ruled could share a similar collective identity.

Michael Herzfeld (2005) developed another innovative perspective on the ways that "cultural intimacy" emerges in the national context. He examined how certain collective customs, considered as authentically national, are a source of both pride and embarrassment to be negotiated inside but not outside. Herzfeld focused on the complex interrelations between localized communities and national-level political forces that cause a "strain between the creative presentation of the individual self and formal image of the national or collective self" (x). Here too, intimacy is extended to the public sphere as a form of communication analyzed through the prism of disclosure and discretion. Similar to other reappraisals of national identity discourse, Herzfeld's approach serves to destabilize collective representations of the national as a fixed identity but does not address intimacy as a form of relationship and hence does not directly address questions of national solidarity. Where his work centers on the meanings that various actors in the national community assign to their shared customs, the framework of public and collective intimacy shifts attention to the social interactions taking place between actors and the meanings that they assign to these interactions.

INTRODUCING PUBLIC INTIMACY

My strategy for studying public intimacy in institutional contexts draws on the understudied dimension of intimacy as a relationship rather than as a form of communication. Simmel (1950) noted that exclusivity is a basic factor in defining and shaping the boundaries of intimate relationships and friendships in that it privileges access to private information (369–370). However, it is the public staging of relationships that are usually kept private that actually defines them as intimate and differentiates them from more casual interactions (Schwarz 2011). In this sense, the concept of public intimacy emphasizes that bonds acquire a sense of exclusivity and, consequently, a sense of intimacy only as the end result of the publicly staged performance.

I initially identified the mechanisms of public intimacy in a previous study of personal friendships among Israeli men (Kaplan 2005). I explored how male confidants maintained social ties that evolved in particular institutions (school, workplace, and military) and carried them over to other settings through the constant outward performance of their friendship (see Chapter 9 for examples pertaining to military friendships). The men staged their bonds in everyday life in front of peers, colleagues, and complete strangers by employing a humorous, ambiguous, and often unintelligible code language which involved nicknames, curses, nonsense talk, and affectionate-aggressive physical gestures. As studied by Fine (1984), the humorous interaction does not by itself create meanings; rather it plays off implicit meanings to present novel, situational ones (97). The ambivalence created by this provocative speech and gestures suspends a clear-cut emotional reaction by the respondents but, at the same time, practically forces them to respond and to engage deeper in the interaction. Thus, this homosocial (male-to-male) coded communication does not so much convey explicit meaning as it teases the participants and seduces those who qualify to be participants to get involved.

Marta Dynel (2008) noted the dichotomous nature of teasing and banter which, similar to other expressions of humor, function in an ambivalent manner (246–247). The humorous utterance can be interpreted as an expression of aggression against the hearer and an act of exclusion from the group but also as an act of inclusion and solidarity, inviting those who find the remark amusing into the group. Ridiculing and pulling pranks on other members of the group place them in a position of inferiority, yet it also works to create a sense of potential equality within the group in comparison with other groups. The principle of rotating roles in these symbolic acts of domination and submission assures that everyone gets to play both attacker and attacked, to be audience and performer. While this kind of staged joking relationship is especially pronounced in male homosocial enclaves (Lyman 1987; Benwell 2004), a similar dynamic can be found in almost any public or semi-public social setting—consider, for example, the historical accounts of sociability in nineteenth-century French cafés described in Chapter 3. Benet Davetian (2009; following Haine 1996) provided a discerning account of the ways in which café etiquette regulated these dynamics of teasing and seduction, exclusion, and inclusion:

> A small group could initiate a discussion and then bring in people from the periphery to participate; meanwhile, a person was expected to observe café etiquette and not interrupt a conversation already in progress (Haine 1996). Witty comments were the best admission ticket to an ongoing conversation. Jibes and remarks were not to be taken too seriously, nor was a person to press the point and request a fight to settle a point of honor. A sense of savoir faire required the wounded party to come back with his own verbal riposte (a fencing term describing the exchange of blows of the sword). Conversation remained a competition of wits, and this verbal competition went a long way in avoiding potential violence. (Davetian 2009, 133)

William Scott Haine (1996) concluded that the small-scale nature of most groups congregating in cafés and the informality and mutability of these groups "permitted individuals to have much more chance of joining in the interaction" and "to find friends and contacts in the café" (177).

On a more general level, these non-utilitarian, humorous interactions correspond to Simmel's (1950) discussion of informal sociability consisting of talk for the sake of talking that derives its significance from the "fascinating play of relations which they create among participants, joining and loosening, winning and succumbing, giving and taking" (52).

At the same time, whereas for Simmel this form of playful sociability temporarily suspends binding social roles and is therefore analytically separated from "real" life, I understand public intimacy as a central building block for wider social ties. Because the meaning conveyed in these playful interactions is open-ended and ambivalent, it encourages both participants and others to engage deeper with the interaction. The triads of public intimacy thus hold a generative quality and enable certain spectators to become participants. In contrast to the aforementioned studies of intimacy-as-communication that focused on intimate self-disclosure by the individual actor as prescribed by the therapeutic discourse, an emphasis on the public staging of intimate relationships between several actors opens up the possibility that spectators not only identify and empathize with the participants but also become involved in the social interaction themselves.

This understanding goes back to yet another aspect of Simmel's (1950, 135–169) work, namely his discussion of the qualitative difference between a dyad and a triad. Once a third party enters a dyad, the tie is no longer dependent solely on the individual will of each member and can continue to exist even if one member departs. Thus, for Simmel, a triad is the cornerstone of larger close-knit cliques. But the key to this, I argue, lies in a dynamic of seduction which, by establishing a sense of exclusivity under the gaze of spectators, teases and invites them to become participants who can, in turn, stage the same performance of exclusivity under the gaze of new actors. In this way, a triad of public intimacy can extend to wider circles and ultimately account for higher-level solidarity—not only because the interpersonal tie expands to a clique or to a large network but also because the underlying feelings of exclusivity, familiarity, and loyalty associated with close friendships are retained even as their reach expands to a larger collectivity.

Sociability as Social Performance

In order to understand how sociability and ties of friendship affect collective-level solidarity, we need to consider acts of public intimacy within a broader theoretical context of social performances and cultural meanings. By this, I am referring to Alexander's (2004) dramaturgical theory of "cultural pragmatics" which theorizes the intersection between performance, ritual, and social action. According to this approach, performers[4] and audiences are embedded in a shared cultural understanding—a symbolic realm that enjoys a level of autonomy and provides a limited context for making sense of the social performance. This approach focuses mainly on collectively shared social drama such as the outbreak of a national crisis or scandal. As noted by Eliasoph and Lichterman (2003), in these sacred events in which performers perform in a style of "high seriousness," the underlying cultural codes may appear relatively evident. But in the variable settings of ordinary life high seriousness is not usually the mode and social interactions allow for diverse group styles that can give different meanings to the same codes (744–745).

Similar to Eliasoph's approach, my interest in interactions of sociability in everyday institutional life may, ostensibly, suggest a much more open-ended interpretation than is implicated in the cultural codes of ritualized social performances. However, in line with Alexander's (2004) cultural pragmatics, the crux of the framework of public intimacy is to consider how the meanings given to everyday interactions rely on underlying cultural codes and beliefs that inform collective sentiments of solidarity. The question to ask, therefore, is how public intimacy—the staged performance of everyday interpersonal sociability—figures in the framework of social performance.

Alexander (2004) defined cultural performance as "the social processes through which actors, individually or in concert, display for others the meaning of their social situation" (529). Social performances are not confined to macro-level phenomena. Alexander (2006) mentioned in passing that just as fused performance is more readily attainable in small (premodern) societies with simplified social organization, fusion in complex societies is also possible in some micro-level relations in which elements of performances can be controlled carefully, such as "between the faithful and their priest," or "between patients and their doctors and therapists" (96).

Regardless of how the performers themselves interpret their situation, what they display is the meaning that they consciously or unconsciously wish to have others believe in. On this point, Alexander (2004) brought up Hans Gerth and Charles Wright Mills (1964) who noted that: "Our gestures do not necessarily 'express' our prior feelings," but rather "they make available to others a sign" (55). In this regard, public intimacy is a particular kind of social performance in which two or more performers display their social situation to others, the meaning of which lies, however, not in any explicit content that this communication signifies to them or to the spectators but rather in the message of exclusivity that is conveyed.

Public intimacy thus follows the metacommunicative logic of secrecy. Secrecy binds together those who share exclusive knowledge by publicly declaring "this is a secret" (Bellman 1981). It binds the confidants not only because they have privileged access to particular content but also because the public declaration signifies and establishes this shared knowledge as an intimate bond. In this sense, secrecy is effectively the opposite of privacy: it is a dramaturgical mechanism for affording personal bonds with public significance.[5] While effective social performance lies "in the ability to convince others that one's performance is true" (Alexander 2004, 529), an effective performance of public intimacy lies not in providing a reasonable, authentic account of some external truth but in signaling that the social performance on display is a close relationship. Whether or not the performers express explicit feelings about their relationship, they need to convince others of their exclusivity, mutual familiarity, and potential loyalty; in other words, to demonstrate that they are confidants and friends.

Going back to the question of how public intimacy figures in the framework of social performance, it might be helpful to think of the relation between everyday sociability and collective performances of solidarity in terms of the basic distinction between "occurrences" and "events" (Mast 2006, 117). Occurrences exist in a social actor's awareness only temporarily and discretely; they do not transcend their original contexts, and they fail to reach public attention. Events, by contrast, are a set of narratively interconnected occurrences that have achieved generalization. Orchestrated and reactively mediated by purposeful performers, they draw public attention as unusually significant meaning constellations, removed from the specificity of everyday life and eventually ingrained in collective memory (Mast 2006; following Alexander 1988).

Underlying this analytic observation is, in fact, a dual shift from a single occurrence to the plurality of narratively interconnected occurrences and from mundane personal life to the sacredness of collective life. A corresponding dual shift from single to plural and from personal to collective experience can be seen in the move from sociability to friendship and from friendship to solidarity. Friendship ties developing in social institutions can be regarded as a series of discrete, fleeting interactions or "occurrences" of sociability between strangers which have achieved generalization and are retrospectively interpreted by the participants as mutually meaningful personal "events" on which their friendship was built. It is, among other things, the dramaturgical mechanism of public intimacy that singles out certain occurrences as exclusive interactions and differentiates them from more casual interactions in the participants' lives.

In the course of their lives, individuals accumulate numerous such friendships—in effect, personal narratives of strangers-turned-friends—across a variety of institutional settings. This may prompt an underlying, collectively shared meta-narrative of strangers-turned-friends operating at the symbolic cultural level and associated with national solidarity discourse, as I describe in Chapter 5. However, for this second move from friendship to solidarity to take shape requires a performative act that captures public attention and could translate the idiosyncratic, personal "events" of individual friendships into the ritualized collective events that make up the bread and butter of mass solidarity; in other words, it requires the staging of a full-blown social performance in the public sphere which could set off and reaffirm the culturally shared meta-narrative. As I discuss below, while the existing literature has addressed solidarity in public events mostly in terms of shared focused attention, it could also be explained in terms of social ties played out in front of the largest public available. To recap, the first move from institutional sociability to friendship entails an accumulation of mundane occurrences of friend-making at the individual level, whereas the second move from friendship to solidarity involves a public event set apart from everyday life in which a collectivity of individuals interact with one another simultaneously and reaffirm the experiences of sociability and friend-making learnt by each of them independently.

COLLECTIVE INTIMACY IN PUBLIC EVENTS: BRINGING SOCIABILITY BACK IN

> Emotion turns the person inside-out, so that totalizing feeling states are evident on persons' exteriors, yet felt as their interiors, such that it is their interiors that are totalized together, rather than their exteriors. Therefore collective effervescence is felt as intimate. This trajectory of emotion… indexes the intimate sharing of solidarity. (Handelman 2007, 123)

In interactional terms, the move from sociability and friendship to solidarity is a move from accumulated acts of public intimacy to simultaneous feelings of collective intimacy. Given the preceding discussion, it would seem only reasonable to examine how interactions of sociability figure in the ritualized public events studied in neo-Durkheimian scholarship and consider the role that past experiences of friendship play in the resultant sense of solidarity. Surprisingly, these issues have, thus far, been ignored in Durkheimian theory.

The Durkheimian tradition highlights how sacred ritualized events reaffirm collective identity and shared values by creating a surge in feelings of solidarity. The basic mechanisms were discussed by Durkheim (2003) in terms of collective "effervescence"—a social energy that strengthens social emotions by bringing "all those who share them into more intimate and more dynamic relationship" (140). The successful performance depends on simultaneous participation and sense of unisonance: "by shouting the same cry, saying the same words, and performing the same action in regard to the same object" (118). This passionate energy produces exaltation, transporting persons outside themselves: "it is no longer a simple individual who speaks; it is a group incarnate and personified" (Durkheim 2008, 210). The common theme in these accounts is that the ritualized event focuses widespread attention such that each participant is assured that others are paying attention to the same object and feeling the same emotions.

Collins' (2004) framework of interaction ritual chains has followed suit and offers the only systematic model of collective effervescence to date that is formulated in interactional terms. Building closely on Goffman's (1967) concept of "interaction ritual," Collins developed a general and highly abstract analysis of group solidarity based on the physical co-presence of the participants who share a contagion of emotion, a common focus of attention and mutual awareness. The ritual invokes the symbolic object to which members of the group become attached. According to Collins, much of social life consists of strings of such group interactions, and groups may cycle between periods of high-intensity rituals that revive the meaning of membership and periods of dispersed existence with little reminder of their commonality. However, due to its radically micro-level focus with no allusion to questions of phenomenology, Collins' framework fails to problematize and address the basic dichotomies and paradoxes underlying the problem of solidarity in society in the first place, namely the public–private divide and the distinctions between strangers and friends. Moreover, according to this mechanistic and context-free model of human interaction, moral sentiments and collective emotions become merely an emergent property of individual-level behavior rather than part of a cultural realm that could give meaning and regulate micro-level interactions (Smith and Alexander 2005, 8).

The aforementioned cultural pragmatics approach (Alexander 2004), on the other hand, underlines how in order for the ritualized performance to be successful and to enhance feelings of solidarity, it must be convincingly authentic and enjoy a widely shared understanding of intention and content. Ideally, the ritual "energizes the participants and attaches them to each other, increases their identification with the symbolic objects of communication, and intensifies the connection of the participants and the symbolic objects with the observing audience, the relevant 'community' at large" (527). However, modern, large-scale collectivities are segmented and differentiated in ways that prevent a social performance from fully resonating with the target audience. In order to attain ritual-like quality, performances need to "re-fuse" their various disentangled elements: performers, audiences, representations (background symbols and foreground scripts), means of symbolic production, social power, and mise-en-scène.

This re-fusion is vital for modern, complex societies, as "even the most democratic and individuated societies depend on the ability to sustain collective belief" and share sacred myths (Alexander 2004, 568). Although this approach does not regard social ties or sociability as a distinct category of analysis, by delineating the relations between performers and audiences it provides some leeway for studying the interactions between various social actors situated at different positions in the social performance but sharing a similar cultural belief system.

Durkheimian perspectives on the cohesive power of ritualized public events are particularly pertinent to national communities and national movements. For instance, Jonathan Wyrtzen (2013) studied a defining moment in the anti-colonial protest that birthed the Moroccan nation, when nationalist activists repurposed a Muslim prayer traditionally recited in local Mosques and linked it to current contentious events. Wyrtzen examined how through social performance selected "patches" of high culture and invented traditions resonated and struck a chord with the mass audience beyond local elites, fusing intense religious emotion with a nascent sense of national identity.

If the ideal of re-fusion is essentially to collapse distinctions between participants and audiences, a case in point can be found in Hizky Shoham's (2009) historical study of the annual Purim festivals celebrated in Tel Aviv prior to the establishment of the State of Israel. At its peak, this site of pilgrimage possibly attracted more than half of the entire Jewish population of Palestine. Shoham suggested that through this periodic gathering the masses could literally encounter the newly formed Jewish nation not as an abstract, discursive construction but physically and visibly as an independent social entity, presented by and to the people. Thus, in a typical Durkheimian circular fashion, the nation became both the subject and object of collective worship.

This Durkheimian tradition continues to have great explanatory power for collective events in late modernity when solidarity (whether affirmed or contested) is enacted mainly through the media sphere (Cottle 2006). The paradigmatic concept of "media events" introduced by Daniel Dayan and Elihu Katz (1992) captured many of these Durkheimian ideas. It provided a systematic theoretical and empirical model for studying live televised coverage of exceptional events as heroic spectacles of contest, conquest, or coronation that draw millions of people together and enable them to take part simultaneously in the event despite their physical dispersion. As noted by Jeffrey Alexander and Ronald Jacobs (1998), media events "erase the divide between private and public" by providing common rituals and symbols which "citizens can experience contemporaneously with everyone and interpersonally with those around them" (27–28). In Chapter 8, I explore the role of media events in generating public and collective intimacy based on a study of the reality TV show *Big Brother*.

Ultimately, despite the role of face-to-face or mediated interactions in mass public events, the analytic focus in Durkheimian scholarship is directed mainly at processes of collective identity formation and pays little heed to interpersonal ties and sociability. Although Durkheim emphasized that emotional life is transpersonal and grounded in interpersonal interactions (Emirbayer 1996), he did not study social ties systematically and, for the most part, considered interpersonal relationships, such as friendship, as capable of joining individuals to one another without being linked to society (Mallory and Carlson 2014). In the same vein, the diverse neo-Durkheimian approaches reviewed above—whether formulating solidarity as interactional chains, as a fusion of differentiated elements in a social performance, or as engagement in media events—did not tackle the actual social ties between participants in the performance and the meanings assigned to these social ties.

Public events are social spaces where participants not only gather together but also interact with one another, engaging in preexisting social ties with friends and acquaintances encountered at the event and forming new interactions with unacquainted participants. Most significantly, these ties are staged and performed in front of all other fellow participants. This is where the concept of collective intimacy differs from related terms such as collective effervescence or fusion. It is not simply an instance of shared focused attention generating involuntary emotional contagion that is at stake but a more complex emotional engagement with fellow participants. By building on past experiences of public intimacy, collective intimacy reflects a dual transition—both interactional and relational—from spectators into participants and from strangers into confidants and friends.

The emotional term that perhaps best captures this transformation is "complicity." Complicity can be applied equally to both individuals and collectives and incorporates the same feelings of exclusivity, familiarity, and loyalty that are characteristic of close friendships, with the added elements of shared secret knowledge and active participation (as well as the negative connotation of conspiracy). It therefore signifies both the interactional position of involvement and the relational role of being a confidant. In the context of audience studies, complicity is sometimes invoked to address the moment when the spectator becomes intimately engaged with the performer, the script, or other elements in the performance (Iser 1993; Barre 2014; Weizman 2013) and may bear moral responsibility (Silverstone 2002; Peters 2009). More specifically, Isaac Reed (2006) highlighted that certain types of social performance are characterized by complicity in that all performers and audiences work from within the same deeply felt set of collective representations, even when offering conflicting views and narratives in the social drama.

Ari Adut (2012) noted that central to ritualized events is, among other things, a sense of mutual awareness, the fact that the group of strangers who assemble realize that they are all spectators or participants in the same event, in other words, "the situation where everyone knows that everyone knows that everyone knows" (245). But what exactly does everyone know? What is the widely shared understanding enacted and revealed by the ritualized performance?

Several options come to mind. The straightforward answer is that the common understanding that redefines the participants as accomplices is the specific news event or public scandal being addressed by the social performance and, more broadly, the underlying cultural belief system shared by all the participants (Alexander 2004; Reed 2006). Herzfeld's (2005) formulation of cultural intimacy poignantly reveals how complicity operates within a national belief system. Shared customs that are considered disreputable constitute a "discretely maintained secret" (60) that local actors are expected to manage internally while, at the same time, presenting a picture of collective unity to outsiders. This shows how a sense of common understanding is accomplished through acts of complicity.[6]

But from the perspective of collective intimacy (as opposed to cultural intimacy) feelings of complicity may also point to a more fundamental grasp on common understanding—a revelation that pertains to the performance itself and not to some independent, predetermined knowledge base (similar to how the meaning of public intimacy lies not in any explicit content or predetermined feelings held by the actors but in the message of exclusivity conveyed to the spectators). Thus, two additional options can be suggested here. One is that the ritualized performance reveals and reaffirms the collective body of the community itself. Through the mass public gathering, anonymous individuals become momentarily tangible to the participants as a distinct, collective group of people. The other possibility, however, is that what becomes tangible for participants is not the public news and common belief system nor the existence of a collectivity of individuals but the existence of cohesive social ties between these individuals, an imagining of the community as a network of friends.

Although, in practice, these three forms of collective revelation and understanding are bound to overlap, it is analytically important to distinguish between them. While the first two may account for the way in which a national community is formed around shared knowledge, values, customs, and group boundaries—in other words, around a collective identity—it is only through the third aspect of social ties experienced as collective intimacy that we can begin to explain people's sense of national solidarity.

Let me illustrate this point with a final Durkheimian account of a ritualized social performance. Anderson's (1991, 35–36) renowned analysis of the newspaper reading ritual is a brilliant example of a mediated public event, foreshadowing Dayan and Katz's (1992) paradigm of televised media events. The appearance of modern newspapers in mass circulation ("one-day best-sellers") occasioned daily mediated encounters between fellow citizens who share the same news stories. Although the stories are read in silent privacy, each reader gathers visible reassurance about the existence of like-minded readers in public spaces and is, ultimately, confident about the existence of millions of others "of whose identity he has not the slightest notion" (Anderson 1991, 35). These insights can serve to explain the emergence of national solidarity in terms of the first two forms of common understanding noted above. First, newspapers formed the basis for common public knowledge, linking unrelated yet concurrent events and assigning them new cultural meanings rooted in the readers' lives and collective beliefs. Second, thanks to mass circulation, readers could imagine themselves living their lives in parallel with millions of anonymous fellow readers with whom they shared a common history and destiny. In other words, through the act of reading, the ontological existence of the national community is dramatized and reaffirmed.

But what is missing from Anderson's account is the third common understanding: the significance of familiarity and sociability for forging solidarity. For even though he presented this virtual communion as a "community in anonymity" (36), it actually illustrates the opposite, namely the shift from anonymity to familiarity. Newspaper readers become intimately familiar with the actions and motivations of fellow individuals—politicians and laypeople, successful heroes and failed antiheroes. The readers not only learn of individuals who have come to fame but also sympathize with the way that these strangers interact and perform socially. Along these lines, in her study of early American novels, Elizabeth Barnes (1997) noted how literary and political texts began to represent sociopolitical issues and concerns through the vocabulary of personal life staged as family dramas. Amit Rai (2002) went on to highlight how this increasingly intimate language enabled readers to sympathetically identify with public strangers shown to be like themselves. He noted that this combination of sympathy and familiarity became the definitive way of "practicing human relations" in American national culture (11) or, rather, in my words, of forming solidarity by observing how others perform these social relations. Thus, when readers share public stories, the common understanding that emerges pertains not only to shared knowledge, values, customs, and group boundaries but also to shared sociability.

To summarize, in public events, participants encounter a multitude of others who are all privy to the same social performance. As they become aware that they share practices of sociability—that they went or go to the same clubs—they may become a collective group of accomplices experiencing feelings of collective intimacy. Unlike the gradual transformation of strangers into friends in everyday life, such public gatherings occasion a unique and alchemic instant transformation of spectators into participants and strangers into confidants, a magical enactment of the meta-narrative of strangers-turned-friends. However, in order for this leap of confidence to take place, participants must have reassurance in the ability of others to form close-knit mutual ties—a reassurance that could only develop through successful past experiences of making friends as accumulated in everyday life in a variety of social institutions, in other words, through mundane staged performances of public intimacy. In this way, the public event becomes a proxy for successful past experiences of choosing one's friends in the life of each member. These interactional and relational dimensions of solidarity as contemporaneous complicity and its dependence on accumulated experience with public intimacy were not addressed by Durkheimian studies of collective effervescence and related terms.

The concepts of public and collective intimacy differ in how they relate to the separation between private and public life. Public intimacy is built on the separation between insiders and outsiders, celebrating both the exclusivity of interpersonal ties and the selectivity of admission. Pure instances of collective intimacy, on the other hand, imagine a unified whole and hence eliminate the very distinction between private and public life. Nevertheless, both constructs capture the particularist and preferential sentiments of familiarity, exclusivity, and loyalty that characterize both friendship and national attachment. If public intimacy underlines how at the micro level exclusive bonds are the end result of a publicly staged interaction, the end result of collective intimacy is similarly an exclusive bond but at the macro level.

Notes

1. While these terms are often indistinguishable in their common usage in English, the equivalent Hebrew adjectives *pumbi* (in public) and *tziburi* (collective, by or of the public) readily differentiate between these two denotations. It is this blind spot in the English usage that motivated me to delve deeper into these analytic distinctions.
2. "Visibility" refers to what is hidden or withdrawn in contrast to what is revealed or accessible. "Collectivity" refers to what is individual or pertains only to an individual in contrast to what is collective or affects the interests of a collectivity of individuals (Weintraub 1997, 5).
3. This phrasing could have easily opened up an alternative reading of intimacy as a new form of relationship between citizens rather than a new form of communication as Ringmar intended, if only it were to read "interaction taking place *between* friends" rather than "in a company of friends." This is but one example of how a seemingly subtle slippage in the meaning of intimacy may conceal an important distinction between national attachment as an identity and as a social tie.

4. For the sake of analytic clarity, I have substituted Alexander's specific allusion to an "actor" in a social performance with the term "performer" in order to avoid confusion with the wider meaning of actor or social actor as any individual who exercises agency including members of the audience.
5. For additional discussion of the relation between secrecy and privacy see Herzfeld's (2009) analysis of the performances of secrecy in public spaces.
6. As an example, Herzfeld brings up the case of a collectivity as large as the European Union: when EU officials act in a defensive manner in the face of a political crisis and subscribe to a cultural intimacy in which old myths can be advantageously redeployed—for instance, that the Greeks are corrupt, whereas the British and the Scandinavians are corruption-free—then one could say that the EU has achieved a measure of cohesion and a sense of collective European identity (Herzfeld 2013). Here, too, what accomplices share is some form of tacit knowledge: "…that of winks and nudges, of 'what everyone knows'…[a] common ground shared by those countries that have been accused of corruption and those countries that sanctimoniously insist that they have largely succeeded in eliminating it" (495).

References

Adut, Ari. 2012. "A Theory of the Public Sphere." *Sociological Theory* 30 (4): 238–262.
Alexander, Jeffrey C. 1988. "Culture and Political Crisis: 'Watergate' and Durkheimian Sociology." In *Durkheimian Sociology: Cultural Studies*, edited by Jeffrey C. Alexander, 187–224. New York: Oxford University Press.
Alexander, Jeffrey C. 2004. "Cultural Pragmatics: Social Performance Between Ritual and Strategy." *Sociological Theory* 22 (4): 527–573.
Alexander, Jeffrey C. 2006. "From the Depths of Despair: Performance, Counter Performance, and 'September 11'." In *Social Performance: Symbolic Action, Cultural Pragmatics, and Ritual*, edited by Jeffrey C. Alexander, Bernhard Giesen, and Jason L. Mast, 91–114. Cambridge: Cambridge University Press.
Alexander, Jeffrey C., and Ronald N. Jacobs. 1998. "Mass Communication, Ritual and Civil Society." In *Media, Ritual and Identity*, edited by Tamar Liebes and James Curran, 23–41. London: Routledge.
Anderson, Benedict. [1983] 1991. *Imagined Communities: Reflections on the Origins and Spread of Nationalism*. London: Verso.
Arendt, Hannah. 1968. *Men in Dark Times*. San Diego: Harcourt Brace.
Barnes, Elizabeth. 1997. *States of Sympathy: Seduction and Democracy in the American Novel*. New York: Columbia University Press.
Barre, Nelson. 2014. "'It's Crazy, That Was Us': The Implicated and Compliant Audience in the Boys of Foley Street." *Comparative Drama* 48 (1): 103–116.

Bellah, Robert N., Richard Madsen, William Sullivan, Ann Swidler, and Steven Tipton. 1985. *Habits of the Heart: Individualism and Commitment in American Life*. Berkeley: University of California Press.
Bellman, Beryl L. 1981. "The Paradox of Secrecy." *Human Studies* 4: 1–24.
Benwell, Bethan. 2004. "Ironic Discourse: Evasive Masculinity in Men's Lifestyle Magazines." *Men and Masculinities* 7 (1): 3–21.
Calhoun, Craig. 1997. "Nationalism and the Public Sphere." In *Public and Private in Thought and Practice*, edited by Jeff Weintraub and Krishan Kumar, 75–93. Chicago: University of Chicago Press.
Collins, Randall. 2004. *Interaction Ritual Chains*. Princeton: Princeton University Press.
Cottle, Simon. 2006. "Mediatized Rituals: Beyond Manufacturing Consent." *Media, Culture and Society* 28 (3): 411–432.
Davetian, Benet. 2009. *Civility: A Cultural History*. Toronto: Toronto University Press.
Dayan, Daniel, and Elihu Katz. 1992. *Media Events: The Live Broadcasting of History*. Cambridge, MA: Harvard University Press.
Durkheim, Emile. [1915] 2003. "The Elementary Forms of Religious Life," translated by Karen E. Fields. In *Emile Durkheim: Sociologist of Modernity*, edited by Mustafa Emirbayer, 109–121, 140–141. Malden, MA: Blackwell.
Durkheim, Emile. [1915] 2008. *The Elementary Forms of the Religious Life*. Translated by Joseph W. Swain. Mineola, NY: Dover.
Dynel, Marta. 2008. "No Aggression, Only Teasing: The Pragmatics of Teasing and Banter." *Lodz Papers in Pragmatics* 4 (2): 241–261.
Eliasoph, Nina, and Paul Lichterman. 2003. "Culture in Interaction." *American Journal of Sociology* 108 (4): 735–794.
Emirbayer, Mustafa. 1996. "Useful Durkheim." *Sociological Theory* 14 (2): 109–130.
Fine, Gary Alan. 1984. "Humorous Interaction and the Social Construction of Meaning: Making Sense in a Jocular Vein." *Studies in Symbolic Interaction* 5: 83–101.
Fine, Gary Alan, and Harrington Brooke. 2004. "Tiny Publics: Small Groups and Civil Society." *Sociological Theory* 22 (3): 341–356.
Furedi, Frank. 2004. *Therapy Culture: Cultivating Vulnerability in an Uncertain Age*. London: Routledge.
Gerth, Hans Heinrich, and Charles Wright Mills. 1964. *Character and Social Structure: The Psychology of Social Institutions*. New York: Harcourt, Brace, and World.
Giddens, Anthony. 1991. *Modernity and Self-identity: Self and Society in the Late Modern Age*. Stanford: Stanford University Press.
Goffman, Ervin. 1967. *Interaction Ritual: Essays on Face-To-Face Behavior*. Chicago: Aldine.

Greenfeld, Liah. 1992. *Nationalism: Five Roads to Modernity*. Cambridge, MA: Harvard University Press.
Haine, William Scott. 1996. *The World of the Paris Café: Sociability Among the French Working Class, 1789–1914*. Baltimore: John Hopkins University Press.
Handelman, Don. 1990. *Models and Mirrors: Toward an Anthropology of Public Events*. Cambridge: Cambridge University Press.
Handelman, Don. 2007. "The Cartesian Divide of the Nation-State." In *The Emotions: A Cultural Reader*, edited by Helena Wulff, 119–140. Oxford: Berg.
Herzfeld, Michael. [1997] 2005. *Cultural Intimacy: Social Poetics in the Nation-State*. New York: Routledge.
Herzfeld, Michael. 2009. "The Performance of Secrecy: Domesticity and Privacy in Public Spaces." *Semiotica* 175: 135–162.
Herzfeld, Michael. 2013. "The European Crisis and Cultural Intimacy." *Studies in Ethnicity and Nationalism* 13 (3): 491–497.
Illouz, Eva. 2007. *Cold Intimacies: The Making of Emotional Capitalism*. Oxford: Polity Press.
Iser, Wolfgang. 1993. *Prospecting: From Reader Response to Literary Anthropology*. Baltimore: John Hopkins University Press.
Jamieson, Lynn. 2005. "Boundaries of Intimacy." In *Families in Society: Boundaries and Relationships*, edited by Linda McKie and Sarah Cunningham-Burley, 189–206. Bristol: Policy Press.
John, Nicholas A. 2013. "The Social Logics of Sharing." *Communication Review* 16 (3):113–131.
Kaplan, Danny. 2005. "Public Intimacy: Dynamics of Seduction in Male Homosocial Interactions." *Symbolic Interaction* 28 (4): 571–595.
Lichterman, Paul, and Nina Eliasoph. 2014. "Civic Action." *American Journal of Sociology* 120 (3): 798–863.
Livingstone, Sonia, and Peter Lunt. 1993. *Talk on Television: Audience Participation and Public Debate*. Oxford: Routledge.
Lyman, Peter. 1987. "The Fraternal Bond as a Joking Relationship: A Case Study of the Role of Sexist Jokes in Male Group Bonding." In *Changing Men: New Directions in Research on Men and Masculinity*, edited by Michael Kimmel, 148–163. Newbury Park: Sage.
Mallory, Peter, and Carlson Jesse. 2014. "Rethinking Personal and Political Friendship with Durkheim." *Distinktion: Scandinavian Journal of Social Theory* 15 (3): 327–342.
Mast, Jason. 2006. "The Cultural Pragmatics of Event-ness: The Clinton/Lewinsky Affair." In *Social Performance: Symbolic Action, Cultural Pragmatics, and Ritual*, edited by Jeffrey C. Alexander, Bernhard Giesen, and Jason Mast, 115–145. Cambridge: Cambridge University Press.

Peters, John Durham. 2009. "Witnessing." In *Media Witnessing: Testimony in the Age of Mass Communication*, edited by Paul Frosh and Amit Pinchevski, 23–24. Basingstoke: Palgrave Macmillan.
Putnam, Robert. 2000. *Bowling Alone*. New York: Simon and Schuster.
Rai, Amit S. 2002. *Rule of Sympathy: Sentiment, Race, and Power, 1750–1850*. New York: Palgrave.
Reed, Isaac. 2006. "Social Dramas, Shipwrecks, and Cockfights: Conflict and Complicity in Social Performance." In *Social Performance: Symbolic Action, Cultural Pragmatics, and Ritual*, edited by Jeffrey C. Alexander, Bernhard Giesen, and Jason L. Mast, 146–168. Cambridge: Cambridge University Press.
Ringmar, Erik. 1998. "Nationalism: The Idiocy of Intimacy." *British Journal of Sociology* 49 (4): 534–549.
Schwarz, Ori. 2011. "Who Moved My Conversation? Instant Messaging, Intertextuality and New Regimes of Intimacy and Truth." *Media, Culture & Society* 33 (1): 71–87.
Sennett, Richard. 1977. *The Fall of Public Man*. Cambridge: Cambridge University Press.
Shoham, Hizky. 2009. "'A Huge National Assemblage': Tel Aviv as a Pilgrimage Site in Purim Celebrations (1920–1935)." *Journal of Israeli History* 28 (1): 1–20.
Silver, Allan. 1990. "Friendship in Commercial Society: Eighteenth-Century Social Theory and Modern Sociology." *American Journal of Sociology* 95 (6): 1474–1504.
Silverstone, Roger. 2002. "Complicity and Collusion in the Mediation of Everyday Life." *New Literary History* 33 (4): 761–780.
Simmel, Georg. [1915] 1950. *The Sociology of Georg Simmel*. Translated by Kurt H. Wolff. Glencoe, IL: Free Press.
Smith, Anthony D. 1991. *National Identity*. Reno: University of Nevada Press.
Smith, Philip, and Jeffrey C. Alexander. 2005. "Introduction: The New Durkheim." In *The Cambridge Companion to Durkheim*, edited by Jeffrey C. Alexander and Philip Smith, 1–40. Cambridge: Cambridge University Press.
Weintraub, Jeff. 1997. "The Theory and Politics of the Public/Private Distinction." In *Public and Private in Thought and Practice*, edited by Jeff Weintraub and Krishan Kumar, 1–42. Chicago: University of Chicago Press.
Weizman, Elda. 2013. "Political Irony: Constructing Reciprocal Positioning in the News Interview." In *The Pragmatics of Political Discourse: Explorations Across Cultures*, edited by Anita Fetzer, 167–190. Amsterdam: John Benjamins.
Wyrtzen, Jonathan. 2013. "Performing the Nation in Anti-colonial Protest in Interwar Morocco." *Nations and Nationalism* 19 (4): 615–634.

CHAPTER 5

The Meta-Narrative of Strangers-Turned-Friends

Friendship is forward-looking. Unlike passing interactions between strangers, close personal relationships entail an "expectation of future events" (Hinde 1997, 38). Similarly, when individuals see each other as belonging to the same national community, they expect that in the course of future events they will treat each other in ways that differ from relations between strangers. Whether or not this expectation is warranted, national attachment can be understood as a cultural expectation for future interactions with compatriots and as reassurance (often in an unreflective and taken-for-granted manner) that in times of trial these fellow strangers will act as friends. At the same time, both friendship and nations are also backward-looking. As noted by Bhabha (2013), despite the historical association between the emergence of national ideology and "modern" social life, "nations, like narrative, lose their origins in the myths of time and only fully realize their horizons in the mind's eye" (1).

In this chapter, I discuss how this belief in a shared destiny with individual strangers viewed in the mind's eye as a long-standing, collective group of friends is central to the discourse of national solidarity. I outline the overarching meta-narrative of strangers-turned-friends; a sense of emergent intimacy between two or more individuals that develops gradually or instantaneously and combines the institutional logic of the state—which prescribes cooperation between anonymous citizens—with the mythic logic of the nation—which considers interaction between citizens as a modern incarnation of tribal-fraternal ties.

© The Author(s) 2018
D. Kaplan, *The Nation and the Promise of Friendship*, Cultural Sociology,
https://doi.org/10.1007/978-3-319-78402-1_5

Before I unpack this cultural structure, it is worth quoting a beautifully articulated argument made by Zygmunt Bauman (1991) on the role of friendship, strangership, and enmity in national ideology:

> The national state is designed primarily to deal with the problem of strangers, not enemies. It is precisely this feature that sets it apart from other supra-individual social arrangements. Unlike tribes, the nation-state extends its rule over a territory before it claims the obedience of people. If the tribes can assure the needed collectivization of friends and enemies through the twin processes of attraction and repulsion, self-selection and self-segregation, territorial national states must enforce the friendship where it does not come about by itself. National states must artificially rectify the failures of nature (to create by design what nature failed to achieve by default). In the case of the national state, collectivization of friendship requires conscious effort and force. Among the latter, the mobilization of solidarity with an imagined community...and the universalization of cognitive/behavioural patterns associated with friendship inside of the boundaries of the realm, occupy the pride of place. The national state redefines friends as natives; it commands to extend the rights ascribed "to the friends only" to all—the familiar as much as the unfamiliar—residents of the ruled territory....Were the national state able to reach its objective, there would be no strangers left in the life-world of the residents-turned-natives-turned-patriots. There would be but natives, who are friends, and the foreigners, who are current or potential enemies. The point is, however, that no attempt to assimilate, transform, acculturate, or absorb the ethnic, religious, linguistic, cultural and other heterogeneity and dissolve it in the homogeneous body of the nation has been thus far unconditionally successful. (63–65)

In this quote, Bauman identified the basic logic of nationalism, which he described as "a religion of friendship," as transforming strangers into friends. Unlike tribal ties based on the binary politics of friendship versus enmity, nation-states deal with the problem of anonymous strangers under its rule. Ideally, all state residents are to turn into natives and natives into patriots through the expressive dimension of friendship. However, Bauman offered limited insights as to *how* this is accomplished, except to assume a conscious effort and force by state authorities engaged in an "artificial" project of social engineering, since, in his words, collectivization of friendship cannot happen "naturally" or "by default."

In contrast, I believe that rather than being simply a deliberate effort by state authorities (who use the idea of extended family far more than the trope of friendship to mobilize national solidarity), this process is a forceful yet banal outcome of modernity itself—a byproduct of the fragmentation and rationalization of institutional life. Thus, throughout this book, I discuss the mundane institutions where strangers practice social club sociability and become confidants and friends. This entails a twofold process of socialization and cultural interpretation; it depends not only on the interactionist mechanisms of public intimacy that mobilize spectators to become participants but also on the symbolic lens of national solidarity discourse that gives meaning to certain instances of sociability, conferring on them an aura of friendship and solidarity.

The Friendship and Family Tropes in National Solidarity Discourse

The rise of modern nationalism is closely related to the partial decline of kinship ties as a central organizing principle of the social order and a displacement of the family as a historically situated political institution (McClintock 1994). In turn, I argue that nationalism is equally related to the emergence of friendship as an alternative organizing principle of society and a potent symbol of collective solidarity. Political friendship is the main social construction that energizes and galvanizes national awareness, whereas strong localized kinship networks and tribal ties often hinder nation-building. Perhaps precisely because of this need to override tribal loyalties, national rhetoric actually invokes the family imagery more than it does the imagery of friendship.

Studies have repeatedly noted the use of family metaphors in the discourse of national solidarity, summoning the warmth and support of kin relations and the stability of an inter-generational structure with common ancestry and a shared future (e.g., Handelman 2004, 125; Lauenstein et al. 2015; McClintock 1994; Smith 1991, 78). Family imagery is also employed to describe historic moments of national dissent and dissolution. Struggles for independence are depicted as an inter-generational conflict between children and parents (e.g., the American Revolution framed as a revolt of the "Sons of Liberty" against "Father England," see Nelson 1998, 35) and civil wars as instances of fratricide (e.g., the American and Spanish civil wars, see Anderson (1991, 201–202).

Much less attention, however, has been given to the rhetoric and imagery of friendship. George Mosse (1982) examined the historical correspondences between the rise of nationalism and the cultural discourse of friendship in the writings of modern German intellectuals, noting a shift from an emphasis on the individualistic-humanistic values of friendship to a focus on comradeship—a mode of sociability subscribing to the higher cause of nationalism. My own work on Israeli men's friendship (Kaplan 2006) is one of the few studies to systematically examine some narrative parallels between retrospective accounts of the development of personal bonds over time and prevalent cultural frames used in national solidarity discourse to account for the strength of the collective bond. A central framing of their ongoing friendships which emerged from the men's stories was the notion of a "shared past," namely, the idea that their friendship had grown gradually through shared experiences and activities. Colored by a familial rhetoric, the friend is perceived in such accounts to have been part of the family for years and to have become as close as a brother. An alternative framing, however, was that of "shared destiny," set in the context of a dramatic encounter with a stranger who immediately and miraculously transformed into a friend. This encounter was tinged with a romantic rhetoric, highlighting mutual "chemistry" and flowing communication, emotional thrills, and exclusive spaces where the confidants can enjoy their intimate bond as best friends forever (Kaplan 2006, 2011).

National discourse incorporates parallel cultural framings of "shared past" and "shared destiny" as a way to make sense of the temporal dimensions of solidarity. As famously noted by Anderson (1991), the nation is "imagined to loom out of an immemorial past" and "glide towards a limitless future" (11–12). More specifically, the symbolism of friendship is apparent in declarations of national independence or commemoration, bonding between alienated groups or uniting between the living and the dead. Anderson (1991) provided striking examples of revolutionary junctures in national history when interactions between groups of strangers were reframed as familial/fraternal unions. Thus, in 1821, Latin American liberator Jose San Martin invited marginalized and alienated groups into the newly formed Peruvian nation by declaring: "in the future the aborigines shall not to be called Indians or natives; they are children and citizens of Peru and they shall be known as Peruvians" (quoted in Anderson 1991, 193). By the same token, violent conflicts between rival groups who had little in common but reached a degree of political reconciliation were reframed in collective memory as instances of "fratricide," as in the American and Spanish so-called civil wars: the former effectively a war between two sovereign states and the latter between European cosmopolites and local Fascists (201–202).

This allusion to strangers as fraternal friends appears also in grassroots initiatives of commemoration. As I describe in Chapter 9, in solidarity campaigns for Israeli soldiers missing in action citizens expressed feelings of familiarity and loyalty to soldiers they have never known and participated in public awareness campaigns projecting exclusive intimacy with the soldiers and their families. By turning anonymous citizens into familiar national heroes, rituals of commemoration epitomize the ways that the meta-narrative of strangers-turned-friends juxtaposes and intersects interpersonal and collective experiences; it prescribes a sense of instantaneous familiarity between individuals who were personally indifferent to one another but turned into friends at the collective level.

The discourse of national solidarity elaborates on the family and friendship tropes in a way that echoes the pervasive analytic distinction between the ethno-cultural and civic-contractual models of nationalism, respectively (Kaplan 2007). On the one hand, ongoing ties of solidarity between citizens are made meaningful through the notion of a primordial (ethnic-tribal) past and are inscribed in collective memory through rituals of commemoration, education, popular culture, and the like. This shared past is encapsulated in the prevailing imagery of the nation as an extended family (Smith 1991). On the other hand, these ties are also made meaningful through the notion of shared destiny and are dramatized and romanticized through the magical transformation of strangers into friends. The trope of friendship stresses civic-like qualities of national attachment such as voluntary, horizontal relations between citizens and mutual cooperation rather than vertical, authoritative relations as in traditional family ties (Kaplan 2007).

What is particularly striking is how the national discourse reconciles these two opposing tropes. The only way to construe a relationship as both familial and a friendship is by invoking the figure of the "brother," one who is a family member yet who signifies the mutual ties and equal status of a friend (Kaplan 2011). It is for this reason that "fraternity" and "brotherhood" are perhaps the most common relational terms to appear in national rhetoric.[1] Thus, the magic of the national imagination lies not simply in the transformation of strangers into friends but in imagining these newly found friends as lost brothers and sisters of the same primordial tribe. This second transformation is located on a longer mythological timeline. And while we may think of "shared past" as preceding the notion of "shared destiny," the causal sequence is more likely the other way around: only after going through the initial move from strangership to a forward-looking friendship, can the friend gradually transform into a brother, and as the tie becomes tinged with familial rhetoric, it eventually becomes a timeless familial bond. It is precisely this fusion of romantic (civic) redemption with primordial (ethnic) origins, destiny, and ancestry that explains the attraction of national solidarity.

Friendship as an Imagined Social Construct

Common among scholars of nationalism is the assumption that the association of national attachment with the emotional bonds of family or friendship is merely a metaphor, in other words, that a comparison of national ties to interpersonal interactions is mostly a "rhetorical device" or form of social engineering utilized by state authorities or nationalist elites and activists and not a legitimate account of what national identity or national attachment really comprise (e.g., Breuilly 1982, 349; Hobsbawm 1983, 13). Similarly, it is assumed that contrary to face-to-face interactions the interactions that characterize large-scale entities such as nations are not a "genuine" form of solidarity (Malešević 2011, 284).

However, this premise is problematic on many levels. First, while attributing familial qualities to a large-scale society could indeed be considered metaphoric given the limited size of an actual family unit, the structure of friendship ties is more amorphous to begin with and can more readily accommodate a larger number of participants (Kaplan 2007). Second, in terms of emotional experience more generally, Schwarzenbach (1996) noted that one should be cautious not to confuse emotions, which must by necessity be concrete, with being by necessity also personal; sharing a personal bond with others is not a prerequisite for caring for them in concrete ways. Indeed, just as we readily acknowledge the role of hatred and fear in collective action, so too should we recognize the role of collective affection and care.

Third, according to the strong program of cultural sociology (Alexander and Smith 2001), metaphors should not be dismissed as fabricated representations dwelling outside the objective social world. On the contrary, precisely because culture should be considered analytically as relatively autonomous from social structures, metaphors should be taken as part of the cultural realm that gives meaning to social life in the first place. This holds true not only for the way in which symbolic representations shape collective ties such as national solidarity but also for how they shape interpersonal ties such as friendship. It is, therefore, wrong to assume that national sentiments of solidarity are somehow more socially constructed than interpersonal ties or that the latter are more "genuine" than the former. The fact that friendships and family ties are more universal than national ties does not imply that they are somehow more natural, spontaneous, or less constructed.[2]

Fourth, while on some level it can be argued that personal friendships are constructed differently than national attachments, they may also share some similar narrative building blocks (Kaplan 2011). Thus, cultural constructs such as "shared past" and "shared destiny," as in the aforementioned stories of men's friendships (Kaplan 2006), are retrospectively employed to explain why a certain bond began or why it endured, irrespective of actual historical contingencies. It is not the actual accumulation of random-shared activities but rather the shared rituals of recollecting these shared activities that gives meaning to their ties, moving them into the realm of folklore. In this sense, personal friendships are, like national attachments, partly premised on "invented traditions" (Hobsbawm 1983), illustrating the effect of collective memory played out in the smallest of possible collectives—the intimate group and even a dyad.

Finally, one of the reasons that scholars tend to dissociate national attachments from friendship is connected to the distinction between interpersonal trust and generalized social trust. For example, Florencia Torche and Eduardo Valenzuela (2011) argued against the assumption of a gradual quality of trust situated on a continuum between personal and impersonal interactions. Such an assumption underlies influential works on trust, such as by Piotr Sztompka (1999) and by Putnam (2000), who both posited that relationships can extend from strong, thick ties between friends to weaker or thinner ties among strangers. Torche and Valenzuela, on the other hand, asserted that personal reciprocity between friends should be clearly distinguished from general trust among strangers: "Building personal relations requires, by necessity, time, but once they are established, trust ceases to be a conscious choice, becomes embedded in reciprocity, and usually acquires the taken-for granted character of familiarity" (187).

It is true that at the interpersonal level strangers rarely become instant reciprocal friends. However, when it comes to the collective sphere, at important junctures in national life compatriots draw on the meta-narrative of strangers-turned-friends and do come to perceive each other in that instance as friends. These are occasions when generalized trust in strangers transforms into feelings not only of familiarity and mutual exclusivity, as described by Torche and Valenzuela (2011), but also of loyalty. In Jack Barbalet's (1996) compelling differentiation between trust and loyalty, trust has to do with cooperation and the confidence that the actions of others will live up to our expectations of them. In contrast, loyalty, like friendship, is forward-looking; it is the confidence that trust can be maintained in the long term. Actors can feel loyalty to a person, relationship, or institution even in the absence of individual trust in those they rely on. For "it is precisely the feeling of loyalty which maintains relationships when they might otherwise collapse, and which assumes, implicitly or explicitly, that irrespective of present circumstances, the thing to which one is loyal will be viable in the future" (Barbalet 1996, 79).

Thus, the notion of a continuum between personal and impersonal interactions criticized by Torche and Valenzuela (2011) is actually key to understanding the national imagination as a move from generalized trust between individual strangers to feelings of loyalty to the nation incarnated in a collectivity of friends. And as with Torche and Valenzuela's description of the shift from general trust to personal reciprocity, one could say that once national solidarity is established, trust ceases to be a conscious choice and becomes embedded in a collective experience of friendship that acquires the taken-for-granted character of familiarity, exclusivity, and loyalty. This shift can be gradual or sudden; the meta-narrative of strangers-turned-friends may create magical shortcuts along the way.

Since both friendships and national attachments are socially constructed emotions, the interesting question is not simply *whether* the framing of national solidarity as a close-knit bond is a metaphor, a rhetorical strategy, an invention by national elites, or an analytical extension of the meaning of trust—for these are all epistemological devices inevitably used in the social construction of all types of emotions—but *how* interactions between strangers are culturally constituted so as to acquire national meanings.

The Cultural Codes of Strangers-Turned-Friends

In order to explore how interactions between strangers acquire collective and, specifically, national meanings, we need to consider how they tap into an underlying cultural expectation of solidarity. As discussed by

Alexander (2003, 12) and demonstrated in the studies of civil society discourse (Alexander and Smith 1993), cultural structures operating through symbolic codes and narratives form a relatively autonomous realm independent of social practice and can, therefore, shape social life in powerful ways. However, unlike the rich and systematic scholarship on civil society discourse, cultural sociology literature has remained virtually silent on the cultural codes of national solidarity.

The meta-narrative of strangers-turned-friends represents what Alexander (2003) identified as the continuing demand for immediate, transformative salvation in modern social life—the existential concern with "how to be saved, how to jump to the present from the past and into the future" (8). Family members are expected to share a common future no less (if not more) than close friends; only the friendship trope, however, can account for the fact that compatriots actually form new ties on daily basis. Thus, recalling that the very raison d'être of nationalism is to legitimize cooperation between citizens by construing civic interactions as potentially newly formed friendships, this political project becomes a quest for transcendence. The liberal account of citizenship and civil society, as discussed by Maurice Roche (1994), presupposes a community of strangers whose members share equal status, civic rights, and duties and negotiate common interests, obligations, and expectations. But they also "accept that in principle and in fact they are and will remain strangers to each other" (90). In contrast, the national account of citizenship presupposes a community of strangers-turned-friends who not only cooperate for common interests but who also share their lives, passions, and destiny.

More empirical research is required in order to identify and establish a comprehensive set of binary codes that would best encapsulate and elaborate on this transformation from individual strangers to collective friends. However, from the breadth of the arguments presented thus far—and building on the recurring allusions to feelings of familiarity, exclusivity, and loyalty in the previous illustrations—five such binary codes can be pinpointed that give meaning and structure to the rhetoric and discourse of solidarity as well as to mundane institutional practices of sociability. These comprise a shift from intangibility (or abstractedness) to tangibility (or concreteness), anonymity to familiarity, inclusivity to exclusivity, indifference to loyalty, and interest (or instrumentality) to passion (or expressivity).

From a semiotic and epistemological perspective, this set of cultural codes operates on multiple levels. First, at the most basic level, it functions as both a key "summarizing symbol" and an "elaborating symbol" (following Ortner 1973, 1338–1345). It not only encapsulates, synthesizes, and collapses complex and ambiguous social experiences in an emotionally powerful way, but through the overarching meta-narrative of strangers-turned-friends it also dramatizes and orders culturally appropriate modes of action.

Second, the meta-narrative operates not only in sacred moments of national life but is incarnated in everyday practices of sociability in institutional life, investing them with an aura of idealized friendship. The move from strangership to friendship epitomizes this Durkheimian distinction between the mundane and the sacred, and, most crucially, it highlights the oscillation between the two spheres (Kaplan 2006; Mallory and Carlson 2014). The meta-narrative could be conceptualized as a symbolically potent carrier of feelings operating in a recursive and cyclic fashion; everyday interactions of sociability generate ambiguous feelings that are then understood through the meta-narrative and its underlying cultural codes. This background understanding, in turn, prompts and reproduces further attempts to engage in interactions between strangers and to consider them as friendship. Thus, the first of each pair of binary codes depicts mundane relations between individuals in any social institution; the second represents sacred relations between fellow nationals. As discussed by Peter Mallory and Jesse Carlson (2014), a Durkheim-inspired perspective must take into account the vacillation between the sacred ideal of friendship and the profane practices of sociability in concrete social institutions and to consider how "moral ideals and beliefs could be produced, sustained, and given force in everyday life" (338). Moreover, theorizing stranger relations through the idealized norms of friendship opens the possibility for understanding "the symbolic and ethical qualities of bonds between strangers" (330).

Third, as part of the moral dimension of national discourse more generally, as it appears, for example, in commemoration rituals, the shift from stranger to friend is codified as a unidirectional movement from low to high, from the ordinary and the morally inferior, to the extraordinary and morally superior (Handelman 1990). However, it is important to note that "friend" and "stranger" are not morally antithetical in the sense that "friend" is antithetical to "enemy" or "evil" is to "good." This is because, unlike the coding system of civil society discourse (Alexander and Smith 1993), in this meta-narrative the "sacred" is juxtaposed to the mundane and not the profane.[3] Consequently, from a normative perspective, some of the mundane countercodes in this typology, in particular "intangibility" and "inclusivity," need not carry a strictly negative connotation in order for them to be subordinated to the opposing code.

Finally, and related to the previous observation, it is important to bear in mind that this meta-narrative does not address the "enemy" as an explicit countercode. Although the category of the enemy is central to national identity discourse (e.g., Bauman 1991; Nagel 1998) and has been researched extensively in interactional and social psychology studies (e.g., Druckman 1994; Eriksen 1993), in this specific and highly idealized narrative of strangers-turned-friends excluding hostile strangers and targeting them as enemies is not part of the story. Unlike the politics of friendship and enmity in premodern societies, the underlying rationale is to turn strangers into friends not to keep them from becoming enemies (Silver 1990) but to overcome the fear of alienation in mass society, the growing perception that citizens are strangers to themselves.

In this, I draw on Sennett's (1977) illuminating distinction between two types of strangers in urban life: strangers as "outsiders" and strangers as "unknown" (48–49).[4] Strangers are readily identified as outsiders and foreigners when group identities are well-defined and distinctions between "us" and "them" can be easily made. But in periods when social identities are in flux and traditional rules of distinction no longer apply, strangers are all those experienced as "unknown"; for example, the new social class of mercantile bourgeoisie which emerged in eighteenth-century London and Paris and formed "a milieu of strangers in which many people are increasingly like each other but don't know it" (Sennett 1977, 49). Thus, to return to the quote by Bauman (1991) that opened this chapter, the modern nation-state was "designed primarily to deal with the problem of strangers, not enemies" (63), because it faced a flood of unknown (rather than foreigner) strangers who did not consider themselves similar to each other, at least not until they imagined themselves as a nation. This is where the national meta-narrative comes into play, seeking to re-enchant modern social life and resurrect this community of unknown strangers as a community of friends. Indeed, the meta-narrative becomes truly magical once we consider how the underlying binary codes reverse the basic qualities said to distinguish between interpersonal and collective ties; for it is the latter which suddenly become tangible, familiar, exclusive, faithful, and passionate.

To conclude, compared to premodern communities, occasions for turning strangers into friends are far more pertinent to modern societies in which the intensity and fragmentation of everyday life requires people to engage socially in a wide range of different institutions. In this respect, whether or not one considers the nation as a modern phenomenon, the meta-narrative of strangers-turned-friends presents a uniquely modern aspect of the national imagination. It transpires in sacred public events, when the social performance attains fusion and gives rise to feelings of collective intimacy, which is, in effect, an alchemic transformation of all members of the community from strangers to friends. At the same time, these feelings are the result of the less magical individual acts of friend-making that accumulate in the course of a person's daily participation in social institutions mediated by the mechanisms of public intimacy. In Part Two, I demonstrate empirically how these interactionist mechanisms operate in specific social clubs, each providing a different manifestation of the symbolic meta-narrative.

Notes

1. A good example is the extensive of use of fraternal terms in national anthems (Lauenstein et al. 2015). It is also striking that despite decades of feminist critics pointing to the gendered and exclusionary implications of the term "fraternity," it is still pervasive in popular discourse. Carole Pateman (1989) and Dana Nelson (1998) have described how the term fraternity was employed in both the French Revolution and the American Revolution to convey a move from absolute paternal rule to a civic-national "rule of the brothers," retaining male supremacy by endorsing a fraternal social contract.
2. Alexander (2006, 48) noted a similar claim made by Claude Lévi-Strauss (1963) who insisted, in opposition to functionalist and reductionist anthropological accounts, that kinship exists "only in human consciousness; it is an arbitrary system of representations, not the spontaneous development of a real situation" (50).
3. More specifically, if we follow Dmitry Kurakin's (2015) suggestion to consider the opposition between the sacred and profane in Durkheim's sociology as totally different than the opposition between the sacred pure and the "sacred impure" (or polluted) (381) then the profane might in fact be better understood as simply the mundane or banal, because it is not actively sacrilegious. As Kurakin put it, the profane "originates from the individual sphere of experience, which is characterized by low intensity, ordinariness, and subordinated position" as compared with the collective mode of life associated with the sacred, which is characterized by extraordinarily intense emotions (384). A similar comment has been made

by Bryan Rennie (2007, 188) with regard to Mircea Eliade's perception of the sacred. According to this logic, unlike the binary cultural codes of good and evil (the sacred pure and the impure), the sacred and profane in Durkheim's work do not stand in a mutually transformable relationship: the sacred can transform the profane into the sacred but not the reverse (Kurakin 2015, 381). This coincides with how the national meta-narrative reflects a unidirectional movement from mundane interactions between strangers to a sacred community of friends but not the other way around.
4. This distinction echoes Simmel's (1950) discussion of the role of the stranger not only as a non-native or foreigner but as a constructive social role which can unify society (either by linking the separate elements of the group or by taking on a special task) and which may form a universal otherhood (see Karakayali 2016).

References

Alexander, Jeffrey C. 2003. *The Meanings of Social Life: A Cultural Sociology*. New York: Oxford University Press.

Alexander, Jeffrey C. 2006. *The Civil Sphere*. New York: Oxford University Press.

Alexander, Jeffrey C., and Philip Smith. 1993. "The Discourse of American Civil Society: A New Proposal for Cultural Studies." *Theory and Society* 22 (2): 151–207.

Alexander, Jeffrey C., and Philip Smith. 2001. "The Strong Program in Cultural Theory: Elements of a Structural Hermeneutics." In *Handbook of Sociological Theory*, edited by Jonathan H. Turner, 135–150. New York: Springer.

Anderson, Benedict. [1983] 1991. *Imagined Communities: Reflections on the Origins and Spread of Nationalism*. London: Verso.

Barbalet, Jack. 1996. "Social Emotions: Confidence, Trust and Loyalty." *International Journal of Sociology and Social Policy* 16 (9–10): 75–96.

Bauman, Zygmunt. 1991. *Modernity and Ambivalence*. Ithaca, NY: Cornell University Press.

Bhabha, Homi K., ed. [1990] 2013. *Nation and Narration*. London: Routledge.

Breuilly, John. 1982. *Nationalism and the State*. Manchester: Manchester University Press.

Druckman, Daniel. 1994. "Nationalism, Patriotism, and Group Loyalty: A Social Psychological Perspective." *Mershon International Studies Review* 38 (1): 43–68.

Eriksen, Thomas Hylland. 1993. *Ethnicity and Nationalism: Anthropological Perspectives*. London: Pluto.

Handelman, Don. 1990. *Models and Mirrors: Toward an Anthropology of Public Events*. Cambridge: Cambridge University Press.

Handelman, Don. 2004. *Nationalism and the Israeli State: Bureaucratic Logic in Public Events.* Oxford: Berg.
Hinde, Robert A. 1997. *Relationships: A Dialectical Perspective.* Hove: Psychology Press.
Hobsbawm, Erik. 1983. "Introduction: Inventing Traditions." In *The Invention of Tradition*, edited by Erik Hobsbawm and Terence Ranger, 1–14. Cambridge: Cambridge University Press.
Kaplan, Danny. 2006. *The Men We Loved: Male Friendship and Nationalism in Israeli Culture.* New York: Berghahn Books.
Kaplan, Danny. 2007. "What Can the Concept of Friendship Contribute to the Study of National Identity?" *Nations and Nationalism* 13 (2): 225–244.
Kaplan, Danny 2011. "Chemistry and Alchemy: Narrative Building-Blocks of Friendship and Nationalism in Israeli Culture." In *Varieties of Friendship: Interdisciplinary Perspectives on Social Relationships*, edited by Bernadette Descharmes, Eric A. Heuser, Caroline Krüger, and Thomas Loy, 119–141. Göttingen: Vandenhoeck & Ruprecht Unipress.
Karakayali, Nedim. 2016. "The Uses of the Stranger: Circulation, Arbitration, Secrecy, and Dirt." *Sociological Theory* 24 (4): 312–330.
Kurakin, Dmitry. 2015. "Reassembling the Ambiguity of the Sacred: A Neglected Inconsistency in Readings of Durkheim." *Journal of Classical Sociology* 15 (4): 377–395.
Lauenstein, Oliver, Jeffrey S. Murer, Margarete Boos, and Stephen Reicher. 2015. "'Oh Motherland I Pledge to Thee…': A Study into Nationalism, Gender and the Representation of an Imagined Family Within National Anthems." *Nations and Nationalism* 21 (2): 309–329.
Lévi-Strauss, Claude. 1963. "Structural Analysis in Linguistics and in Anthropology." In *Structural Anthropology*, Vol. 1, translated by Claire Jacobson and Brooke Grundfest Schoepf, 31–54. New York: Basic Books.
Malešević, Siniša. 2011. "The Chimera of National Identity." *Nations and Nationalism* 17 (2): 272–290.
Mallory, Peter, and Carlson Jesse. 2014. "Rethinking Personal and Political Friendship with Durkheim." *Distinktion: Scandinavian Journal of Social Theory* 15 (3): 327–342.
McClintock, Anne. 1994. "Family Feuds: Gender, Nationalism and the Family." *Feminist Review* 44: 61–80.
Mosse, George L. 1982. "Friendship and Nationhood: About the Promise and Failure of German Nationalism." *Journal of Contemporary History* 17: 351–367.
Nagel, Joan. 1998. "Masculinity and Nationalism: Gender and Sexuality in the Making of Nations." *Ethnic and Racial Studies* 21 (2): 242–269.
Nelson, Dana D. 1998. *National Manhood: Capitalist Citizenship and the Imagined Fraternity of White Men.* Durham, NC: Duke University Press.

Ortner, Sherry B. 1973. "On Key Symbols." *American Anthropologist* 75 (5): 1338–1346.
Pateman, Carole. 1989. *The Disorder of Women: Democracy, Feminism and Political Theory*. Stanford: Stanford University Press.
Putnam, Robert. 2000. *Bowling Alone*. New York: Simon and Schuster.
Rennie, Bryan. 2007. "Mircea Eliade and the Perception of the Sacred in the Profane: Intention, Reduction, and Cognitive Theory." *Temenos: Nordic Journal of Comparative Religion* 43 (1): 73–98.
Roche, Maurice. 1994. "Citizenship, Social Theory, and Social Change." In *Citizenship: Critical Concepts*, Vol. 1, edited by Bryan S. Turner and Peter Hamilton, 80–110. London: Routledge.
Schwarzenbach, Sibyl. 1996. "On Civic Friendship." *Ethics* 107: 97–128.
Sennett, Richard. 1977. *The Fall of Public Man*. Cambridge: Cambridge University Press.
Silver, Allan. 1990. "Friendship in Commercial Society: Eighteenth-Century Social Theory and Modern Sociology." *American Journal of Sociology* 95 (6): 1474–1504.
Simmel, Georg. [1915] 1950. *The Sociology of Georg Simmel*. Translated by Kurt H. Wolff. Glencoe, IL: Free Press.
Smith, Anthony D. 1991. *National Identity*. Reno: University of Nevada Press.
Sztompka, Piotr. 1999. *Trust: A Sociological Theory*. Cambridge: Cambridge University Press.
Torche, Florenica, and Eduardo Valenzuela. 2011. "Trust and Reciprocity: A Theoretical Distinction of the Sources of Social Capital." *European Journal of Social Theory* 14 (2): 181–198.

CHAPTER 6

Can We Really Distinguish Between Civic and National Solidarity?

> To speak of "citizenship" without simultaneously speaking of "nation" is to utter an abstraction. (Davetian 2009, 508–509)

Although the theoretical approach presented in this book mainly centers on the question of national solidarity, the actual bottom-up practices of social club sociability do not in themselves differentiate between the various forms of mass solidarity. In particular, since much of the micro-level sociability formed in social clubs operates within and is circumscribed by the existing international state system, it could be just as relevant to civic solidarity as it is to national solidarity. While most sociologists presuppose and take for granted the analytic differences between civic and national attachments, one should bear in mind how both forms of solidarity reflect the same expectation that compatriots will overcome the differentiation and fragmentation of modern institutional life and socialize with one another.

There are, of course, other contemporary forms of mass solidarity below and beyond the level of the state, such as local ethnic and religious enclaves or transnational religions and social movements, which may likewise build on relations between strangers-turned-friends. When membership in social clubs is strictly confined to such sectarian enclaves or to transnational networks, then participants' sense of solidarity is likely to be geared toward these particular collectivities.[1] However, when a significant number of the social institutions that people attend are nonsectarian and operate within a relatively bounded national community—which, I suspect, is what has occurred and is continuing to occur since the emergence and dissemination of nation-states—then each of these institutions becomes one of many social clubs that contribute to people's feelings of both civic and national solidarity.

Rogers Brubaker et al. (2004, 48–49) argued convincingly that from the perspective of collective identification and classification, there is little reason to stick to conventional distinctions between nation, ethnicity, and race and suggested treating these categories as one integrated domain of study which examines how people construct their commonalities. But once we shift attention from the ways in which actors assume a common identity to the question of social ties between actors, national attachments stand out as quite distinct from ethnicity or race. For whereas ethnicity can be conceptualized with little regard for the quality of the ties between members, a central rationale of nationalism is to account for cooperation between citizens (e.g., Gellner 1983; Smith 1986), and it thus requires the formulation of an appropriate theory of national attachment.

At the same time, by shifting from identity to solidarity, we face another challenge, namely how to distinguish between national and civic attachment. This question is far more complex than conventional sociological wisdom would have it. In fact, when it comes to the question of solidarity (as opposed to identity), it is only at the symbolic cultural level that civic and national forms of attachment can really be distinguished, shaped by a specifically civic or national discourse of solidarity. I accordingly spelled out in the previous chapter how the symbolic meta-narrative of strangers-turned-friends figures in national solidarity discourse. But once the symbolic, discursive dimension is bracketed, it is, I believe, not easy to distinguish between civic and national solidarity.

Phenomenological Considerations

I illustrate this point on several levels. To begin with, there are very few studies that make explicit analytic distinctions between civic and national solidarity. Rather, political theorists tend to contrast civic solidarity with national *identity*. A telling example is the previously mentioned work by Honohan (2001), one of the few scholars to systematically discuss the difference between civic and national attachments through a vocabulary of friendship. Honohan claimed that civic attachments (which she compared to relations between colleagues but not close friends) may entail special obligations without being radically exclusive, whereas national attachments may elicit commitment at the cost of excluding outgroups. Citizens can thus cooperate in political interaction despite diversity, dislike, and emotional distance. At the same time, a closer examination of her account reveals a division of meaning such that national attachments (or obligations) are taken to mean national identity while civic attachments are forms of mutual interactions: "Obligations to co-nationals require feelings of shared identity, those to citizens reflective recognition of interdependence....The key feature of nationality is a collective sense of a common identity...and [it] does not intrinsically require interdependence in practices between co-nationals" (Honohan 2001, 64–65). In other words, at no point did Honohan actually compare or distinguish between civic and national solidarity; similar to most scholars, her understanding of national attachment shifts inadvertently to the dimension of identity formation and has little to do with questions of social interaction.

Moreover, from a phenomenological standpoint and contrary to scholarly convention, the common usage in English of the term "compatriot" does not differentiate between co-citizens and fellow nationals (Honohan 2001). This lack of distinction between the civic and the national in folk understanding is revealing, and scholars should give it further consideration rather than trying to prove its analytic fallacy. Although in most political cultures it is common practice to differentiate between citizenship (associated with the state and society) and a more exclusive national primordial core (often a combination of ethnicity and religion), the extent of this differentiation depends on how the national community is defined in the collective imagination.

In some cases, the cultural boundaries of the nation are indeed formulated independently of citizenship status, for example, in officially multinational states like Canada and Switzerland or in states like Israel where unofficial distinctions between Jewish and non-Jewish citizens prevail. In such cases, we can expect the meta-narrative of strangers-turned-friend to map onto the (ethnic) national core rather than the civic body. However, countries that lack an explicit definition of national membership beyond citizenship may offer a more inclusive cultural understanding of the nation, which comprises all citizens of the country, as in the case of the USA. This is not to deny that certain (growing) factions in American society and elsewhere promote a more purified version of the national core. But the very fact that they frame their advocacy in terms of a revitalization of society as a whole (e.g., President Trump's election slogan, "Make America Great Again") means that even they partly conflate the civic with the national. Indeed, they have no choice but to conflate them, because when it comes the social institutions that people attend in their everyday life there is little reason to make an analytic distinction between society and nation (even when, in practice, some institutions may systematically exclude certain citizens). As noted by Alexander (1997), since nation-states continue to form the most effective boundaries for solidary ties, it is not surprising that civil society might be considered, on some levels, as isomorphic with the national community.

This phenomenological ambiguity between state, society, and nation can be partly explained by tracing the historical shifts in the meanings assigned to patriotism in Western political vocabulary. Mary Dietz (2002) and Maurizio Viroli (1995) both suggested that until the mid-eighteenth century, patriotism was understood as a love for members of one's community and concern for the common good along the lines of the (Greek/Roman) republican legacy of civic friendship. The patriot battled in the name of his people against the tyranny and corruption of the throne and was often associated with radical politics in the defense of liberty. By the nineteenth century, however, the rhetoric of patriotism had been adopted by more conservative circles in ways that stressed particularist attachment to one's country, a love for its uniqueness, and cultural homogeneity rather than civic virtue (Viroli 1995). As "patriotism" was increasingly assimilated into the emerging fusion of "state" and "nation," it became an attribute, no longer of the "rebel" against the (old) social order but of the "loyalist" to the (new) national social order (Dietz 2002). As national consciousness spread deeper and more broadly throughout society, the nation and its embodiment in state institutions gradually became the ultimate object of loyalty. In this sense, the locus of solidarity shifted from care for the people in the face of authoritarian rule to care for a community understood to be governed by the people, thus confounding civic and national solidarity.

Empirical Considerations

Turning to empirically grounded research, prominent bottom-up approaches to mass solidarity also evade a clear distinction between civic and national meanings. For example, Fine's framework of tiny publics (Fine 2012; Fine and Harrington 2004) considers how small-group interactions align local frames of reference with broader ideologies and symbols and shows how collective concepts such as citizenship or national sacrifice are linked by the localized group to its specific norms and standards of interaction. It is noteworthy, however, that Fine and Harrington's (2004) account alternates between a civic and national vocabulary, as they themselves observed: "while our argument is not fundamentally about the construction of nationalism, we propose that whether we examine civic involvement or national identity, small groups generate the identity and the socialization processes involved in creating citizens" (347).

Another bottom-up approach that is perhaps closer to mine in its focus on institutionally mediated sociability is Putnam's (2000) associationalism. Putnam underscored how localized social interactions in civic associations contribute to a community's "social capital" (social-organizational features that facilitate mutual cooperation) and therefore enhance democracy and civic solidarity. But it remains unclear why associational life and social capital should not be just as significant for national solidarity. For instance, in Putnam's description of the rise of civic activity during bursts of American patriotism in the wake of World War II (268), there is nothing to distinguish between civic and national attachments. He did make a distinction between "bonding" and "bridging" social capital; the former reinforces "exclusive identities and homogeneous groups," whereas the latter encompasses "people across diverse social cleavages" (22). Yet, while this distinction might seem to mirror the dichotomy between exclusive national ties and inclusive civic ties, Putnam made no such claim and confined his discussion to the qualitative difference between "weak" and "strong" ties (Granovetter 1973), in other words, to the structural level of social networks that has no bearing on the realm of meaning through which categories of collective attachments are formulated.

A final case in point is Collins' (2004a) framework of interactional ritual chains. Some of his work (e.g., Collins 2004b, 2012) presents what is perhaps the only bottom-up account of national solidarity per se. Building on Durkheim's (2003) notion of collective effervescence, Collins examined the surge in feelings of solidarity during public events such as the 9/11 terrorist attacks and the 2011 Egyptian Revolution, both of which generated widespread focused attention accompanied by national symbolism. These feelings of solidarity operate as a capsule of collectively experienced time that dissolves within a three- to six-month period. And yet, it is, once again, unclear what in the actual interactional account (as opposed to the symbolic, discursive dimension) distinguishes between civic and national solidarity.

The Debate Over Civic Nationalism

Having laid out phenomenological and empirical considerations for the lack of differentiation between civic and national solidarity, I now turn to a critical examination of two central debates pertaining to the epistemology of nationalism, debates that presuppose a distinction between civic and national solidarity despite the limited evidence for such differentiation in practice.

The first debate is the ongoing scholarly critique of the civic-contractual model of nationalism, commonly referred to as "civic nationalism." Originating primarily in the writings of Hans Kohn (1944), civic nationalism emphasizes the political contract between fellow citizens and conceives of the nation as a community of equal, rights-bearing citizens, united in their attachment to a shared set of political practices and universalistic values and to a common territorial homeland (Brown 2000, 51; Ignatieff 1993). It is contrasted with an ethno-cultural model, which foregrounds perceived primordial origins and shared cultural customs and traditions. While Kohn linked these ideal models to a distinction between Western and Eastern forms of nationalism, historical analysis suggests that a mixture of both ethnic and civic models prevails over time in most nation-states (Kuzio 2002; Singer 1996).

The ethno-cultural model draws on characteristics of the national imagination that render it similar to deterministic and vertical ties of kinship and tribal structure, invoking the notion of an extended family. The civic-contractual model, on the other hand, emphasizes those characteristics that place it in the context of a voluntary and horizontal solidarity between members, thus invoking the notion of friendship. These structural characteristics suggest that friendship could potentially serve not only as a metaphor for national solidarity but also as a deeper account for some of its emotional and cultural underpinnings, once the stress is on the civic-contractual aspects of the nation.

In recent years, the fundamental viability of the civic national model and its universalist vision has been called into question (Brubaker 1999; Xenos 1996; Yack 1996). Bernard Yack (1996) rejected the civic-national emphasis on voluntary contractual ties and accused its proponents of propagating a political myth. Social contract alone could not set the boundaries of the national community or account for political sovereignty. Without an established cultural legacy associated with a predetermined, prepolitical community, people would find no reason to seek agreement with one group of individuals over another. Contingent communities of collective memory cannot be reduced to voluntary associations united by moral and political principles; they require collective boundaries that predate the formation of political sovereignty.

A crucial point, however, has gone unnoticed in this critique. Definitions of civic nationalism include among other things "a collective enterprise based upon common values and institutions, and patterns of social interaction" (Keating 1997, 690). By rejecting this model, we are left with no account of the interactions and patterns of cooperation and solidarity between compatriots, issues which do not play any part in the definitions of the ethno-cultural model of the nation. I thus argue that instead of distinguishing between these models as ideal types of national ideologies or identities, we would be better to reframe them as two complementary epistemological dimensions of national attachments: processes of collective identity formation and processes of social bonding and solidarity. The former dimension is indeed an extension of ethnic and cultural considerations of commonality, and in this respect, critics were correct to point to the futility of a civic-contractual model of national identity. The latter, solidarity-related dimension, however, addresses the issue of cooperation between citizens and therefore demands a civic-contractual model of national solidarity.

The Critic of Methodological Nationalism

A second debate that reveals misguided assumptions about clear-cut distinctions between the civic and the national has to do with the bias of "methodological nationalism" and to some of the attempts to avoid it. As discussed by Andreas Wimmer and Nina Schiller (2002), methodological nationalism describes the tendency in much of social science scholarship until recently to take for granted the nation/state/society as one natural social and political form of the modern world. Because societies were structured according to the principles and contours of the nation-state, these contours became so routinely assumed and banal that they vanished from sight altogether. Paradoxically, in their pursuit of the grand schemes of modernity, classical sociological theorists, among them Weber and Durkheim, ignored the national framing of states and societies in the modern age.

Yet, even as contemporary scholars have attempted to avoid such misconceptions of the nation-state as equivalent to society, they have often reproduced another variant of the methodological nationalism bias in their assumption that civil society and democracy can be studied independently of nationalism and their disregard for the historical links between democratic state-building and the rise of nationalism (Wimmer and Schiller 2002). For when nation and state become two separate objects of enquiry—the former discussed as a domain of identity, rooted in common history and shared culture, and the latter as a system of government and a playground for different interest groups—what once again becomes invisible is "the fact that the modern state itself has entered into a symbiotic relationship with the nationalist political project" (Wimmer and Schiller 2002, 306).

In fact, it is not only the question of methodological bias on the part of social scientists that is at stake; as noted previously, this bias is also central to the way laypeople understand nation/state/society as a single entity such that the civic and the national become one. If, therefore, researchers want to account for the phenomenology of mass solidarity in modern nation-states, they should work from within these folk perceptions rather than against them. They should explore, for example, the pragmatic meanings of civic nationalism as its values are negotiated in certain social clubs and not preoccupy themselves with the analytic contradictions of this model (see Kaplan 2014). This, if nothing else, might help us understand why state politics cannot be divorced from nationalism any time soon.

Normative Considerations

Given the above, it would appear that the sociological distinction between civic and national solidarity is based not on phenomenological, empirical, or epistemological grounds but on a normative stance that distinguishes between "good" civic and "bad" national ties. The civic is characteristically associated with a universalist, inclusivist ethos and with values of individual autonomy, rational choice, and abstract reasoning, while the national is associated with a "primordial core group" and thus with an exclusivist ethos and more emotionally-laden bonds (Alexander 1988, 80). Furthermore, national struggles, unlike civic struggles, are often associated with intensive and irrational passions (Walzer 2002).

That said, when put into practice the notion that citizenship is more inclusive than national belonging is misleading. For one thing, citizenship forms a barrier to immigration, which, on a global scale, is a stronger source of inequality than the inner, ethnic-based exclusions associated with national solidarity. For another, even within the body of citizens, opponents of the dominant political order often suffer from exclusion (Brubaker 1999). In fact, from a cultural sociological perspective, one could argue that although the normative idea and the values of civil society may be more universal than the themes of national ideology (Alexander 1997), the kind of purifying solidarity generated by the discourse of civil society is no less exclusive. Indeed, Alexander and Smith (1993) stressed that the discourse of civil society is premised on a fundamental and exclusionary binary logic of good versus evil, friend versus enemy—the very same logic that we much more readily associate with national discourse. In both cases, the purifying discourse of sacred friendship necessitates a profane side, the point beyond which membership and hospitality cannot be extended.

One should also bear in mind that despite its particularist and exclusivist connotations, the ideal of national solidarity carries with it also universalistic principles to overcome pervasive social and sectarian distinctions. Alexander's (1997) definition of solidarity is particularly telling in this regard. Perhaps inadvertently,[2] he located his universalist account of solidarity in civil society within a national framework:

> it is the 'we-ness' of a national community taken in the strongest possible sense, the feeling of connectedness to 'every member' of that community that transcends particular commitments, narrow loyalties and sectarian interests. Only this kind of solidarity can provide a thread of identity uniting people dispersed by religion, class or race. (118)

Brubaker (2004) made a similar point, noting how the normative critique of the nation-state feeds into "the prevailing anti-national, post-national, and trans-national stances in the social sciences and humanities," and "risk[s] obscuring the good reasons—at least in the American context—for cultivating solidarity, mutual responsibility, and citizenship at the level of the nation-state" (120). Here too, Brubaker's discussion of solidarity employs an undifferentiated civic-national vocabulary, perhaps more intentionally than other scholars.

All told, despite my claim that national solidarity and civic solidarity are equivalent in many respects, I have chosen to center my argument on national solidarity because it is associated with stronger, passionate emotions and is thus more clearly linked to friendship. As persuasively analyzed by Honohan (2001), civic attachments are more directly comparable to relations between colleagues than to friendship in that they may uphold special obligations and enable cooperation even in conditions of diversity, dislike, and emotional distance. Moreover, from a scholarly standpoint, given the extreme scarcity of work which attempts to theorize and investigate solidarity in national context (unlike the scope and depth of such work in civic context), it seems imperative that we focus the inquiry on national solidarity.[3]

Finally, and most importantly for the present discussion, it is in the symbolic dimension that the meanings of national solidarity differ from those of civic solidarity. The gist of the national imagination lies not only in the transformation of strangers into friends; it is in imagining these newly found friends as rediscovered brothers and sisters of the same primordial tribe. As discussed in Chapter 5, it is precisely this fusion of primordial ethnicity and civic redemption, this weaving together of ancestry and destiny, which not only distinguishes between national and civic solidarity but also gives the former its seductive appeal.

Notes

1. Because such enclaves or networks are typically associated with specific social institutions and more explicit in defining their common denominator from the outset (ethnic origin or ideological/religious belief), the transition from micro-level interactions to macro-level solidarity is analytically more straightforward in such cases and requires less explication.
2. In an updated formulation, Alexander (2006) expanded the definition to include "the 'we-ness' of a national, regional and international community" (43).
3. The gap in theoretical interest in national solidarity compared with civic solidarity seems even more striking considering the actual prevalence of the two phrases. A search in Google Scholar conducted on September 29, 2017, yielded 29,800 references to "national solidarity" and only 4160 references to "civic solidarity" and "civil solidarity" (combined). This suggests that a focused theoretical and empirical work on solidarity in the national context is long overdue.

References

Alexander, Jeffrey C. 1988. "Core Solidarity, Ethnic Out-Group, and Social Differentiation." In *Action and Its Environment: Towards a New Synthesis*, edited by Jeffrey C. Alexander, 78–106. New York: Columbia University Press.

Alexander, Jeffrey C. 1997. "The Paradoxes of Civil Society." *International Sociology* 12 (2): 115–133.

Alexander, Jeffrey C. 2006. *The Civil Sphere*. New York: Oxford University Press.

Alexander, Jeffrey, and Philip Smith. 1993. "The Discourse of American Civil Society: A New Proposal for Cultural Studies." *Theory and Society* 22 (2): 151–207.

Brown, David. 2000. *Contemporary Nationalism: Civic, Ethnocultural and Multicultural Politics*. London: Routledge.

Brubaker, Rogers. 1999. "The Manichean Myth: Rethinking the Distinction Between 'Civic' and 'Ethnic' Nationalism." In *Nation and National Identity: The European Experience in Perspective*, edited by Hanspeter Kriesi, Klaus Armingeon, Hannes Siegrist, and Andreas Wimmer, 55–71. Zurich: Verlag Ruegger.

Brubaker, Rogers. 2004. "In the Name of the Nation: Reflections on Nationalism and Patriotism." *Citizenship Studies* 8 (2): 115–127.

Brubaker, Rogers, Mara Loveman, and Peter Stamatov. 2004. "Ethnicity as Cognition." *Theory and Society* 33 (1): 31–64.

Collins, Randall. 2004a. *Interaction Ritual Chains*. Princeton: Princeton University Press.

Collins, Randall. 2004b. "Rituals of Solidarity and Security in the Wake of Terrorist Attack." *Sociological Theory* 22 (1): 53–87.

Collins, Randall. 2012. "Time-Bubbles of Nationalism: Dynamics of Solidarity Ritual in Lived Time." *Nations and Nationalism* 18 (3): 383–397.

Davetian, Benet. 2009. *Civility: A Cultural History*. Toronto: Toronto University Press.

Dietz, Mary G. 2002. "Patriotism: A Brief History of the Term." In *Patriotism: Philosophical and Political Perspectives*, edited by Igor Primoratz, 201–215. Amherst, NY: Humanity Books.

Durkheim, Emile. [1915] 2003. "The Elementary Forms of Religious Life," translated by Karen E. Fields. In *Emile Durkheim: Sociologist of Modernity*, edited by Mustafa Emirbayer, 109–121, 140–141. Malden, MA: Blackwell.

Fine, Gary Alan. 2012. *Tiny Publics: A Theory of Group Action and Culture*. New York: Russell Sage Foundation.

Fine, Gary Alan, and Harrington, Brooke. 2004. "Tiny Publics: Small Groups and Civil Society." *Sociological Theory* 22 (3): 341–356.

Gellner, Ernst. 1983. *Nations and Nationalism*. Oxford: Blackwell.

Granovetter, Mark S. 1973. "The Strength of Weak Ties." *American Journal of Sociology* 78 (6): 1360–1380.
Honohan, Iseult. 2001. "Friends, Strangers or Countrymen? The Ties Between Citizens as Colleagues." *Political Studies* 49 (1): 51–69.
Ignatieff, Michael. 1993. *Blood and Belonging: Journeys into the New Nationalism*. New York: Farrar, Straus & Giroux.
Kaplan, Danny. 2014. "Jewish-Arab Relations in Israeli Freemasonry: Between Civil Society and Nationalism." *Middle East Journal* 68 (3): 385–401.
Keating, Michael. 1997. "Stateless Nation-Building: Quebec, Catalonia and Scotland in the Changing State System." *Nations and Nationalism* 3 (4): 689–717.
Kohn, Hans. 1944. *The Idea of Nationalism: A Study in Its Origins and Background*. New York: Collier-Macmillan.
Kuzio, Taras. 2002. "The Myth of the Civic State: A Critical Survey of Hans Kohn's Framework for Understanding Nationalism." *Ethnic and Racial Studies* 25 (1): 20–39.
Putnam, Robert. 2000. *Bowling Alone*. New York: Simon and Schuster.
Singer, Brian C. J. 1996. "Cultural Versus Contractual Nations: Rethinking Their Opposition." *History and Theory* 35 (3): 309–337.
Smith, Anthony D. 1986. *The Ethnic Origins of Nations*. Oxford: Blackwell.
Viroli, Maurizio. 1995. *For Love of Country: An Essay on Patriotism and Nationalism*. Oxford: Clarendon Press.
Walzer, Michael. 2002. "Passion and Politics." *Philosophy & Social Criticism* 28 (6): 617–633.
Wimmer, Andreas, and Nina Glick Schiller. 2002. "Methodological Nationalism and Beyond: Nation-State Building, Migration and the Social Sciences." *Global Networks* 2 (4): 301–334
Xenos, Nicholas. 1996. "Civic Nationalism: Oxymoron?" *Critical Review* 10 (2): 213–231.
Yack, Bernard. 1996. "The Myth of the Civic Nation." *Critical Review* 10 (2): 193–211.

PART II

The Case Studies

This section presents three in-depth, empirical case studies of social club sociability and discusses how they contribute to national solidarity: friendship ties in Masonic lodges, ties between viewers and contestants in the *Big Brother* reality TV show, and military friendship and commemoration rituals. Each of these institutions presents its own structural characteristics that form "folds" in the veil separating outsiders from insiders and therefore represents a different way of transforming strangers into friends. The case studies draw on extensive ethnographic fieldwork conducted in Israel (as elaborated in each chapter). An analytic comparison between these cases is presented in the concluding part of the book.

CHAPTER 7

Sacred Brotherhood: Freemasonry and Civic-National Sociability

Freemasonry is a worldwide fraternity practicing an elitist stance of civilizing the self (Hoffmann 2007), which is translated into a collective mission of society-building that is premised on a civic-democratic political vocabulary (Jacob 1991). Though not a national movement, Freemasonry was implicated in national struggles against imperial rule in the Americas and the Middle East (Dumont 2005; Harland-Jacobs 2003). It provided a secluded social space for negotiating a national consciousness set in a civic context, one which can be associated with the principles of civic nationalism. Drawing on ethnographic fieldwork in the lodges of the Israeli Freemasons, this chapter examines how Masonic organizational practices and rituals shape members' personal friendships and collective solidarity. Unlike most civic organizations, the Order lacks any concrete instrumental goal beyond the exercising of friendship. In addition, a halo of secrecy restricts the flow of information and reinforces the distinction between members and nonmembers. The organization operates therefore as a pure social enclave, seemingly isolated from wider society.

At the same time, Freemasons view the individual ties of friendship formed in the lodge as a sacred project that carries collective significance and consider Freemasonry as a way of life that disseminates civic virtue for the good of society at large. In the absence of external and instrumental influences on members' sociability, this unique organizational setting provides a promising "ethnographic laboratory" for exploring how members extend the logic of strangers-turned-friends from their

© The Author(s) 2018
D. Kaplan, *The Nation and the Promise of Friendship*, Cultural Sociology, https://doi.org/10.1007/978-3-319-78402-1_7

individual experience in the organization to societal solidarity. Already in the Constitutions of 1723, the first publication to formalize and standardize the practice and norms of Freemasons, James Anderson (1923) noted that "Masonry becomes the Center of their Union, and the happy Means of concilating Persons that must have remain'd at a perpetual Distance" (144).

In contrast to the rich historical scholarship on Masonic sociability, ethnographic research on contemporary Masonic social clubs is exceedingly scarce (for one exception, see Mahmud 2012), and the question of how members conceive and practice their ties as a collective union remains largely unaddressed. A systematic phenomenological inquiry is therefore called for, one which attends explicitly to how members make sense of their collective ties as a bond of friendship and, in turn, how they come to venerate concrete bonds of friendship as instances of sacred solidarity.

Following a brief description of the international history of Freemasonry and its development in Ottoman Palestine/Israel, the chapter goes on to tackle the social "architecture" of contemporary Masonic clubs: first, by considering members' emic formulations of personal ties of friendship, fraternity, and occasions of strangers-turned-friends; second, by describing instances of public intimacy whereby members communicate through an elaborate coding system which both seduces and excludes nonqualified audiences; and finally, by exploring organizational instances of collective intimacy. As lodge administrative and democratic procedures undergo ceremonial dramatization, the juxtaposition of mundane sociability and sacred rituals serves to collapse the distinction between actors and audiences, between personal and collective affairs, and casts each member simultaneously in the roles of citizen, bureaucrat, priest, and president. I conclude by suggesting how these intersections of intimacy can provide a model for collective attachments along the lines of civic-nationalism.

INSTITUTIONALIZING FRATERNITY: THE ORDER OF FREEMASONS

The Order of Freemasons adheres to an explicit ideology of fraternity, viewed as "a system of morality veiled in allegory and illustrated by symbols" (Mackey 1898, 37). The central mythology of Freemasonry goes back to the biblical King Solomon and the construction of the First Temple. Scenes from this mythology are staged and performed during the ritual activity, termed "lodge work," which is accompanied by elaborate metaphors of stonemasons' craftsmanship inherited from medieval builder guilds.

In its modern form, Freemasonry was established in London in 1717, when preexisting stonemason lodges admitted a growing number of middle-class professionals, aristocrats, and intellectuals and soon evolved into an elitist social club structured as a loosely coupled network of lodges (Bullock 1996). Schaich (2008, 128) noted Masonic lodges as one of a vast array of associations (reading clubs, philanthropic organizations, religious and scientific societies, etc.) that mushroomed throughout eighteenth-century Europe as part of a rising bourgeois public sphere. These institutions were distinct from traditional corporations and guilds in that membership was voluntary rather than ascribed. Schaich reported that in London alone by 1750 some 20,000 men would meet daily in such clubs and associations; by the end of the century an estimated third of all English townsmen belonged to at least one such society.

Freemasonry spread worldwide with the advent of British and French imperialism, forming perhaps the first social network of global scope in modern times. Margaret Jacob (1991) has suggested that Masonic lodges in eighteenth-century Europe provided an organizational network that translated the theoretical ideals of the Enlightenment into tangible practices of sociability. Within the safe bounds of the lodges, men of diverse occupational, religious, and ethnic backgrounds could practice a new democratic political vocabulary, negotiating issues of constitution, self-governance, and social order. Masonic-style fraternalism reached its peak in nineteenth-century America, serving as a widespread organizational model for various civic, professional, and political movements (Clawson 1989), at times contributing to alliances formed between hegemonic and marginalized groups in society (Porter 2011). A growing body of literature has also examined women's participation in Masonic and Masonic-related organizations across the world (Heidle and Snoek 2008; Mahmud 2012).

However, historians have also stressed the ways that, despite a rhetoric of universal humanism, the elitist and gendered implications of Masonic fraternalism inevitably led to continual and variable restrictions on universal participation. Not only were women categorically excluded from membership in mainstream Freemasonry but also, in certain periods and regions, local lodges did not readily accept men from marginalized or divergent groups (Catholics, Jews, Hindus, etc.). This resulted in an upper-class, Anglocentric, and at times particularistic-nationalist understanding of civility (Clawson 1989; Harland-Jacobs 2003; Hoffman 2007).

The Case of Israeli Freemasonry

Between 2006 and 2008 I conducted fieldwork among Israeli Masons. Besides stating my academic interest in Freemasonry, I expressed personal curiosity in joining the Order, and after a prolonged candidacy period I was admitted to Urim Lodge (pseudonym), located in central Israel and catering to Jewish members. I participated in formal lodge work and took part in lodge social life and informal activities.[1] In addition, I held 40 in-depth interviews with Masons from lodges across the country and with selected family members.[2]

Israeli Freemasons refrain from advertising their activities, and new members are recruited mostly through social networks and family ties. Unlike in the Americas where the historical and cultural impact of Freemasons is not only well-documented but also publicly acknowledged, media coverage of Israeli Freemasonry is extremely scarce, with, to date, only one scholarly study of local Masonic early history (Campos 2005).

Masonic activity began in the Middle East in the late nineteenth century, stimulated by the growing influence of British and French colonial interests in the region. Men of free professions and bureaucrats of the Ottoman Empire found in Masonic lodges opportunities for professional networking (Campos 2005). Some also engaged in political activism, particularly those who followed French Freemasonry, which assumed a more active anticlerical position in the pursuit of civic rights than its British counterpart (Wissa 1989).

Masonic activity in Palestine spread in the early twentieth century and increased under the British Mandate government. Members were mainly Jews, Christians, and Muslim Arabs of local commercial and social elites. Freemasonry typically spread as a system of autonomous "Grand Lodges" which united local lodges formed in various regions and countries. Because new lodges depend on formal recognition from an established Grand Lodge, local lodges in Palestine worked separately under the charter of diverse foreign jurisdictions (Fuchs 2003). In 1953, following the establishment of the Israeli state, local lodges united under the umbrella organization of the Grand Lodge of the State of Israel (hereafter, GLSI). The new organization was recognized by the Grand Lodge of Scotland and supported by the English and Irish Grand Lodges (Fuchs 2003). Accordingly, GLSI adopted the orthodox principles of British Freemasonry, among them a stated belief in God (dubbed the "Grand Architect of the Universe") and a categorical exclusion of women from becoming members, though members' wives often assume active roles in lodge social life and charity activities.

Currently GLSI operates around 55 active lodges across Israel, consisting mainly of Jewish members and a minority of Arab members who are mostly Christians (Israeli citizens who may or may not identify as Palestinians). In its formative years local lodges attracted primarily members from the upper echelons of society (Campos 2005), however in recent decades membership has become more heterogeneous and increasingly includes men of middle-class and lower-middle-class backgrounds.[3]

Lodge activities take place alternately in closed and semi-open spaces. Masonic ritual activity is practiced in the lodge room, the place of worship laden with symbolic ornamentation that is open to members only. The lobby adjacent to the lodge room is open to visitors. Social events, primarily the "White Table" dinner and lecture that follow each lodge work session, take place in the lobby in the company of members' wives and friends and potential candidates. Additional activity occurs in public, including dining out at restaurants, weekend family picnics, and excursions to tourist sites, as well as charity activities in various institutions. During lodge work members are expected to suspend any personal disputes or internal lodge politics and to express themselves according to the formal rules of conduct associated with temperance and politeness (Kieser 1998). They are to sit and stand in certain postures, talk according to a prearranged order, and avoid interrupting one another. This emotional disciplining during lodge work comes in stark contradiction to the informal manners that I observed at White Table gatherings and semipublic events, during which food, drink, and playful behavior provide a sudden shift of mood in lodge sociability.

Like the historical studies of Freemasonry (Jacob 1991; Kieser 1998), my ethnographic observations of contemporary Israeli Freemasonry revealed a meticulous preoccupation with Masonic constitutional and administrative procedures, including quasi-democratic decision-making processes in which members voted to admit new candidates, elected lodge presidents, or approved the protocols of prior meetings. At the wider organizational level, lodge presidents from around the country served as official representatives at the general GLSI assembly and elected the president of GLSI (the Grand Master). Members are encouraged not only to advance in Masonic degrees but also to assume ceremonial roles, lodge administrative jobs, or other positions in the higher administration and educational arms of GLSI.

These multiple positions, some of which can be attained soon after joining a lodge, are open to all members, depending on rank and seniority. In fact, in smaller lodges there are sometimes more positions available than personnel to fill them. Such opportunities offer members hands-on experience in lodge and higher-level organizational involvement, which may serve as a symbolic model for civic engagement and leadership at the national level. A good example is the office of lodge president, officially termed "Worshipful Master." Any member who has reached the third degree of a Master Mason can run for this office, which is limited to a one- or two-year period. Hanoch, a Jewish-Israeli Mason of a northern lodge who was interviewed for this study, described the underlying democratic principle of the Order: "A street cleaner could become president...of a local lodge; hard-working people who struggle to make ends meet can become [presidents], because [being] lodge president is not something you buy with money." The president enjoys significant autonomy in governing the lodge. The system of local lodges forming around a Grand Lodge, as in the case of GLSI, is a loosely coupled structure based on bottom-up governance, with each individual lodge acting as a sovereign unit, a mini-state in its own right. Beyond established Masonic rituals and regulations, lodges are free to choose their own topics for discussion during lodge work, shape the content and format of all social events, and launch independent charity projects. Given this bottom-up structure, the elected lodge president holds a mandate for shaping the lodge's year-long policies.

In the case of Urim, I noticed that the president's wife was particularly active in managing the informal social activities alongside her husband. During formal lodge work the president would typically make a speech on Masonic moral philosophy and discuss matters of administration. Then, during the ensuing White Table dinner, his wife would sometimes make speeches of her own, urging brothers to volunteer for new charity projects initiated by the lodge. I was struck by how lodge sociability stages this gendered division of roles between them in ways that are reminiscent of the traditional divide in state leadership between the male head of state who deals with political affairs and the First Lady who often leads charity initiatives. This analogy marks the men's involvement in Masonic ritual and lodge administration as symbolically equivalent to national-political engagement. In the following I address the various ways that Masonic social "architecture" serves to produce a strong sense of continuity between personal interactions, organizational practices, and collective meanings.

Personal Ties: Strangers Turned into Virtuous Friends

I begin by describing how lodge members idealized their personal friendships and how these ideals informed their collective and moral consciousness. An average-sized lodge consists of approximately 40 members. Even in such a close-knit group individuals cannot maintain close ties with all the other members. Pinhas, a functionary in the administration of GLSI, illustrated in plain spatial terms how dyadic bonds and fraternal bonds coexist in these circumstances:

> There are some members who bond [with others] more, there are some who bond less, but we are all bonded together, no doubt about that…you cannot break ties; look, I can't sit next to everyone; I can only sit in a specific table…there's someone on my right and someone on my left, so I can talk to them. I can't talk with a guy who sits at a distant table, but he's still my brother.

Many interviewees made similar distinctions between personal bonds that they shared with particular lodge members and broader Masonic ties. As in typical accounts of personal friendships in everyday life, members described how individual friendships evolved through a gradual process of familiarity and growing intimacy. Rami, a Christian Arab member of a northern lodge, explained:

> Some people you connect with more than others, and then the bond develops beyond the confines of the lodge…I met this guy 11 years

ago, we were total strangers....We met by chance and he asked me a few questions [about the Order], the way you're asking me now, and after a while he decided to join....Our ties could have stayed on a more formal basis, meeting once every two weeks in lodge gatherings and that's that. But, as I told you, there's the personal attraction, and so today we've become very close, we speak on a daily basis...so, the relationship is very warm and sympathetic and very personal.

Rami's account draws on two presumed understandings about close relationships: first, that they carry stronger attachments than collective ties, and second, that the transformation from strangers to friends is a gradual process.

Although most of the members I talked with acknowledged these basic distinctions, their accounts also highlighted how Masonic sociability overturned some of these social constraints. First, lodge members who were not close friends were ascribed qualities associated with close friendship, particularly in terms of trust, immediate availability, and support. As Zohar, an Urim member, noted:

> No doubt, if I need help from someone, I know for sure that I can trust those people, even those who aren't really friends of mine. I can pick up the phone and ask for help and they'd do whatever they could....The Masons are always there for you, even financially. Whenever there's a problem...if it's 2 a.m. and you're stuck somewhere or just depressed and you don't know what to do, you can always pick up the phone and they'd answer and try to help you.

This expectation of active support and immediate availability reiterates a pervasive "folk model" of friendship that I noticed in my study of Israeli men's friendship in everyday life (Kaplan 2006). It depicts a scenario of total and immediate availability for the sake of one's friends, ranging from instrumental aid when stranded on the road in the middle of the night to emotional support during times of crisis. Culturally associated with life and death situations, Israeli men often transform this hegemonic national-military logic of emergency into a test case for close personal friendships. Local Masons alluded to this hegemonic model not simply to describe a personal bond but to illustrate the essence of Masonic fraternity, and in doing so, they established a continuity between personal and fraternal aspects of care and support.

In addition to extending qualities associated with close friendship to broader fraternal ties, some of the interviewees described face-to-face encounters with unfamiliar members that defied the commonplace understanding of a gradual transformation from strangers to friends. Instead, Masonic sociability occasioned random encounters that formed almost instant friendships. Rafi, a member of a lodge in Tel Aviv, recalled one such meeting when, traveling abroad, he entered a restroom at a US airport:

> The janitor was this old black guy. He was standing there with his broom and cleaning gear, when suddenly I saw on his finger a symbol of Freemasonry…so I ask him, "What's that ring you're wearing?" and he says, "It's the Freemasons." And I couldn't believe that this person, a restroom janitor, is a Freemason. How does he even relate to it?....Of course, at the end, we hugged and kissed and remained in touch for many years until he passed away. A lawyer and a restroom cleaner. I was amazed to find out that this person held the highest degree in Freemasonry, degree 33....Of course at the time [as we signaled each other] I got stuck with how to do the signs and couldn't meet him on the level....It was amazing to talk to him. The rituals are all identical in every country. It doesn't matter what language people speak. It's amazing how you can walk down the street and meet someone you don't know, and it takes you just 20 s to hug and kiss him as if he were your brother.

Rafi's story of his instant bonding with an African-American restroom janitor with whom he would have never interacted under regular circumstances conveys a sense of fascination with how Masonic sociability can miraculously turn strangers into friends. Indeed, the suspension of social boundaries and the transformation of nonequals into equals reflects a central Masonic moral principle commonly referred to as "meeting on the level," symbolized by the spirit level used by traditional masons. Rafi's account, however, demonstrates the double-edged nature of this elitist civic morality: first, the patronizing presumption that men of certain racial, ethnic, class or occupational backgrounds are less compatible with Masonic membership and not as likely to advance in the hierarchy of degrees, and, second, a celebration of the Masonic propensity to overcome such barriers and attain universal inclusion.

Another way in which Masonic sociability produces a sense of continuity between personal, organizational, and collective attachments can be inferred from lodge members' engagement in philosophical and symbolic musings over the moral virtue of their social ties and activities. When I asked my informants directly what their friendships meant to them, their reactions often turned inadvertently from the question of personal friendship to the collective and moral sphere, as in the following response by one young member:

> This question came up for discussion [at the lodge]: who's closer—personal friends (from school or work), or fellow Masonic brothers? I always say that fellow Masons are not necessary "better" people—that would be too idealized—but they do work harder on themselves, trying to set an example for others.

Throughout my discussions with fellow Masons at Urim and other lodges, it became clear to me that they viewed their personal participation in what is technically a social club as a moral project, one which derives its hidden meanings from a rich body of symbolic imagery, literature, and discourse. During my very first visits to Urim, I participated in an introductory study group on Masonic philosophy and history. Our teachers were senior lodge members. One of them, Maor, noted that there were two ways to approach Masonic teachings: some consider Freemasonry a form of philosophical "enlightenment," while others see Freemasonry as a path toward "society-building." He introduced us to a particular Masonic doctrine developed by the American occult philosopher (and Confederate general) Albert Pike (1871), who interpreted the Masonic Scottish Rite as a moral allegory for citizenship and statesmanship.[4] Each of the 33 degrees in this rite, Maor explained, represented in Pike's view good governance and virtuous leadership, qualities symbolized by the Ashlar stone.[5]

The blurring between interpersonal ties and civic virtue draws also on the Masonic ideal of active self-improvement, perceived as contributing to the betterment of society at large. In a sense, this ideal brings together a commitment to both enlightenment and society-building and is often invoked by the metaphor of light and candles. Sharon, a senior member from a lodge in southern Israel, explained how the candle metaphor implies that every member can conduct himself in a virtuous manner and enlighten his everyday environment beyond the confines of lodge sociability:

We believe…that each of us, each essentially a good person, carries a candle. We want to spread this light…not by slogans or propaganda…just by taking an unlit candle and lighting it. And the more candles are lit, the better things will be for everyone.

Public Intimacy: Secrecy and Masonic-Coded Communication

The Masons' experiential and moral apprehension of instant social transcendence between unequal strangers is enhanced by mechanisms of public intimacy that enable them to communicate in public with fellow members through a coded sign system, as in Rafi's aforementioned encounter in the restrooms. Although contemporary Freemasons repeatedly stress that they are no longer a secret society (Mahmud 2012), Masonic organizational structure and norms still build on secrecy. An elaborate system of code words and bodily gestures derived from Masonic mythology are practiced during ritual work. New initiates pledge not to reveal the primary codes used for membership identification and learn additional Masonic codes and symbolism only through sustained social participation in lodge activities as they gradually climb the hierarchy of degrees. At the same time, members habitually communicate in public or semipublic settings through this coding system or through Masonic symbolism more broadly. Beyond the official identification codes learned during ritual work, members often wear inconspicuous visual markers of identification, such as rings, watches, or lapel pins carrying the universal Masonic logo (a square and compass with the letter G inscribed at the center).

Underlying this secretive communication is a mechanism of inclusion and exclusion shaped by complex relations between intimacy, privacy, and secrecy. As Simmel underscored in his foundational discussion of secrecy and secret societies (1906), a secret is best understood not in terms of its substance or content, but in terms of its form and the strategies through which it is managed and exchanged among members of the group. Along these lines, one member explained to me that the secrecy of the Order has nothing to do with the content of the rituals, which are freely displayed on the internet, but with the "commitment" that develops between members as they manage their shared knowledge. In other words, the notion of secrecy translates into patterns of sociability and a sense of intimacy within the group as members negotiate—both inwardly and outwardly—different levels of access to the ritual system. The power of secrets rests on the public knowledge that they exist. Secrecy operates as kind of "adornment," enhancing the social distinction of those in possession of the concealed knowledge and surrounding them with an aura of mystery, awe and power (Urban 2001, 1; following Simmel 1906). Ultimately, secrecy serves to bind members of the group, not only by privileging their access to knowledge and excluding others from it but by signifying that they share an intimate bond; indeed the bond becomes intimate precisely by publicly staging it as a secret (see also Bellman 1981). In this sense, secrecy is effectively the opposite of privacy; it encapsulates the function of public intimacy as a dramaturgical mechanism for affording personal bonds with public significance.

The coded communication is directed both externally and internally. Externally, the coded signs capture the curiosity of bystanders, sending them a message that they are missing out on something. Sharon, a senior member in a lodge in southern Israel, explained why he always wore a Masonic ring:

> Because one of our principles is to be available to others. How would they know I was a Mason if I didn't have a sign?…And it serves another purpose. If someone is not part of us but could be worthy [of joining], then as soon as they ask about [the ring], I can tell him about the meaning of this sign.…Many people look and ask about it.

In this respect, the wearing in public of a partly veiled Masonic sign, such as a pin or a ring, becomes a strategy of seduction.

But coded communication in the presence of unqualified audiences is directed also internally, reinforcing members' sense of inclusion. One evening I participated in an informal study group initiated by Urim members to discuss Masonic principles in a more relaxed setting. The meeting took place at a member's home located in a working-class town. The apartment was situated at street level and was relatively exposed to the exterior surroundings. One of the senior members was concerned that the neighbors might overhear our lively conversations. The other participants reassured him that even if the neighbors could make out what we were saying, our talk would remain meaningless to them. One member added, half-jokingly, that no one in this locality would be able to grasp our discussions and referred to the locals in derogatory terms.

Later that evening, I spoke to Asaf, a recent initiate already well versed in Freemasonry mythology. He told me that he had volunteered to give a lecture at the next lodge meeting, a special annual ceremony held in the presence of members' wives. He planned to discuss Masonic content concerning the story of King Solomon but to frame it in such a manner that only the men would understand the Masonic connotations with the women remaining oblivious to such meanings. Asaf was concerned that if, at any point during his talk, other members were to become wary of exposure and openly warn him that there were women in the audience, then the women might begin to realize that a secretive mythology was being transmitted in their presence. This suggests that Asaf's main concern was inward, toward his fellow members; his challenge in compartmentalizing the story had less to do with the question of exposure than with his friends' reactions to the alleged threat. In other words, his lecture was intended to provoke and tease them as a way of negotiating their intimacy in front of an audience.

Underlying these rare moments when secrets are explicitly exposed and yet concealed is a pervasive logic of staged exclusion that reinforces members' sense of inclusion and extends to everyday lodge sociability. As family members and guests habitually participate in informal social events, Masons are constantly preoccupied with the compartmentalization of Masonic content. The attendance of this unqualified audience continually provokes the in-group to negotiate and reaffirm their intimacy. It also asserts their social supremacy, demarcating boundaries based on gender, class, or cultural background. Even when an unqualified audience is not actively present, it must be imagined (as in the aforementioned reference to eavesdropping lower-class neighbors) so that members can publicly stage their intimacy.

COLLECTIVE INTIMACY: STAGING AND COLLAPSING THE PERSONAL AND THE COLLECTIVE

Interactions between Masons extend beyond personal ties of friendship and coded communication in public to ties of fraternity that connect the Masonic Order as a whole. The following account by Rami provides a good starting point for examining the experience of fraternity at the organizational level, especially as it comes from a Christian Arab member who may, in other circumstances, face social barriers when interacting with members of the Jewish-Israeli majority. In addition to his aforementioned description of a personal friendship with a fellow Mason at his northern lodge, Rami noted the periodic national GLSI meetings he attended in central Tel Aviv:

> Here people come and meet from all over the country...I'm not always interested in their first names; the fraternal bond is what's interesting. When we meet here, at our meeting place, there are no barriers; you speak to your brothers in the clearest, most honest way, in the sense that you have trust in them, and trust is the fundamental principle in all of this.

These notions of trust and the overcoming of barriers during interactions at the collective-organizational level echo preceding accounts of strangers-turned-friends at the interpersonal level. The interviewees thus conceived Masonic collective solidarity as a community of strangers who are trusted as friends.

Masonic rituals provide a central vehicle for forging this sense of cohesive fraternity. Observance of the rich, elaborate ritual system reinforces participants' sense of collective identity as belonging to a long-standing tradition. It also inscribes collective meanings of solidarity onto their mutual interactions. John, a member of another northern lodge, compared the functions of ritual to those of friendship:

> The ritual is a friend....It's a basic tool [we have] for connecting with one another. If we had no rituals, forget it, what would we do? So the ritual helps, otherwise there would be no connection, nothing to talk about.

The question therefore remains, how does collective ritual activity, the locus of sacred experience, become equated with ties of friendship, typically associated with personal experience in mundane everyday life? To begin with, although much of lodge work involves a sequence of essentially bureaucratic or administrative procedures, its theatrical staging as a social performance of ritualized role-playing serves to stimulate members' emotional experiences and reinforces their organizational involvement and commitment. Some members play elaborate ceremonial roles, while others serve mostly as audience; yet all recite Masonic scripts and liturgy and engage to some degree in a role-playing steeped in pomp and ceremony. In this respect, Masonic lodge work brings to the fore the kind of ritualized, symbolically-laden performance of focused interactions that takes place in all social movements and helps channel members' emotions into a collective display of solidarity, enthusiasm, and morality (Summers-Effler 2005). A social performance is likely to instantiate such an effective integrative process provided the social actors work through symbolic and material means and orient toward fellow members as if they were actors on a stage, seeking identification and understanding from their audience (Alexander and Mast 2006). As noted by Ron Eyerman (2006) in his analysis of mobilization processes in social movements, such ritualization and theatrical staging "are transformative in that they help blur the boundaries between individual and collective, between the private and public, and help fuse a group through creating strong emotional bonds between participants" (196).

From the perspective of friendship these emotional reactions during social performance merit a closer look at how they blur not only the boundaries between the individual and the collective but specifically between personal and collective ties, often collapsing these very distinctions. Masonic social life is premised on stark spatial and temporal mood shifts between ritualized lodge work and informal sociability. This is reminiscent of the ways in which ritualized distinctions between the sacred and the profane provide confirmation of collective values shared by members of the community (Durkheim 2003). A similar tendency for rapid shifts between periods of worship and periods of engagement in mundane activities has been noted in other institutions of worship, such as Samuel Heilman's (1982) interactionist study of synagogue life. Heilman further suggested certain parallels between these instances of "shifting involvements" during worship among American Modern Orthodox Jews and their propensity in everyday life to display allegiance to multiple collective identities at the same time, for example, an American civic identity and a religious Jewish identity (14–15).[6]

In lodge social architecture, however, this context shifting affects not only each member as an individual but also the interpersonal ties between members; personal friendships thus constantly alternate between the profane and the sacred, and the two realms of sociability become closely linked. Following I discuss two specific cases in point: shifting modalities of sociability with lodge officials and the amalgamation of personal and collective attachments in Masonic rituals.

During one of the lodge work sessions at Urim, the Grand Master of GLSI made a grand entrance as our honored guest. Clad in a unique cloak, apron, and vest laden with ribbons and medals, he was followed by an entourage of senior brothers. They marched slowly in solemn majesty as we stood in tribute. I was reminded of the Israeli President reviewing the honorary guard during Independence Day ceremonies. Then, some 50 min later, there he was, sitting with all of us at the White Table dinner, dressed in an ordinary suit, sharing some banal jokes. By differentiating between the sacred and the profane but juxtaposing them in close proximity to one another, lodge architecture alters social distinctions. The fact that the same individual could personify both conditions in such a short period of time and within the same building shows how the revered can become familiar and the familiar revered.

An observation of how members perform standard Masonic rituals can provide yet another demonstration of the continuity between personal and collective attachments. A straightforward example is the brief toast that opens each White Table dinner—a series of blessings paying tribute to the president of the State of Israel, the president of GLSI, representatives of the GLSI assembly, the brothers of the lodge, and new lodge candidates. Through this simple gesture, interpersonal identification between lodge members is linked to organizational identification with the Order's functionaries and, ultimately, to collective identification with the head of the state. Once again, all levels of identification become infused with a dual emotional quality of solidarity as consisting of both reverence and familiarity.

A similar juxtaposition of the personal and the collective emerges in a central ritual celebrating the Masonic ideal of fraternity—the "Chain of Brothers" (also called the "Chain of Union"). The ritual takes place at the closing of each lodge work. The participants gather in a circle in the center of the lodge room. Each brother crosses his arms and joins hands with his neighbors, his right hand holding the left hand of the neighbor on his left, his left hand holding the right hand of the neighbor on his right. The ritual represents a transformation of sociability from the concrete interactions between lodge members to the abstract connections among the worldwide fraternity of Freemasons. As the brothers interlace their hands, they evoke an image of this collective entity as a cohesive, harmonic, and unified body.

When Urim members performed the Chain of Brothers, the lodge president would give a brief address relating to fraternity. The topic of the address varied every meeting. On one occasion, one of the participants asked the president to add a special plea for the return of "kidnapped Israelis," referring to the soldier Gilad Shalit who was being held captive in Gaza at the time, arousing national concern and extensive displays of public solidarity. Another member told the group that the son of a close friend had been seriously injured in a car crash and asked for his name to be included in the plea. As the group incorporated both requests in the Chain of Brothers ritual, it symbolically connected care for personal acquaintances with care for national symbols of solidarity and associated both with the universal sentiment of fraternity. Moreover, the inclusion of a tribute to Israeli soldiers within formal lodge work demonstrates both how Zionist affiliations permeate lodge social life, as might be expected among Jewish-Israeli Masons, and how the official Masonic symbolism of fraternity sanctifies—even if inadvertently—members' local civic and national attachments.

The ceremonial examples of White Table toasts and Chain of Brothers rituals illustrate how, through the theatrical staging and rescaling of larger society to an average-sized lodge of 40 members, bureaucracy and ceremony are brought together, attaching collective significance to lodge administrative procedures and conferring Masonic sanctity on national life. Moreover, the spontaneous choices and gestures made by lodge members as they enact and interpret the rituals reveal the reproduction of this juxtaposition of mundane sociability and sacredness through bottom-up initiatives.

Overall, Masonic sociability seems to collapse the analytic distinction between the private and the personal on the one hand and the public and collective on the other. This becomes all the clearer when one tries to map the spatial and temporal shifts between formal lodge work and informal lodge interactions onto the public-private divide. The official and ceremonial gathering in the lodge room may resemble the public sphere of politics and the state, but it is public only in the sense of simulating a collective body and not in the sense of displaying and negotiating public concerns. On the contrary, because Masonic regulations forbid any controversial discussion of politics or religion and, furthermore, lodge members refrain from bringing up internal organizational disputes during lodge work, this ceremonial space is kept pure from political negotiations. Instead, such negotiations take place primarily during White Table dinners and other social events framed as informal sociability, personal gossip, and jovial relations.

The lodge assembly room thus emerges as both the most private space in the organization, secretive and hidden from view, and the most collective, fostering an intimacy shared by all lodge members. The purified, disciplined, conflict-free, and depoliticized assembly becomes a symbol of collective intimacy. Like the rituals of the nation-state, it magnifies the quality of "selfless unisonance" experienced during national ceremonies (Anderson 1991, 145) and presents a moral order of unity and singularity (Handelman 2004).

Unlike the atmosphere of inclusion fostered by this sacred space of collective intimacy, the secular spaces and mundane interactions of everyday life provide an arena for staging the exclusionary functions of public intimacy, as described in the previous section. By being constantly displayed in public, secrecy forms a multilayered boundary-generating mechanism, at once seducing and excluding out-groups to sustain and fuel the in-group experience. While pure instances of collective intimacy eliminate the public-private distinction by imagining a unified whole, they also build on accumulated experiences of public intimacy where the public-private divide is continually reproduced.

A Playground for Forging Civic-National Attachment

The foregoing analysis demonstrated how Masonic social architecture provides members with an experiential model for connecting social ties at the interpersonal and organizational level with collective attachments at the wider societal level. But what form does this collective attachment take? Israeli Freemasons hold fast to the official policy of political non-involvement in line with the founding tradition of English Freemasonry. However, on occasions, as evident in some of the previous examples, members' rhetoric and symbolic activities did relate to political issues and signaled their identification with state and nation.

To begin with, some interpreted the traditional prohibition on discussions about politics and religion as an injunction on talking against one's country. This, in turn, unfolded into a declared duty to be loyal to the state, as explained by Yonah, a Mason from a lodge in central Israel:

> One may not talk against religion or against the state, and one shouldn't stir up disputes or do anything that opposes the state. The country comes above all! If you live in this country, you need to respect it and its rules, so you shouldn't do anything against it.

The significance of state loyalty reappeared when I applied to become an official member of Urim in 2007. Two lodge representatives paid me a home visit and interviewed me in order to prepare an official letter of recommendation for the lodge assembly. I was given an admission form and requested to answer several philosophical questions about my understanding of morality, justice, mutual relief, and good citizenship. Interestingly, my visitors elaborated only on the last, explaining that since the Freemasons avoided engaging in political issues, obedience to the state is of prime importance. In other words, they reinterpreted the question of good citizenship as loyalty to the state and, in addition, connected it to the Masonic principle of nonpolitical engagement, overlooking the fact that claiming allegiance to the state is an inherently political act.

Beyond the issue of citizenship and state loyalty, nationalism serves as another source of collective attachment; this, however, was rarely addressed directly by members but rather taken for granted. Zionist-national values, such as support for military service, partly carried over into Masonic rituals. In one of the presidential sermons concluding lodge work, the Urim president preached about Masonic and civic participation. After providing some exemplary stories of individuals who had contributed to society, he brought up a negative example of military service dodgers, who were at the center of a prevailing public debate after it had been discovered that local celebrity singers in a reality TV show had evaded the draft. An animated debate began among the lodge members as many rallied to speak against draft dodgers. One member noted other groups who disobeyed military orders, recalling an event from earlier that day in which religious Jewish soldiers had refused to participate in the forced eviction of two Jewish families who had settled in Palestinian territory in the city of Hebron. He hedged his remarks, however, by saying that he didn't want to comment on a political issue.

A few days later, Yoav, one of my friends at the lodge, called me to exchange views on the event, troubled that a controversial political issue had been raised during the ritual work. We recalled the previous meeting when the president included in the "Chain of Brothers" ritual a special plea for the return of Israeli captive soldiers, a gesture that had not raised any reservations. We speculated whether commemorating soldiers during an official Masonic ceremony was not on a continuum with debating military service. Weren't all of these issues ultimately political? I tried to imagine how Arab Masons, officially exempted from military service due to their potential Palestinian allegiances, would respond to this consecration of military participation.[7] The unexpected debate during the president's sermon against military dodgers merely exposed what the plea for captive soldiers had concealed: as members explicitly advanced issues of state loyalty and civic participation in and through formal Masonic practices, they concomitantly sanctioned local national values. This depoliticized national attachment went unnoticed precisely because of the local members' preoccupation with preventing explicit political controversies.

What emerges from these observations is that despite a stance of universal humanism and a cosmopolitan vision, Freemasons associate civic virtue with a declared loyalty to the state and an unstated identification with the nation. Masonic sociability thus provides a "playground" for negotiating the vocabulary, ideals, and tensions of civic-nationalism. The common definition of civic-nationalism, as discussed in Chapter 6, refers to a contractual form of collective attachment that considers the nation a community of equal citizens, sharing a set of political practices and universalistic values (Brown 2000, 51; Ignatieff 1993; Kohn 1944).

Freemasonry relates to these principles on various levels. First, the international spread of Freemasonry provided secluded settings where local lodge members could engage in performative enactments of administrative democratic principles associated with civil society such as a constitution, elections, and self-governance. In each locality, these ceremonial, theatrical performances served to solidify and make tangible for participants a cultural script for imagining their nation-state as a civic democracy. Freemasonry per se was not involved in the rise of national movements.[8] However, historical records suggest that individual members of Masonic lodges played important roles in advancing national revolutions with distinctly civic aspirations, such as the 1776 American Revolution (Triber 2001; York 1993), the 1908 Young Turk Revolution (Dumont 2005), and the 1919 national democratic revolution in Egypt (Wissa 1989). Masonic circles were also implicated in struggles for national independence in the 1830 Belgian Revolution (Maes 2010), the Mexican and various other Latin American national movements (Uribe-Uran 2000), and the 1905 Iranian Constitutional Revolution (Bayat 2009). While these historical studies by no means provide a causal link between participation in Masonic lodges and the rise of civic-national revolutions, they do suggest that Masonic sociability provided not only a semi-democratic political vocabulary (Jacob 1991) but also a playground for negotiating national consciousness in a civic context.

Second, Masonic sociability highlights the unique qualities of a purely civic understanding of the national community. It posits friendship, rather than kinship, as a central organizing moral principle and construes group membership in universal terms of allegiance to shared contractual principles rather than shared ethnic descent. Similar to Masonic ceremonial acts of admission, the civic-contractual model of nationalism embraces a ceremonial oath of allegiance that demonstrates commitment to shared principles and highlights the importance of consent in line with liberal and civic republican traditions of citizenship (Smith 1997). Finally, Freemasonry emphasizes civic virtue and an active stance of self-improvement as a path to good citizenship and the building of an enlightened society.[9]

In this, it echoes a central aspect of civic nationalism proposed by Kohn (1944). As elaborated by Calhoun (2007, 43, 132), a key principle in Kohn's theory is a transformative, redemptive self-fashioning through active participation in the community and a collective effort to shape a common culture (rather than merely receiving it as inheritance as in the ethno-cultural model of nationalism).

The Nation as a Club of Chosen Friends

In this case study I described how the negotiation of personal ties among Freemasons and their experience of strangers-turned-friends is structured by Masonic social architecture and extends to collective life through the mechanisms of public intimacy. First, members apply an elaborate coding system to compartmentalize Masonic content from nonqualified audiences. This secretive communication is directed both externally, in order to seduce outsiders to attend, and internally, in order to reaffirm members' intimacy in front of excluded audiences. Second, members engage in administrative and democratic practices that undergo ceremonial dramatization derived from Masonic mythology. This theatrical staging serves to blend personal and collective attachments. The official-ceremonial and the personal-mundane become closely linked, each acquiring an aura of both familiarity and reverence. Underlying this understanding of interpersonal ties as sacred fraternal ties is a Masonic meta-narrative veiled in allegory and symbolism, according to which personal participation in what is essentially a social club becomes a collective moral project of building an enlightened society through active self-improvement.

Although esoteric and secretive, Masonic lodges were historically influential civic associations (Jacob 1991). From the eighteen century onwards lodge sociability enabled members to develop a hands-on understanding of the novel and seemingly abstract conception of "the people," the new popular sovereign of the nation-state (Yack 2012). Central to the notion of self-governing people is not only a sense of subjective agency but also of transparency between the individuals and the collective (Gaonkar 2002). In present-day lodges set within the bounds of contemporary nation-states Masonic sociability continues to uphold such transparency by dissolving distinctions between personal ties and collective forms of solidarity and enabling members to take on the symbolic roles of a citizen, a bureaucrat, a priest, and a president all in one.

The distinct patterns of sociability fostered in Masonic clubs cultivate a civic-national attachment and reveal how this form of national solidarity combines a universalist ethos of fraternity with a particularist preference for a selected group of citizen-friends. Premised on the logic of social clubs, this solidarity binds participants through both ties of mutual trust and consent and feelings of exclusiveness and privilege. It is a boundary work that is at stake, accomplished by official rules of admission and by ongoing negotiation and interpretation of the limits of collective sentiments of fraternity. Both social clubs and nation-states vary in the kinds of boundaries that they draw; even Masonic systems vary in their rules of admission. But all social clubs and all national communities are premised on such boundary work. Freemasonry simply underscores how underlying the universal, contractual rhetoric of civic nationalism is a particular form of boundary maintenance that defines the limits of civic membership not through an ancestral lineage of "brothers," as in the ethno-cultural model, but by venerating a voluntary yet privileged formation of civilized "brother-friends."

Notes

1. As Freemasonry is characterized by an organizational culture of learning and members are encouraged to actively seek knowledge about the Order, my own position as both member and researcher was not particularly remarkable. Although I did not identify with certain attitudes conveyed around me, particularly with respect to the exclusion of women, upon

official initiation I suddenly felt a stronger attachment to my fellow lodge members and more involved as a participant.
2. Interviewees from other lodges were chosen so as to reflect diverse age, ethnic, and religious backgrounds. Some interviews were conducted by my students participating in a research seminar on fraternal societies during Winter and Spring 2006. For more details on research methods and analysis see the Book Outline and Methodology section in Chapter 1.
3. For a more detailed account of Israeli Freemasonry with a focus on relations between Jewish and Arab members, see Kaplan (2014).
4. The Scottish Rite, amalgamated from several Masonic traditions and disseminated worldwide by Albert Pike, is one of several appendant bodies of Freemasonry that members can join in order to advance to higher degrees after attaining the three principal Masonic degrees. The ceremonial practice of each degree involves dramatic reenactments of scenes from Masonic mythology.
5. In Pike's (1871) original wording: "[The] perfect Ashlar, or cubical stone, symbol of perfection, is the State. ...[The cube] is an appropriate symbol of the Force of the people, expressed as the Constitution and law of the State; and of the State itself the three visible faces represent the three departments—the Executive, which executes the laws; the Legislative, which makes the laws; the Judiciary, which interprets the laws, applies and enforces them, between man and man, between the State and the citizens. The three invisible faces, are Liberty, Equality, and Fraternity, the threefold soul of the State—its vitality, spirit, and intellect" (5–6).
6. Iddo Tavory (2016, 147–148) offered an alternative interactionist approach to this shifting involvement among Ultra-Orthodox Jews that is based on the concept of "summoning." This approach explores the relationship between processes of individual identification and the construction of social worlds by attending to the intersection of actors' actions and their multiple interactions with (and invocations by) other members of their community.
7. In Israeli-Zionist discourse the term military "dodgers" runs the gamut from conscientious objectors to individuals discharged from service for personal difficulties, deliberate draft evaders who fake mental problems, and Ultra-Orthodox Jews who are exempted from service through legal and administrative arrangements (Livio 2012). It does not, however, normally extend to Arab citizens who, like Ultra-Orthodox Jews are officially exempted from the military. Thus, while this discourse is framed in civic terms as a contribution to the common good, it masks an underlying nationalist logic that excludes groups of citizens who are not part of the Jewish nation.

8. Contrary to popular impressions, there is little evidence of direct Masonic involvement in either the French Revolution (Loiselle 2010) or the American Revolution (York 1993).
9. As Stefan-Ludwig Hoffmann (2001) noted in his detailed study of nineteenth-century German Freemasonry, lodge sociability fostered an active stance of "civilizing the self" as part of its "enlightened-liberal utopia of a virtuous self-improvement through sociability" (226).

REFERENCES

Alexander, Jeffrey C., and Jason L. Mast. 2006. "Introduction: Symbolic Action in Theory and Practice: The Cultural Pragmatics of Symbolic Action." In *Social Performance: Symbolic Action, Cultural Pragmatics, and Ritual*, edited by Jeffrey C. Alexander, Bernhard Giesen, and Jason. L. Mast, 1–28. Cambridge: Cambridge University Press.
Anderson, Benedict. [1983] 1991. *Imagined Communities: Reflections on the Origins and Spread of Nationalism.* London: Verso.
Anderson, James. ed. [1746] 1923. *The History and Constitutions of the Most Ancient and Honourable Fraternity of Free and Accepted Masons*, vol. 1. London: J. Robinson.
Bayat, Mangol. 2009. "Freemasonry and the Constitutional Revolution in Iran: 1905–1911." In *Freemasonry and Fraternalism in the Middle East*, edited by Andreas Önnerfors and Dorothe Sommer, 109–150. Sheffield: University of Sheffield.
Bellman, Beryl L. 1981. "The Paradox of Secrecy." *Human Studies* 4: 1–24.
Brown, David. 2000. *Contemporary Nationalism: Civic, Ethnocultural and Multicultural Politics.* London: Routledge.
Bullock, Steven C. 1996. *Revolutionary Brotherhood: Freemasonry and the Transformation of the American Social Order, 1730–1840.* Chapel Hill: University of North Carolina Press.
Calhoun, Craig. 2007. *Nations Matter: Culture, History, and the Cosmopolitan Dream.* New York: Routledge.
Campos, Michelle. 2005. "Freemasonry in Ottoman Palestine." *Jerusalem Quarterly* 22–23: 37–62.
Clawson, Mary Ann. 1989. *Constructing Brotherhood: Class, Gender, and Fraternalism.* Princeton: Princeton University Press.
Dumont, Paul. 2005. "Freemasonry in Turkey: A By-Product of Western Penetration." *European Review* 13 (3): 481–493.
Durkheim, Emile. [1915] 2003. "The Elementary Forms of Religious Life." Translated by Karen E. Fields. In *Emile Durkheim: Sociologist of Modernity*, edited by Mustafa Emirbayer, 109–121, 140–141. Malden, MA: Blackwell.

Eyerman, Ron. 2006. "Performing Opposition Or, How Social Movements Move." In *Social Performance: Symbolic Action, Cultural Pragmatics, and Ritual*, edited by Jeffrey C. Alexander, Bernhard Giesen, and Jason L. Mast, 193–217. Cambridge: Cambridge University Press.

Fuchs, Ephraim (ed.). 2003. *Jubilee Book of the Grand Lodge of the State of Israel of Ancient Free and Accepted Masons*. Tel Aviv: Grand Lodge of the State of Israel.

Gaonkar, Dilip Parameshwar. 2002. "Toward New Imaginaries: An Introduction." *Public Culture* 14 (1): 1–19.

Handelman, Don. 2004. *Nationalism and the Israeli State: Bureaucratic Logic in Public Events*. Oxford: Berg.

Harland-Jacobs, Jessica. 2003. "All in the Family: Freemasonry and the British Empire in the Mid-Nineteenth Century." *Journal of British Studies* 42 (4): 448–482.

Heidle, Alexandra, and Jan A.M. Snoek (eds.). 2008. *Women's Agency and Rituals in Mixed and Female Masonic Orders*. Leiden: Brill.

Heilman, Samuel C. 1982. "Prayer in the Orthodox Synagogue: An Analysis of Ritual Display." *Contemporary Jewry* 6 (1): 2–17.

Hoffmann, Stefan-Ludwig. 2001. "Civility, Male Friendship and Masonic Sociability in Nineteenth-Century Germany." *Gender and History* 13 (2): 224–248.

Hoffmann, Stefan-Ludwig. 2007. *The Politics of Sociability: Freemasonry and German Civil Society, 1840–1918*. Ann Arbor: University of Michigan Press.

Ignatieff, Michael. 1993. *Blood and Belonging: Journeys into the New Nationalism*. New York: Farrar, Straus & Giroux.

Jacob, Margaret C. 1991. "The Enlightenment Redefined: The Formation of Modern Civil Society." *Social Research* 58 (2): 475–495.

Kaplan, Danny. 2006. *The Men We Loved: Male Friendship and Nationalism in Israeli Culture*. New York: Berghahn Books.

Kaplan, Danny. 2014. "Jewish-Arab Relations in Israeli Freemasonry: Between Civil Society and Nationalism." *Middle East Journal* 68 (3): 385–401.

Kieser, Alfred. 1998. "From Freemasons to Industrious Patriots: Organizing and Disciplining in 18th-Century Germany." *Organization Studies* 19 (1): 47–71.

Kohn, Hans. 1944. *The Idea of Nationalism: A Study in Its Origins and Background*. New York: Collier-Macmillan.

Livio, Oren. 2012. "Avoidance of Military Service in Israel: Exploring the Role of Discourse." *Israel Studies Review* 27 (1): 78–97.

Loiselle, Kenneth. 2010. "Living the Enlightenment in an Age of Revolution: Freemasonry in Bordeaux, 1788–1794." *French History* 24 (1): 60–81.

Mackey, Albert G. 1898. *A Manual of the Lodge*. New York: Maynard, Merrill & Co.

Maes, Anaïs. 2010. "Freemasonry as a Patriotic Society? The 1830 Belgian Revolution." *Revista de Estudios Históricos de la Masonería Latinoamericana y Caribeña* 2 (2): 3–17.
Mahmud, Lilith. 2012. "'The World is a Forest of Symbols': Italian Freemasonry and the Practice of Discretion." *American Ethnologist* 39 (2): 425–438.
Pike, Albert. 1871. *Morals and Dogma of the Ancient and Accepted Scottish Rite of Freemasonry*. New York: Masonic Publishing.
Porter, Joy. 2011. *Native American Freemasonry: Associationalism and Performance in America*. Lincoln: University of Nebraska Press.
Schaich, Michael. 2008. "The Public Sphere." In *A Companion to Eighteenth-Century Europe*, edited by Peter H. Wilson. 125–140 Malden, MA: Blackwell.
Simmel, Georg. 1906. "The Sociology of Secrecy and of Secret Societies." *American Journal of Sociology* 11 (4): 441–498.
Smith, Rogers M. 1997. *Civic Ideals: Conflicting Visions of Citizenship in US History*. New Haven, CT: Yale University Press.
Summers-Effler, Erika. 2005. "The Emotional Significance of Solidarity for Social Movement Communities." In *Emotions and Social Movements*, edited by Helena Flam and Debra King, 135–149. New York: Routledge.
Tavory, Iddo. 2016. *Summoned: Religious Life in an Orthodox Jewish Neighborhood*. Chicago: Chicago University Press.
Triber, Jayne E. 2001. *A True Republican: The Life of Paul Revere*. Amherst, MA: University of Massachusetts Press.
Urban, Hugh B. 2001. "The Adornment of Silence: Secrecy and Symbolic Power in American Freemasonry." *Journal of Religion & Society* 3: 1–29.
Uribe-Uran, Victor M. 2000. "The Birth of a Public Sphere in Latin America During the Age of Revolution." *Comparative Studies in Society and History* 42 (2): 425–457.
Wissa, K. 1989. "Freemasonry in Egypt 1798–1921: A Study in Cultural and Political Encounters." *British Society for Middle Eastern Studies* [Bulletin] 16 (2): 143–161.
Yack, Bernard. 2012. *Nationalism and the Moral Psychology of Community*. Chicago: University of Chicago Press.
York, Neil L. 1993. "Freemasons and the American Revolution." *Historian* 55 (2): 315–360.

CHAPTER 8

Big Brother: Viewers Turned Accomplices on Reality TV

Nowhere is the transformation of strangers into friends (and rivals) perhaps more evident—and its collective dimension more explicit—than in the reality TV show *Big Brother*. The series gathers a diverse group of individuals to live together for three months in a specially constructed house that is isolated from the outside world but continuously monitored by live television cameras and microphones. The successful format has been aired in roughly 80 countries to date. The Israeli version of *Big Brother* earned top prime-time ratings, and its first few seasons became an ongoing "media event" (Dayan and Katz 1992) of national scale, second only to "real" national news in arousing public interest. Communication studies in the Durkheimian tradition have critically examined the importance of ritualized media events for mobilizing feelings of solidarity (Cottle 2006; Couldry 2003; Dayan and Katz 1992; Sonnevend 2016). Understood as a social performance, media events can be said to accomplish fusion when viewers identify with performers and background cultural scripts achieve verisimilitude (Alexander 2004). However, despite the centrality of face-to-face or mediated interactions between actors in the social performance (performers and viewers) scholars have largely remained silent on the role of social ties in media events and on the meanings that actors assign to these ties.

This chapter is based in part on an article written with Yoni Kupper and published in 2017 in *Journal of Communication* 67 (5): 758–780.

© The Author(s) 2018
D. Kaplan, *The Nation and the Promise of Friendship*, Cultural Sociology,
https://doi.org/10.1007/978-3-319-78402-1_8

Similar inattention to relational-interactional considerations can be noted in the growing body of research on reality TV. While much of this literature has centered on the public staging of an authentic self (Aslama and Pantti 2006; Corner 2002; Hill 2002), it has not considered the public staging of social ties between actors as an equally important category of analysis. Reality viewers are invited not only to identify with individual contestants but also to affiliate with them—both symbolically and practically (Tincknell and Raghuram 2002).

Drawing on qualitative data from a doctoral study of the reality show *Big Brother Israel* (Kupper 2015), this chapter demonstrates various practices of "mediated public intimacy" taking place between two (or more) contestants with the audience as an absent third party. As I elaborate below, certain structural features and interactional dynamics built into the Big Brother format and orchestrated by its local production create atypical "folds" in the veil that separates insiders from outsiders. These conditions serve to mobilize viewers' sense of participation, moving them from a position of casual bystanders to one of privileged confidants and potential companions of the contestants.

As I further show, this sense of "audience-turned-participant" can explain the intensity of audience involvement as reflected in interactions between viewers in everyday life and in online forums and social media. Once attention is shifted from the actual show to the discourse about the show, it is the audience who become the active participants in the social performance and the contestants who assume the role of an absent third party, a role that carries a totemic, symbolic presence in the social life of the audience. In this way, the social performance mobilizes feelings of solidarity among viewers not only by orchestrating instances of focused attention but by staging interpersonal interactions and fomenting a dynamic of seduction that culminates in feelings of collective complicity. From a Durkheimian perspective, it is through such emergent feelings of complicity that reality television comes close to capturing the essence of media events, namely, that the object of worship serves as a personification of the collective.

Global Format, National Meaning

Big Brother is a reality game show in which a group of contestants (referred to as "housemates") are brought together in a specially designed house that is isolated from the outside world but continuously monitored by live television cameras and microphones.[1] The housemates live together for about three months and are joined by additional contestants in the middle of this period. Each week contestants secretly nominate other contestants whom they wish to evict, and viewers vote to keep their favorite contestant in the house. The last remaining housemate wins a substantial cash prize.

The Big Brother house is designed as a spacious residential home. The contestants share all the facilities and rooms of the house including the sleeping area. At the same time, this simulated home is also a television studio which broadcasts live 24/7 from every corner of the house. In this regard, the show conforms with the growing trend in the late modern era to blur commonly held distinctions between the domestic, personal, and private sphere on the one hand and the collective and public sphere on the other. In this case, it is the very structural and architectonic features of the show that serve to materially eliminate the physical and conceptual divides between the spheres.

The Israeli version of *Big Brother* began airing in 2008 on Channel 2 and instantly gained top ratings (Kupper 2015). The main broadcast consists of edited episodes aired twice a week on prime time. In addition, unedited live coverage from the in-house cameras is aired on a designated cable channel and streamed on Channel 2's official Web site. The prime-time episodes showcase developments and occurrences that have taken place in the house over the previous days and are heavily edited by the production team in order to draw viewers' attention. The episodes also feature live interactions between the housemates and the show's hosts who stand right outside the Big Brother house in the company of a live audience. Once a week the hosts announce the contestant selected for eviction.

The contestants are typically selected to reflect diverse social groups in terms of class, age, ethnicity, sexual orientation, and religion, although the sizable Jewish ultra-Orthodox and Arab Palestinian minorities within Israeli society tend to be underrepresented. Some contestants join the show on a self-proclaimed mission to advocate for a particular agenda (veganism, a specific political ideology, religious conviction, etc.). The social diversity and ideological rifts between contestants often serve to spark debates inside the house and among the viewers. But it is mostly the personal friendships and rivalries formed in the house that attract audience attention.

The current analysis draws on findings derived from Yoni Kupper's (2015) study of Big Brother Israel conducted between 2008 and 2012.

The study included a semiotic analysis of four seasons of the show, an analysis of online discussions about the show that appeared on major news Web sites and on related Facebook pages, 41 semi-structured personal interviews with viewers, 10 focus groups with a total of 70 viewers, and selected participant observations with a live audience.[2]

The worldwide success of the reality genre is part of the rising trade in TV formats since the early twenty-first century and is considered an exemplary case of media globalization (Fung 2015). At the same time, even as viewers across the world watch the same TV format, they may engage with it in culturally distinct ways, such that local adaptations of each show acquire national meanings (Moran 1998; Waisbord 2004). Local producers do, in fact, tend to tailor program formats to fit local tastes. In order to achieve popular and commercial success, they capitalize on the legitimacy of local national discourse by strategically invoking perceived national sentiments (Kaplan and Hirsch 2012; Livio 2010). Although these local productions are often explicitly presented to the audience as an imported, internationally successful format, on some level the viewers nonetheless experience and perceive the show as nationally unique. Elsewhere, I called attention to this paradox of "isomorphic national uniqueness," whereby local actors in fields of popular culture systematically "erase" the exogenous source of a given genre or organizational model, considering it a local invention and authentic manifestation of local national culture despite its dependence on global isomorphism (Kaplan 2012, 218–219).

The case of *Big Brother* is particularly illuminating in this regard. The format was created in 1999 by Dutch TV producer John de Mol and distributed worldwide (Hill 2002; Mathijs and Jones 2004), aired to date in roughly 65 countries mostly by means of franchises granted to individual countries. In each country, the local production is situated within national boundaries: using a local cast, which is often diverse and reflective of the country's native population, and catering to the local national audience who typically share a common language.[3] Because the show is confined to this national framework, producers often tap into shared national themes. For instance, the format prescribes weekly tasks in which the housemates divide into groups and undergo some entertaining assignment designed to test their team spirit. In *Big Brother Israel*, some of these weekly tasks bring up common themes from national life. In one case, contestants participated in a trivia game and responded to questions drawn from Israel's history and folklore. On another occasion, they played roles in a "pioneers' assignment," in which living conditions in the house were refashioned after the British Mandate period and the contestants were required to fight the British military who supposedly interfered and sabotaged their tasks.

Even more telling is the way in which the global reality format acquires national meaning in the eyes of the local audience. When set in the context of the Big Brother house, daily routines that are essentially universal human activities achieve national significance, as demonstrated in the following comment made by Ronit, an executive secretary who was interviewed for this study: "The lunch bit. How they [the housemates] make lunch, how they eat it. It's just like we do at home, it's usually schnitzels and sausages and *pireh*...which is basically our daily Israeli food."

Schnitzel and *pireh* (the Hebrew word for mashed potatoes which is derived from the French *purée*) are common in many countries. Even their spoken Hebrew names, which retain the German and French wording, show that there is nothing uniquely Israeli about them. What in Ronit's eyes makes this standard meal into "Israeli food" isn't the menu, but the intimate exposure to and sense of familiarity with daily practices taking place in the house of strangers, which are nonetheless so similar to her own.

This point becomes even clearer from the observations of Lee, who pointed out that watching American *Big Brother* while on a visit to the USA didn't feel as stimulating as viewing the Israeli version:

> It was less interesting. [Consider] our slang and the little things that Israelis have....They have their own customs, their own silly things and we have ours. For example, sometimes you laugh at TV series, movies, and all sorts of joke and punchlines that Israelis share, and Americans will laugh at their own. You connect to it better because you know it better. They [the housemates] speak about places you know. They speak about experiences that you can say, "I was there, I also had something like that happen to me."

Lee's reflections reveal how the cultural nuances surrounding personal interactions between housemates—their specific style of humor or use of slang, their allusion to shared experiences and customs—vary in each country, and her ability to enjoy the show and identify with the participants depends on this cultural commonality. This is reminiscent of Herzfeld's (2005) discussion of collective discretion in terms of cultural intimacy, by which he referred to the ways that distinctive customs and practices shared by members of the national community are a source of both pride and embarrassment and form their experience of national identity. However, I would argue that the feelings of closeness that develop while watching the show and that engender national solidarity have less to do with specific customs than with the social interactions that give rise to these customs and the meanings assigned to these interactions. In other words, it is less about cultural intimacy than about collective intimacy; it is about the fact that ordinary people on the screen interact and present common patterns of communication and sociability that seem relatively similar to the viewers' own practices of sociability.

It is therefore clear that when a global television format is adapted locally and acquires national meaning, it is not just exogenous practices and customs, such as preparing mashed potatoes and schnitzel, that become appropriated as nationally unique; the exogenous source of the media event as a whole is practically erased and interpreted by the viewers as national, because, among other things, it is mediated by everyday interactions of sociability, interactions which are banal and yet intimately familiar. The very art of social bonding, itself a universal phenomenon, becomes an expression of national attachment, indeed the very glue of national attachment.

Of course, not all viewers feel close to the participants, and various events on the screen may cause some of them to experience rejection and exclusion. But assuming that national solidarity is based not only on identification with the content and boundaries of collective identity but primarily on the experience of shared sociability, we need to understand how this happens: What are the interactional mechanisms of sociability to which audiences respond, and how do they mold and engineer an experience of national solidarity? There is a fascinating process going on here between viewers and participants and among the viewers themselves—a process of strangers turning into friends.

Televised Media Event as a Social Club

Durkheim's idea of collective effervescence in ritualized public events has been taken up by communication scholars who recognized how solidarity (whether affirmed or contested) is enacted in late modernity mainly through the media sphere (Cottle 2006). The paradigmatic concept of media events introduced by Dayan and Katz (1992) captured much of the Durkheimian argument. They provided a systematic model for studying live televised coverage of exceptional events as sacred ceremonies that draw millions of people together and enable them to take part in the event simultaneously despite their physical dispersion. Media events erase the divide between private and public by providing common rituals which viewers can experience contemporaneously with everyone and interpersonally with those around them (Alexander and Jacobs 1998, 27–28).

Dayan and Katz's (1992) model has been widely discussed and often criticized for presupposing a totalizing view of society as consensual and uniform with little regard for conflictual power relations. Scholars have noted various ways in which media events reinforce social differentiation, contestation, and national disintegration (Cottle 2006; Couldry 2003; Kellner 2010; Mihelj 2008; Yadgar 2003). These various discussions, however, leave a basic lingering question that remains unanswered even in Durkheim's initial model of solidarity: How does the ritualized event attempt to connect the private and the public, the interpersonal and collective, and how does it purport to bring a mass of individuals who are technically strangers "into more intimate and more dynamic relationship" (Durkheim 2003, 140)? Whether or not an event actually succeeds in mobilizing solidarity, we still know too little about the underlying interactionist mechanisms set to turn strangers into a collective group of friends. For in order to develop feelings of solidarity, each member of the community must have some reassurance in the ability of fellow members to follow shared codes of sociability and to form socially significant ties. The theoretical framework of this book attempts to tackle this issue by suggesting that people in modern societies live the greater part of their lives in a range of nationally bounded social institutions which, regardless of their instrumental purpose, operate as social clubs where members negotiate modes of cooperation through informal interactions of sociability.

The question then is whether a televised media event can qualify as such a social club. The archetypical social club is based on a network infrastructure that potentially enables all members to be active participants but makes clear-cut distinctions between insiders and outsiders. The mass media, on the other hand, is typically accessible to wider publics but draws a clearer line between the position of performers and audiences. As powerfully argued by Frosh (2012), televised media events epitomize the live, monological, and centralized system of broadcast television, an infrastructure of attention that links individuals to a social and political center in synchronous time. This form of connectivity can be contrasted with midrange associational formations—in other words, social clubs—that are based on close-knit interpersonal ties and exhibit a networked connectivity that is decentralized, dialogical, and interactive. Hence, network-based communication (such as online social media sites) is more reflective of participatory civic society than the hierarchical and unaccountable structure of traditional mass communication. From this standpoint, the connection between televised media events and collective solidarity becomes all the more puzzling; how can such events foster integration and mobilize solidarity in the absence of interactive, participatory, and intimate social interactions between all actors in question, both performers and viewers alike?

That said, in recent decades electronic media technology has enhanced the capacity for active audience participation. Whereas Anderson's (1991) famed analysis of the newspaper reading ritual (see Chapter 4) provided little occasion for actual interactions between the audience and the protagonists, interactive media practices in which the output is partly determined by audience input blur distinctions between viewers and performers and pave the way for stronger feelings of solidarity. Thus, on radio shows listeners are invited to share their personal stories with the radio host and with other listeners who go on air, practically performing "group dynamics on the air" (Katriel 2004, 250). Multi-platform television often employed in reality formats is also making growing use of complementary media platforms as "return channels" that enable viewers to communicate back to the broadcaster and participate in the show by, for example, voting by SMS for their favorite contestants or posting comments in designated Web forums and Facebook pages on occurrences taking place in the show (Beyer et al. 2007; Jensen 2005). Consequently, whereas in classic televised media events the audience is physically absent from the scene and can be said to be participating only vicariously, in such multi-platform formats audience participation is clearly more tangible and immediate. Along these lines, Espen Ytreberg (2009) described how sending a text and seeing it appear in a designated chat zone on the television screen enable viewers to feel more intimately part of the live media event.

Rob Cover (2006) discussed how such interactive practices alter the traditionally discrete positions of author (or producer), text, and audience. As the text leaves the hands or real-time control of an author (or content creator), its content becomes partly available to alteration by a reader or content-user. Such interactivity raises complex questions regarding the author–text–audience relationship and the transfer of power and authority to the audience (Holmes 2004). Critical discussions of these implications often assume a conflict perspective, focusing, for example, on the "tactical war of contention for control over the text" (Cover 2006, 141), the economic exploitation of consumers as they "participate in the labor of being watched" (Andrejevic 2002, 231), or the "deliberate construction" of viewers' sense of agency and power by the production team (Holmes 2004, 226).

I, in contrast, opt for a neo-functionalist approach that considers interactive media as another realm of sociability through which we can understand the continuing appeal of national solidarity in late modern societies. Interactive media practices facilitate mechanisms of public intimacy and play a pivotal role in arousing collective intimacy. By enabling audiences to act as participants, such practices mitigate the analytic distinction between the infrastructure of close-knit social networks and of ritualized media events. While lacking the explicit quality of face-to-face interpersonal interactions found in traditional clubs, interactive media practices nonetheless contribute to the concretization of social relations and facilitate familiarity between strangers.

BIG BROTHER AS A MEDIA EVENT

The television reality show *Big Brother* is a good place to carry out an interaction-centered analysis of media events. To begin with, the show resembles Dayan and Katz's (1992) original model of media events on various levels. For one, it includes episodes of live broadcasting which typically attract very large audiences. The fact that a mass of viewers synchronously witness the unfolding of events in the Big Brother house plays a central part in the shows ability to project an image of solidarity, similar to the ways that live media events are considered integrative and effective nation-building tools (Evans 2014). Second, these broadcasts represent an interruption of routine, and some of their scripted moments (such as announcements of contestants nominated for eviction) are presented with ceremonial reverence. Furthermore, as with many reality shows, the Big Brother format unfolds as a social drama that can be said to combine the three scripts identified in Dayan and Katz's (1992) typology: conquests, coronations, and contests (Neiger 2012).

But like other reality formats, *Big Brother* also diverges from the model in various ways. First, rather than focusing on the heroic accomplishments of well-established public figures it "features 'ordinary' people doing 'ordinary' things" (Tincknell and Raghuram 2002, 205). Second, it is not limited to a one-time singular event but instead is aired as weekly or bi-weekly episodes throughout the season. Accordingly, the "upsurge of fellow feeling, an epidemic of communitas" (Dayan and Katz 1992, 196) associated with the singular media event can potentially last the entire season. Third, in its original formulation the production of media events is scripted and planned, hence it could only refer to anticipated events such as presidential debates, inaugurations, sports contests, and so forth.[4] At the same time, these events occur in the real world, ostensibly independent of the media production apparatus. Reality television presents quite the opposite picture: While the specific scenes displayed on the screen are meant to be spontaneous, unexpected, and even shocking, the events as a whole are planned specifically for the purpose of mediation (Ytreberg 2009).

Finally, the ritualized social performance created by reality television goes beyond the idea of a "sacred center" that endows the events "with authority to preempt our time and attention" (Dayan and Katz 1992, 32) and instead stretches across multiple sites and means of communication such as text messaging, the show's official Web site, social media, and Web forums where the audience is invited to be actively involved and to intervene in the narrative (Couldry 2002; Tincknell and Raghuram 2002). These multiple sites for participation provide "pilgrimage points" where the myth of the sacred, mediated center can be reaffirmed and redeemed (Couldry 2003, 90). In this way, reality viewers are invited not only to identify with the contestants but also to become one of them (Tincknell and Raghuram 2002, 205).

From a Durkheimian perspective, it is precisely this final point that qualifies reality shows as a supreme exemplar of media events rather than a substantial variation from it: In attempting to minimize the distance between the object of worship and the audience, it comes closer to fulfilling the Durkheimian idea that the venerated object serves as a personification of the collective and that through this veneration the solidarity of the collective is reaffirmed (Durkheim 2008).

Interactions Between Strangers Under the Gaze of Other Strangers

Having established how *Big Brother* qualifies as a media event, I now address how it can be studied as a social club of sorts and consider the social ties between the different actors involved, namely, the face-to-face interactions between contestants on the show, the mediated interactions between the contestants and the audience, and the face-to-face and mediated interactions between members of the audience. The contestant–audience interaction is of particular interest. Despite the limitations of mutual exchange between the television audience and the performers on the screen, *Big Brother* viewers may either explicitly or symbolically assume participatory roles in this communication process. The possibility that viewers develop actual feelings of "companionship" with a media figure (rather than merely identifying with the figure) has been discussed in psychological media studies under the term "parasocial interactions" (following Horton and Wohl 1956) and measured by such parameters as the style of address of the performer (e.g., Giles 2002; Hartmann and Goldhoorn 2011). However, underlying structural aspects and interactional processes in the televised performance that engender such feelings have rarely been addressed.

Whereas in most reality TV formats the contestants engage in relatively well-defined instrumental tasks such as performing a song, choosing a date, or surviving outdoors, Big Brother contestants do not perform any significant assignments (beyond brief, entertaining weekly tasks) and lack a clear goal other than to outlast the other contestants. The content of the show is mainly informal sociability: Contestants spend most of their time in mutual small talk and expressive, non-instrumental conversations consisting of "talk for the sake of talking" (Simmel 1950, 52). Simmel highlighted how this purely sociable form of interaction derives its significance from the "fascinating play of relations which they create among participants, joining and loosening, winning and succumbing, giving and taking" (52).

Although the show has no script to speak of, three dramatic axes serve to advance a linear sequence of events and draw viewers' attention. The first, noted by Scannel (2002), is the weekly eviction of contestants, which builds up a climactic movement toward the final day of the show when the last person in the house emerges as the ultimate winner. The second dramatic axis is the psychological dimension. Similar to many reality formats, Big Brother contestants indulge in confessional monologues and dialogues involving intimate self-disclosure and the public staging of an authentic self (Corner 2002; Hill 2002), in line with the growing influence of the "therapeutic discourse" (Furedi 2004; Illouz 2003).[5] As the contestants reveal on camera their inner thoughts and feelings about their personal life and their fellow housemates (Aslama and Pantti 2006; Skeggs 2009), the audience looks for performances of authenticity, sanctioned moments when real people are "really" themselves and create empathetic identification (Hill 2002; Livingstone and Lunt 1993). But scholars of talk shows and reality TV have rarely addressed how such acts of self-disclosure are mediated by the interactions taking place between participants and how the public staging of such interactions affect viewers' responses. For no less important than the act of unveiling the self are the questions of who this unveiling is directed at and how it is used to create both a sense of familiarity and feelings of exclusivity and loyalty.

This is where a third axis driving the show becomes of paramount importance: the development of relationships among contestants and between contestants and absent third parties. Big Brother housemates start off as complete strangers to one another and must interact socially under the gaze of millions of other strangers. From this egalitarian starting point of strangership, contestants are scrutinized for how they manage their interpersonal relations. Dyadic and group friendships are soon formed (and occasionally also romantic ties). Personal and group rivalries soon emerge as well, reinforced by the need to outlast others in order to win the show. In addition, contentions on the basis of social and political divides and segregated group affiliations often lead to the formation of cliques that split up the house. These personal and group relations may develop and change over time; contestants who became good friends can turn into rivals and vice versa. All of these evolving relationships become a central topic of conversation among contestants and viewers alike and form the basis of mediated public intimacy.

The viewers judge not only the authenticity of the contestants' performance but also their behavior toward their fellow housemates. They are therefore expected to nominate others for eviction, because that's the rule of the game, but not to nominate someone who has become their friend. A forceful example concerns the relationship between Jackie, the would-be winner of the third season of *Big Brother Israel*, and Lee-Oz

Cohen, another high-profile contestant at the time. Lee-Oz nominated Jackie for eviction despite the close friendship that had developed between the two, sparking immediate uproar and becoming a central topic of public debate.

While the Big Brother format limits viewers' options for direct intervention to voting for their favorite contestants, in this specific case a few of Jackie's fans found an innovative way to influence the outcome of events. They climbed up a small hill facing the Big Brother house, which is located at the Channel Two television studios, and tried to overcome the housemates' physical isolation by reaching out to them through megaphones, shouting out that Lee-Oz had "betrayed" Jackie. Needless to say, this intervention led to a bitter clash between the two contestants. The hardcore fans felt that by nominating his best friend in the house for eviction, Lee-Oz had violated the norms of friendship and, in so doing, betrayed not only Jackie but also them as the absent third party in this relationship.

The fans' response, itself a violation of the rules of the game, illustrates how viewers are not only an absent third party but may also consider themselves active participants in the relationships taking place in the house. Although actual contact between viewers and housemates is minimal, such rare incidents notwithstanding, various structural features of the Big Brother format, discussed below, systematically encourage viewers to change positions in the mediated triad of public intimacy and to gradually feel like the preferred confidants and companions of their favorite contestants.

THE CONFESSION ROOM

The Big Brother confession room is a good starting point for this discussion, providing an architectural example of the reversal of positions between insiders and outsiders. The room is isolated from the rest of the house and can be entered by the housemates only at the production's invitation. With minimal furnishings—a couch, television camera, and screen—the room is designed to simulate a church confessional or a counseling therapy room and thus to spur confessional conversations along the lines of therapeutic discourse. The confessing housemate (usually only one) sits on the couch and converses with the production director referred to as "Big Brother." The director is not physically present, and the housemates fix their gaze on the camera, in other words, on the audience at home. The conversations revolve mainly around emotional issues about their relationships with other housemates and with people from their private lives. Big Brother may ask guiding questions and express his interest and sympathy, but as with a priest or therapist, he refrains from sharing mutual information or expressing personal involvement.

Although the dialogues and semi-monologues taking place in the confession room are aired in public just like all other interactions taking place in the house, they are inaccessible to the other housemates, and therefore they distinguish the viewers as privileged spectators and as the confessing housemate's preferred confidants. The confession room therefore generates two complementary emotional experiences. On the one hand, the disclosure of intimate information by the housemate inspires empathy in the viewer, reminiscent of the empathy that therapists feel for their patients. On the other hand, unlike the private setting of the therapy room, here the confession is public and, furthermore, entails an important element of managing and compartmentalizing one's feelings, that is, choosing to share them with the viewers but not with the other housemates. This preferential treatment draws viewers in and encourages them to feel something beyond empathy, namely, a sense of involvement and closeness. Indeed, it is a prime example of the inclusionary effect of public intimacy: staging an intimate exchange between participants in front of strangers and enticing them to join by sharing secrets that are not disclosed to the other participants.

These unique qualities of the confession room as seen from the audience's perspective were neatly summarized by Ron, a hotel receptionist aged 28 and frequent viewer of the show:

> I think they're more truthful there. It's like a psychologist—they come in, talk, pour their heart out. And they open up just to the viewers at home, in fact, only to the viewers at home and not to their housemates, what they really feel....In the confession room you actually connect to them more because, like I said, they are the most truthful there and they talk about the other housemates and what they think of them. Because sometimes in the Big Brother house you see them facing the cameras like maybe they're a bit fake, no, not a bit, a lot, and you don't know what they're really thinking about the others.

Ron commented that the intimate exposure in the style of the therapeutic discourse allows him as a viewer to identify with the housemates, that is, to feel empathy. But, more than that, he stressed that in the confession room he is able to "connect to them more" than elsewhere in the house, because they become more open and truthful there than in the company of their housemates. In other words, the viewers' sense of involvement intensifies because they have been made party to the secrets that the contestant has chosen not to share with fellow housemates. It is not just the management of secret information that is at issue here but also the management of social relations. These simultaneously inclusionary and exclusionary aspects of public intimacy engender not only the viewers' greater familiarity with the contestant—"I know her better than her housemates because I know more about her private life"—but also position the viewers as exclusive confidants and companions—"I am more like a personal friend to her than the others (even though she spends all her time with them) because she chose me over them."

PARTICIPANTS WHO WERE FORMERLY VIEWERS

Another structural feature of the show that demonstrates the effects of mediated public intimacy relates to the introduction of additional contestants (around five) into the Big Brother house in the middle of the season (after several housemates have already been evicted). This development leads to systematic tensions between the new and existing housemates, as both groups need to win audience affection. The following conversation between Leon Shnaiderovsky and Ranin Bulus, two contestants from the first season, is telling:

> Leon: Personally I can feel the split between the newcomers and the old housemates. We don't mix completely...I mean, we've been here for two months, together, in intimate situations, one on one. We already know each other's nonsense, for better and for worse.
>
> Ranin: They [the new housemates] didn't go through all of that. We haven't seen them yet in situations when they are struggling, when they get homesick, when they begin to fade. They are still fresh.

The newcomers enter as strangers into a house whose current residents have already bonded with each other. As explained by Leon and Ranin, the new housemates have yet to experience harsh situations and expose their real selves. In other words, to qualify as bona fide reality show contestants they must go through the initiation rites of self-disclosure mandated by the therapeutic discourse. Although Leon and Ranin did not say so explicitly, the intrusion of these newcomers is particularly sensitive, because they enjoy the privileged position of an all-knowing absent third party; up until their admittance to the house, the newcomers were familiar with the existing contestants just from viewing them on TV, like the rest of the audience. This means that, as discussed in the previous section, they were privy to the intimate information shared by each of the contestants in the confession room but not revealed to the other contestants on the show.

This creates, once more, an atypical fold in the triad of public intimacy, transgressing the boundaries between participants and audience, insiders and outsiders. The admittance of new contestants into the house entails not simply an encounter between actors who have already been exposed in public and those who haven't; rather, it is an encounter—or rather a collision of sorts—between actors who were hitherto engaged in relationships at the level of *interpersonal* intimacy and actors who hitherto served as absent (but all-knowing) spectators in a triad of *public* intimacy but who have now become full-blown (but still all-knowing) participants at the interpersonal level. The newcomers' privileged position produces an asymmetric power relation that often impinges on their relationships with the existing contestants. Throughout the seasons examined for this study, the new contestants rarely received the support of the existing housemates and were often quick to be evicted from the house. Most tellingly, none of them won the contest. For the most part, the audience seemed to remain faithful to the ties they had already developed with the existing housemates and, like them, looked upon the "foreigners" with reservation and much suspicion.

FAMILY MEMBERS AS SYMBOLICALLY PRESENT

A more symbolic instance of audience-turned-participant can be found in the role of the contestants' family members. The contestants often talk about their feelings toward their families, partners, and friends back home with whom they cannot communicate for the duration of their stay in the house. They express their longing to hear from loved ones and to get some feedback about their performance on the show. This is another case of mediated public intimacy; this time involving the public staging of a relationship not between contestants on the show but between contestants and actors external to the show.

The Big Brother production, for its part, systematically dramatizes the contestants' homesickness by materializing the relatives as actors and semi-participants in the show. Therefore, on rare occasions, the production allows housemates who have succeeded in the weekly task to make a phone call to their significant others, and in this way they admit (the voice of) an outsider into the house as a partial participant. The production also invites the relatives and friends of the contestants nominated for eviction to wait outside the house and greet them as they leave the premises. This weekly reception ceremony depicting a reunion between (evicted) contestants and their families is a concrete demonstration of how each contestant is embedded in a network of ordinary personal ties, a network that is part of the general fabric of Israeli society. In these brief moments, the live, televised broadcast of public intimacy extends from the interactions taking place at the sacred center of the media event inside the Big Brother house to the interactions of ordinary Israelis taking place at the periphery of the house, emphasizing that both forms of social ties are on a par and, in effect, make up the sacred national collective.

Taken together, these appearances of family members render them absentees who are virtually present. This materialization of family members as participants is, in fact, a specific example of the materialization of the audience. When the production presents designated viewers as close companions of the contestants who can indirectly influence the events taking place in the house, it sends out a message to all viewers that they, likewise, are symbolically present actors who can potentially have a close relationship with the contestants. For although regular viewers are merely anonymous strangers, their role in the game is actually far more important than that of the family members. After all, contestants calculate their actions in the show according to how they imagine their viewers will react; they care about the opinions and expectations of the viewers and long for their feedback (which they are not in a position to get). In short, the contestants imagine their viewers not as strangers but as their companions and invite their viewers to do the same.

SOCIAL INTERACTIONS AT HOME AND AT WORK

The experience of becoming the contestants' confidants and virtual companions has important implications for the interactions taking place between the viewers themselves. The various types of interactions between viewers, either while watching the program or in the course of their everyday life, serve to transform the position of audience and contestants. Viewers shift from the role of an absent (but virtually present) party to the role of full participant, while contestants become absent, symbolic figures in the background. Through this process, performances of public intimacy ultimately lead to collective intimacy.

The feelings of closeness that viewers develop toward the contestants have in part to do with the viewing habits and routines that make the program part of their everyday life. As noted by Shir, a 30-year-old financial administrator: "Because you feel part of it, you feel that they are your friends. They're in your living room, they are with you all the time, you feel like you're their friend." In other words, this form of viewing experience means not only that the audience is privy to daily life in the Big Brother house but also that the contestants become part of the fabric of everyday life in the audience's homes, as put succinctly by another viewer Dina, a homemaker aged 57:

> For me they are just like a couple of extra people in the house. The television is always on, so when I'm downstairs they're with me, and I don't have to actually sit and watch them. And if I'm upstairs and let's say I'm folding the laundry, then I can still watch them, they're always there in the background.

The nonstop screening of the Big Brother housemates' activities in Dina's home assigns them a mundane presence, as if they were regular acquaintances or family members hanging around the house. Rather than such round-the-clock daily viewing, many viewers expressed a preference for watching the show (particularly the main prime-time broadcast) with friends or family as part of a weekly or bi-weekly viewing ritual. Shaul, aged 24, described how this viewing experience with his group of friends was a trigger for sealing their friendship:

> Everyone gets together to watch the show, you could say it's an event that draws us closer. After the show we sometimes go out for a drink.... Some of my friends are dealing with similar issues that the contestants are going through, so they feel that they identify with them. And somehow the show just brings us closer, I'm telling you, we're a bunch of friends sitting here on the sofa, each Saturday we go to someone else's house...and it's just something that we enjoy doing together, we sit and talk during the

commercial breaks, talk about other things going on at work or wherever. It's a kind of process, you could say.

Shaul's words point to the two distinct circles of intimacy that emerge from the viewing experience. The first is a triad of mediated public intimacy formed between each viewer and the contestants. As discussed earlier, this triad causes viewers to identify with contestants and to feel as if they have become confidants of their favorite housemates. The second circle is comprised of the feelings of closeness and intimacy that build up within the group of friends who gather regularly to watch the show. The two circles are interconnected. Once viewers share with one another their sense of becoming confidants of the housemates, it redefines their bond, turning them into a group of accomplices. This emerging feeling of being joint accomplices has implications for sustaining and reaffirming collective norms and exerting social control.

This point can be illustrated by the following example. During the third season of *Big Brother Israel*, a group of female coworkers in an insurance company would gather every morning in their office kitchenette to discuss the latest occurrences in the show over their coffee. One morning, the discussion centered on what seemed to be the beginning of a romantic liaison between two popular contestants Lihi Griner and Atay Schulberg. Before joining the show, Lihi had been engaged, and, just to add to the general excitement, the production had announced that her spurned fiancé was among the newcomers scheduled to join the house the following week. Lihi's behavior as well as the production's surprising move had stirred intense public debate about the crossing of moral boundaries (Walla!News 2011). The coworkers were likewise fired up about this turn of events, agreeing that Lihi and Atay's fling was inappropriate. One of the women said, "the people of Israel will never forgive them," and this was met with unanimous approval.

Interestingly, that same morning the women discussed and harshly judged a passing incident between Dana Ron and Frieda Hecht, two other contestants on the show, an incident which seemed far less dramatic. The two housemates had become sworn opponents, and one of the women complained to her colleagues that Frieda was no longer waking Dana up when she came to the living quarters to wake up the housemates. On this issue too, the coworkers concurred that, despite the quarrel between the two housemates, Frieda's behavior was entirely inappropriate.

In both of these cases, the women, still emotionally charged from their previous night's viewing, engaged in a group discussion about the moral conduct of the housemates in terms of interpersonal relations, both romantic and social. This shows how every member of the morning coffee circle was familiar with the ins and outs of the reality show and with the housemates' secrets. It also demonstrates how this sense of complicity brought the group members closer and how such complicity contributed to the women's experience of collective solidarity, as they exerted social control and reaffirmed accepted social norms within Israeli society as a whole.

INTERACTIONS ON SOCIAL MEDIA

Big Brother viewers interact with one another not only in the close circles of family, friends, or work colleagues and not only face to face but also in the wider circles of semi-public social network sites and Internet forums. Like many other television programs in recent years that boast a new participatory relationship between viewer and screen (Holmes 2004), the Big Brother production aims to stay relevant and competitive in the media market by providing a more interactive viewing experience. The production has therefore launched official Web sites, forums, and Facebook pages that encourage viewers to be involved and to communicate with one another about the show.

The official Facebook page of *Big Brother Israel* (Big Brother, n.d.) is highly popular (reaching around 500,000 followers during the eighth season) and provides continuous updates from the house. Significant incidents receive thousands of responses within minutes. Viewers not only comment on the events in the show but also respond to each other's posts. The same holds true for the individual Facebook pages prepared by the production for each housemate, encouraging fans to express their admiration for their favorite contestants. Viewers have themselves created a variety of Web forums (e.g., the Big Brother Forum on the Tapuz Web portal) and independent Facebook pages dedicated to the show. In addition, and perhaps no less significant, is the public discourse about the show that takes place in the viewers' (and non-viewers') personal Facebook accounts. Most viewers holding active Facebook accounts posted comments about the show or responded to friends' comments.

Social media enables viewers' involvement in a much more tangible way than the other examples previously discussed and virtually eliminates the distinction between spectators and participants. Kobi, a frequent viewer of the show and active Facebook user, explained how using social media changes the viewers' position in the equation of presence and absence:

> I'm part of the viewers....You can't watch an episode and stay detached. When you go to see a play in the theater, you share your experiences with other people. Whoever's sitting next to you, or your spouse, or someone else. So here, what's Facebook? It's a social medium to connect with others.

Although watching the show in the privacy of his living room, Kobi expressed his awareness that an entire audience was watching with him, as if they were sitting next to him in the theater, and his need to share his feelings with others. In this respect, the public as a whole is no longer an absent third party in the media event but a virtual participant, present in the living room of every single viewer. In a similar vein, Shai, a 45-year-old freelancer, explained how social media gives him a voice and provides him with a stage, almost as if he himself were one of the contestants:

> It's important for me to express my voice. As far as I'm concerned, it's as if I were a housemate. If I can't talk on television, then I'll just talk on Facebook, because Facebook is the mode of communication for all of these people...it's this Facebook group which unites them all. You've got all kinds of opinions there, and I interact regularly with a few people there from the second season, they call us the old-timers. We always have our arguments, but in the end we find common ground.

The free expression and the exchange of opinions in the Facebook group reinforce the bonds among certain viewers and strengthen their sense of a specialized community ("they call us the old-timers") and solidarity ("we find common ground").

Lilach, a 50-year-old homemaker, provided another example of a virtual community, one which centered around the shared adoration of Ayala Reshef, a prominent contestant from the second season. Ayala's online fan forum remained active well after the end of the season, and Lilach became a central activist in the Web site:

We are a group of 5,000 fans. Ayala and her boyfriend, Tommy, log on every day and greet us, say thank you...it's a social forum, it's not just about Ayala...believe me, I've met people there, I've expanded my circle of friends. It's only virtual, and yet I feel as if it's not virtual. I feel like I've known them for years, and I feel close to them. It's amazing...and we're like a family, we set up meetings, celebrate birthdays together, meet on weekends.

Lilach's story shows how the fan forum turned into a meaningful arena of sociability and a platform for expanding personal ties. The active members of the forum follow one another's private lives and also engage in non-virtual interactions, such as meeting up on weekends and celebrating birthdays. As with the basic logic of the actual show, i.e., bringing strangers together and watching how they become friends (and rivals), so too the virtual ties between viewers reproduce a similar logic of strangers-turned-friends (the interviewees rarely addressed the rivalries that formed in the online communities). At the same time, these newfound friends are perceived to be long-standing. To express her amazement at how close she felt to these newly formed connections, Lilach noted: "I feel like I've known them for years." This is not unlike the way in which a national community is perceived to emerge from an immemorial past despite its modern foundations (Anderson 1991).

The community emerging in this fan forum revolves around activities and interests that go well beyond both the events taking place on the television show and the personal life of their favorite contestant ("it's not just about Ayala"). The forum remained active on a daily basis even a year after the end of the season in which Ayala took part, thus turning their idol into an absent third party in their own relationships; a third party which served as a sort of totem for this community.

This latter point is worthy of further consideration. According to the totemic principle as initially conceived by Durkheim (2008), the totemic emblem is a venerated object or being that represents concretely to the clan its otherwise intangible solidarity. Individuals have the capacity to feel excited by their connection with a totemic figure, precisely because it is widely valued as a personification of the collective (Duffett 2012). In Durkheim's (2008) words, "the god of the clan, the totemic principle, can therefore be nothing else than the clan itself, personified and represented to the imagination under the visible form of the animal or vegetable which serves as totem" (206). Since in Durkheim's view this formulation of religious life basically extends to the cultural life of modern societies (Alexander 2003), it has been readily and widely adapted to studies of secular culture in contemporary societies, such as rock music or sports fandom. Michael Serazio's (2013) study of the US baseball league depicted the role of the team as a totem for its fans. The fans in the stadium cheer not only for the success of their team on the field but also for the togetherness of the experience. The totem reifies social bonds between the fans, as aptly stated by Anthony King (1997) in his study of sports and masculinity: "The team, and the love invested in it, is a symbol of the values and friendships which exist between the lads" (333). Mark Duffett's (2012) wide-ranging study of Elvis fandom noted how keeping Elvis's memory alive by engaging in diverse "boosting" (318) practices is seen as a means of actively maintaining the fan base and energizing the fans' own solidarity.

The current analysis demonstrates how this mediating function of the totemic figure as a proxy for solidarity and its fluctuation between the presence and absence can be accounted for in terms of the basic transformation of social actors from spectators to participants. In the case of *Big Brother* one could say that whereas in the actual show the viewers are the absent third party in the contestants' public lives, once the viewers engage in their own social performances with fellow viewers, it is the contestants who are gradually relegated to the background and become the absent third party, assuming a totemic symbolic presence in the everyday life of their audience. This is yet another example of the ways in which mechanisms of public intimacy consistently blur the distinctions between outsiders and insiders, audience and participants, and strangers and friends and engender feelings of collective intimacy. Such feelings of collective intimacy among millions of viewers who have never met assume an ontological status as a concrete bond, a community that exists in and of itself beyond the initial object of worship—the celebrity-totem or, more broadly, the television show—that started it all off.

A Nation of Accomplices

Whereas previous Durkheimian scholarship explored how televised media events can generate collective effervescence and become a vehicle of solidarity mainly by orchestrating collective instances of focused attention, here I point to the importance of interpersonal interactions for nurturing audience involvement and feelings of solidarity both during and after the mediatized performance. Reality shows rely on small talk sociability, confessional dialogues between participants, and confessional monologues directed at the audience. These televised performances have been studied mainly in terms of the public staging of an authentic self encouraged by the therapeutic discourse (Hill 2002; Illouz 2003). However, such performances are all the more significant in terms of public staging of social ties. Whereas the public display of self turns anonymous strangers into celebrities, the dynamics of public intimacy facilitated by interactive media practices turns anonymous strangers into a collective body of friends.

The case of *Big Brother* illustrates how mechanisms of public intimacy mediate between the centralized, monological infrastructure of media events and the decentralized, dialogical structure of interpersonal networks that are more characteristic of social clubs. I have delineated several structural features of the show that form atypical folds in the veils that separate outsiders from insiders and move viewers from a position of casual bystanders to one of privileged confidants of the contestants. The emergent sense of collective complicity reinforces interactions between viewers and triggers public discourse about the show.

First, the Big Brother confession room encourages contestants to divulge to viewers intimate information not shared with fellow housemates, thus singling out viewers as the preferred confidants. Second, the newcomers admitted to the house in the middle of the season transgress the boundaries between audience and participants, between an all-knowing but absent third party in a triad of public intimacy and a full-blown participant in the interpersonal interactions on the show. Third, a more symbolic instance of audience-turned-participant can be found in the case of family members whose relationships with contestants are dramatized in ways that manifest these viewers as semi-participants in the show.

These various triads of public intimacy convey the message that the entire audience too is symbolically present in the media event as actors who are potentially companions of the contestants. Moreover, this emotional involvement translates into a rich array of rituals practiced among viewers themselves. As the reality show is a prolonged media event stretching across multiple sites, interactions between viewers are not confined to family and friends gathering around the television set but extend to everyday social encounters and to mediated encounters on social media and in Web forums. While these interactions often start off as an exchange of comments about events taking place on the actual show, they may persist independent of the show and develop into bonds in their own right, as in the aforementioned case of the Ayala fan forum. Through their engagement in social media, the viewers form new triads of public intimacy in which they assume an active position as participants, while the totemic media figures become the absent third party. This social exchange becomes part of a wider discourse about the show shared by the general public—even those who don't actually watch it.

As noted by Paddy Scannell (2002), during the first season of *Big Brother UK* it was "the *only* thing that anyone talked about whether at home, in pubs and buses or in the press" (277). He further highlighted how this talk about others is a central mechanism in any society for regulating discursively circulating norms. The cumulative knowledge shared by the audience about the actions of the contestants and the relationships between them forms a "gossip community" (277). However, as I hope to have demonstrated, it is the interactional dynamics and underlying symbolic cultural aspects of such a gossip community that forms the basis of solidarity and is best captured under the notion of complicity.

Being an accomplice is invoked in audience studies in moments when a viewer becomes intimately engaged in the performance (Barre 2014) and signifies the interactional position of involvement, the relational role of being a confidant and the moral issue of taking responsibility and holding others accountable. This latter, moral aspect of complicity can be further explicated through the association between spectatorship and surveillance. Reality TV formats reassert television's power to interfere profoundly in people's private lives. But while the term "Big Brother" alludes directly to George Orwell's (1949) vision of a disciplining and punishing all-knowing gaze of state authority, the image of power portrayed on reality television is one of a compassionate (even when reprimanding) all-knowing gaze of a sympathetic community (Frau-Meigs 2006).

Philip Smith's (2008) made a similar claim from within a broader cultural sociological perspective, in his study of the symbolic meaning of penal institutions and critic of Foucault's (1977) theory of discipline. A case in point is the Panopticon, an utopian prison designed by Jeremy Bentham in the late eighteenth century and often compared both to Orwell's (1949) dystopian society and to the role of surveillance in reality television (Wong 2001). In Bentham's ideal prison, the guards were to be stationed in a central tower and have visual access to all the inmates while remaining invisible to them. Because of this constant sense of being watched by unseen eyes, the inmates were to be disciplined to participate in their own self-surveillance. This panoptic principle became the centerpiece of Foucault's conception of knowledge production as a form of administrative control and internalized surveillance. And yet Bentham did not foresee a closed-up institution oriented around individual reform nor did he reduce the observers to some robotic, abstract power. Rather, the Panopticon was to offer a vivid social performance to a witnessing civil society. Bentham envisaged a public gallery where visitors could see the inmates and even speak to them through tin tubes (Smith 2008). More than simply an observatory for the "cold eye of the one over the many," Smith underscored how Bentham's vision of the Panopticon was of a stage and a theater where "the multitude could look upon a few for both entertainment and edification" (106).

Thus, contra to Foucault's notion of surveillance as a form of disciplinary power and much like reality television viewing, Smith (2008) construed practices of punishment as expressive, communicative, and ritualistic activities that recruit spectacle into surveillance and are central to how civil society engages in moral debate, exchanges information, and narrates its myths of good and evil. In a similar fashion, the Panoptic gaze of the audience in reality shows combine a sense of intrusion, pleasure, and moral judgment. Collaborating within a shared, deeply felt set of collective representations, the spectating and gossiping community act as a group of accomplices who witness, respond to, and exert civic control over the social drama unfolding in the sacred center of the televised performance.

Most studies of media events and solidarity direct attention to the integration of autonomous individuals into a unified collective body made tangible through the ritual activity. In this regard, media events are understood mainly as processes through which society "takes cognizance of itself" (Turner 1974, 239, as cited in Couldry 2002, 285). However, what becomes tangible for the audience-turned-accomplice in these instances of collective intimacy is also the ontological existence of social ties between these individuals; in order to develop feelings of solidarity, each member of the community must have some reassurance in the ability of all other members to form close-knit ties. By staging performances of public intimacy and turning viewers into accomplices, the public event can provide such reassurance; it becomes a proxy for successful past experiences in the life of each member in choosing one's friends (and enemies).

Viewed from this interaction-centered perspective, media events such as reality TV should be considered social institutions that not only interpellate spectators as participants but also transform strangers into friends, affording this transformation collective significance. Although *Big Brother* does not present an explicit plot, it portrays a symbolic meta-narrative of strangers-turned-friends, arousing focused interest in the shared destiny of a group of strangers destined to live in one house under stringent living conditions and to cooperate with each other. They must negotiate how to share their intimate living space, reach a consensus around their strict food budget (which they order each week from the production), reconcile tensions around social, ethnic, religious, and political divides within the group, and, above all, interact with one another in a socially acceptable manner under the gaze of millions of other strangers. Within this collective gaze, the show's meta-narrative symbolizes both the norms of cooperation between citizens and the ideal of fraternity among fellow nationals.

A final example concerning audience voting may shed light on the way in which the show inspires solidarity of a civic-national nature. Several viewers of *Big Brother Israel* referred to the outcome of the voting processes as a calculated expression of public opinion or the will of the people. Shani, a regular viewer who was also very active on the show's Facebook pages, noted that she was "surprised for the better by the nation's voting preferences," arguing that:

> It demonstrates that we are not totally ruined. Justice usually prevails. I mean I usually expect people to do the opposite of what I think, so when I am proven wrong, it is really gratifying. It gives me the feeling that we might still have a chance as a country. It's a kind of patriotic statement that maybe people's priorities are directed at the common good.

The very fact that there are viewers who link voting results in a reality game to the common good and the fate of society at large demonstrates that through their social involvement, which is triggered by the show, they become engaged with issues of collective solidarity, construed in civic-national terms. Indeed, some researchers have suggested that *Big Brother* is partly constructing ideas of civic participation, as viewers are invited to judge morally the contestants' ability to represent the audience and to act upon this judgment (Cardo 2011). The viewing experience would, of course, be far more alienating for viewers who disagree with the audience's choices. However, the question is not to what extent reality shows actually succeed in forging solidarity but rather how they attempt to mobilize such feelings in the first place.

Studies of mass media—Israeli media included—have extensively examined the ways that television reinforces national attachment by reproducing the content of national identity, such as the explicit or nuanced reproduction of local customs, landscape, and collective memory (e.g., Aslama and Pantti 2007; Livio 2010; Meyers et al. 2009), or by redefining the boundaries of the national community through the misrepresentation of minorities (e.g., Bell-Jordan 2008; Elias et al. 2009; Karniel and Lavie-Dinur 2011; Volcic and Andrejevic 2009). But how the television broadcast stimulates national attachment through sociability has not been tackled directly. As I have demonstrated in this chapter, by participating in mediated triads of public intimacy, reality TV viewers implicitly confer national meanings on the social bond in and of itself, and it is this experience of virtual friendship that becomes the glue of national solidarity.

Notes

1. The number of contestants ranges from 10 to 18 depending on the specific production.
2. The interviewees and focus group participants consisted of regular and irregular viewers of the show and were recruited through social networks, flyers placed around a university campus, and an invitation on the Big Brother Facebook page. Although non-representative, the overall sample was relatively diverse in terms of education, household income, geographical area, and religion, but women (61%) and the 20–29 age group (67%) were overrepresented. Arab-Palestinians and ultra-Orthodox Jews were not sampled, as relatively small numbers of these populations watch the show. For more details on research methods and analysis, see section "Book Outline and Methodology" in Chapter 1.
3. In rare cases, a regional franchise encompasses several neighboring countries, such as *Big Brother Africa* in which there are contestants from 17 countries in central and southern Africa and the show is conducted in English.
4. In a subsequent reformulation of media events Katz and Liebes (2007) incorporated the live broadcasting of unplanned and disruptive events such as disaster marathons or terrorist attacks. While initially Dayan and Katz (1992) argued that media events celebrate common values and the promise of reconciliation, they later conceded that disruptive events may reflect division rather than integration and may speak to an increasingly disenchanted and segmented audience (Dayan 2008; Katz and Liebes 2007).
5. Just as the therapeutic discourse challenges individuals to be self-reflective and to present a narrative of personal transformation (Illouz 2003), many reality show formats subscribe to an ideology of self-improvement and are often referred to as "makeover TV" (Bignell 2005; Sender 2012).

REFERENCES

Alexander, Jeffrey C. 2003. *The Meanings of Social Life: A Cultural Sociology.* New York: Oxford University Press.
Alexander, Jeffrey C. 2004. "Cultural Pragmatics: Social Performance Between Ritual and Strategy." *Sociological Theory* 22 (4): 527–573.
Alexander, Jeffrey C., and Ronald N. Jacobs. 1998. "Mass Communication, Ritual and Civil Society." In *Media, Ritual and Identity*, edited by Tamar Liebes and James Curran, 23–41. London: Routledge.
Anderson, Benedict. [1983] 1991. *Imagined Communities: Reflections on the Origins and Spread of Nationalism.* London: Verso.
Andrejevic, Mark. 2002. "The Work of Being Watched: Interactive Media and the Exploitation of Self-Disclosure." *Critical Studies in Media Communication* 19 (2): 230–248.
Aslama, Minna, and Mervi Pantti. 2006. "Talking Alone: Reality T.V., Emotions and Authenticity." *European Journal of Cultural Studies* 9 (2): 167–184.
Aslama, Minna, and Mervi Pantti. 2007. "Flagging Finnishness: Reproducing National Identity in Reality Television." *Television & New Media* 8 (1): 49–67.
Barre, Nelson. 2014. "'It's Crazy, That Was Us': The Implicated and Compliant Audience in The Boys of Foley Street." *Comparative Drama* 48 (1): 103–116.
Bell-Jordan, Katrina. 2008. "Black. White. And a Survivor of The Real World: Constructions of Race in Reality TV." *Critical Studies in Media Communication* 25 (4): 353–372.
Beyer, Yngvil, Gunn Sara Enli, Arnt Johan Maasø, and Espen Ytreberg. 2007. "Small Talk Makes a Big Difference: Recent Developments in Interactive, SMS-Based Television." *Television & New Media* 8 (3): 213–234. Accessed September 29, 2017.
Big Brother. n.d. *Big Brother.* https://www.facebook.com/search/top/?q=%D7%94%D7%90%D7%97%20%D7%94%D7%92%D7%93%D7%95%D7%9C. Accessed September 29, 2017. Hebrew.
Bignell, Jonathan. 2005. *Big Brother: Reality TV in the Twenty-First Century.* Basingstoke: Palgrave Macmillan.
Cardo, Valentina. 2011. "'Voting is Easy, Just Press the Red Button': Communicating Politics in the Age of Big Brother." In *Political Communication in Postmodern Democracy*, edited by Kees Brants and Katrin Voltmer, 231–247. Basingstoke: Palgrave Macmillan.
Corner, John. 2002. "Performing the Real." *Television and New Media* 3 (3): 255–270.
Cottle, Simon. 2006. "Mediatized Rituals: Beyond Manufacturing Consent." *Media, Culture and Society* 28 (3): 411–432.

Couldry, Nick. 2002. "Playing for Celebrity: Big Brother as Ritual Event." *Television & New Media* 3 (3): 283–293.
Couldry, Nick. 2003. *Media Rituals: A Critical Approach.* London: Routledge.
Cover, Rob. 2006. "Audience Inter/Active: Interactive Media, Narrative Control and Reconceiving Audience History." *New Media & Society* 8 (1): 139–158.
Dayan, Daniel. 2008. "Beyond Media Events: Disenchantment, Derailment, Disruption." In *Owning the Olympics: Narratives of New China*, edited by Monroe E. Price and Daniel Dayan, 391–401. Ann Arbor: University of Michigan Press.
Dayan, Daniel, and Elihu Katz. 1992. *Media Events: The Live Broadcasting of History.* Cambridge, MA: Harvard University Press.
Duffett, Mark. 2012. "Boosting Elvis: A Content Analysis of Editorial Stories from One Fan Club Magazine." *Participations* 9 (2): 317–336.
Durkheim, Emile. [1915] 2003. "The Elementary Forms of Religious Life," translated by Karen E. Fields. In *Emile Durkheim: Sociologist of Modernity*, edited by Mustafa Emirbayer, 109–121, 140–141. Malden, MA: Blackwell.
Durkheim, Emile. [1915] 2008. *The Elementary Forms of the Religious Life.* Translated by Joseph W. Swain. Mineola, NY: Dover.
Elias, Nelly, Amal Jamal, and Orly Soker. 2009. "Illusive Pluralism and Hegemonic Identity in Popular Reality Shows in Israel." *Television and New Media* 16: 375–391.
Evans, Martyn. 2014. *Broadcasting the End of Apartheid: Live Television and the Birth of the New South Africa.* London: I.B. Tauris.
Foucault, Michel. 1977. *Discipline and Punish: The Birth of the Prison.* New York: Vintage.
Frau-Meigs, Divina. 2006. "Big Brother and Reality TV in Europe: Towards a Theory of Situated Acculturation by the Media." *European Journal of Communication* 21 (1): 33–56.
Frosh, Paul. 2012. "The Showing of Sharedness: Monstration, Media and Social Life." *Divinatio* 35: 123–138.
Fung, Anthony. 2015. "The Globalization of TV Formats." In *The Routledge Companion to the Cultural Industries*, edited by Kate Oakley and Justin O'Connor, 130–140. London: Routledge.
Furedi, Frank. 2004. *Therapy Culture: Cultivating Vulnerability in an Uncertain Age.* London: Routledge.
Giles, David C. 2002. "Parasocial Interaction: A Review of the Literature and a Model for Future Research." *Media Psychology* 4 (3): 279–305.
Hartmann, Tilo, and Charlotte Goldhoorn. 2011. "Horton and Wohl Revisited: Exploring Viewers' Experience of Parasocial Interaction." *Journal of Communication* 61 (6): 1104–1121.

Herzfeld, Michael. [1997] 2005. *Cultural Intimacy: Social Poetics in the Nation-State*. New York: Routledge.
Hill, Annette. 2002. "Big Brother: The Real Audience." *Television & New Media* 3 (3): 323–340.
Holmes, Su. 2004. "'But This Time You Choose!' Approaching the 'Interactive' Audience in Reality TV." *International Journal of Cultural Studies* 7 (2): 213–231.
Horton, Donald, and R. Richard Wohl. 1956. "Mass Communication and Para-Social Interaction: Observations on Intimacy at a Distance." *Psychiatry* 19 (3): 215–229.
Illouz, Eva. 2003. *Oprah Winfrey and the Glamour of Misery: An Essay on Popular Culture*. New York: Columbia University Press.
Jensen, Jens Frederik. 2005. "Interactive Television: New Genres, New Format, New Content." In *Proceedings of the Second Australasian Conference on Interactive Entertainment*, 89–96. Sydney: Creativity & Cognition Studios.
Kaplan, Danny. 2012. "Institutionalized Erasures: How Global Structures Acquire National Meanings in Israeli Popular Music." *Poetics* 40 (3): 217–236.
Kaplan, Danny, and Orit Hirsch. 2012. "Marketing Nationalism in the Absence of State: Radio Haifa During the 2006 Lebanon War." *Journal of Contemporary Ethnography* 41 (5): 495–525.
Karniel, Yuval, and Amit Lavie-Dinur. 2011. "Entertainment and Stereotype: Representation of the Palestinian Arab Citizens of Israel in Reality Shows on Israeli Television." *Journal of Intercultural Communication Research* 40 (1): 65–87.
Katriel, Tamar. 2004. *Dialogic Moments: From Soul Talks to Talk Radio in Israeli Culture*. Detroit: Wayne State University Press.
Katz, Elihu, and Tamar Liebes. 2007. "'No More Peace!': How Disaster, Terror and War Have Upstaged Media Events." *International Journal of Communication* 1 (2): 157–166.
Kellner, Douglas. 2010. "Media Spectacle and Media Events: Some Critical Reflections." In *Media Events in a Global Age*, edited by Nick Couldry, Andreas Hepp, and Friedrich Krotz, 76–91. New York: Routledge.
King, Anthony. 1997. "The Lads: Masculinity and the New Consumption of Football." *Sociology* 31 (2): 329–346.
Kupper, Yoni. 2015. "The Construction of National Solidarity on Mass Media in the Era of Globalization: A Case Study of the Television Show Big Brother in Israel." PhD dissertation, Department of Sociology and Anthropology, Bar-Ilan University, Ramat Gan, Israel, Hebrew.
Livingstone, Sonia, and Peter Lunt. 1993. *Talk on Television: Audience Participation and Public Debate*. Oxford: Routledge.

Livio, Oren. 2010. "Performing the Nation: A Cross-Cultural Comparison of Idol Shows in Four Countries." In *Reality Television: Merging the Global and the Local*, edited by Amir Hetsroni, 165–187. New York: Nova Science Publishers.

Mathijs, Ernest, and Janet Jones. 2004. "Big Brother International: Format, Critics and Publics." In *Big Brother International*, edited by Ernest Mathijs and Janet Jones, 1–9. London: Wallflower.

Meyers, Oren, Eyal Zandberg, and Motti Neiger. 2009. "Prime Time Commemoration: An Analysis of Television Broadcasts on Israel's Memorial Day for the Holocaust and the Heroism." *Journal of Communication* 59 (3): 456–480.

Mihelj, Sabina. 2008. "National Media Events: From Displays of Unity to Enactments of Division." *European Journal of Cultural Studies* 11 (4): 471–488.

Moran, Albert. 1998. *Copycat TV: Globalization, Program Formats, and Cultural Identity*. Luton: University of Luton Press.

Neiger, Motti. 2012. "Cultural Oxymora: The Israeli Idol Negotiates Meanings and Readings." *Television & New Media* 13 (6): 535–550.

Orwell. George. 1949. *Nineteen Eighty-Four*. London: Secker and Warburg.

Scannell, Paddy. 2002. "Big Brother as a Television Event." *Television & New Media* 3 (3): 271–281.

Sender, Katherine. 2012. *The Makeover: Reality Television and Reflexive Audiences*. New York: New York University Press.

Serazio, Michael. 2013. "The Elementary Forms of Sports Fandom: A Durkheimian Exploration of Team Myths, Kinship, and Totemic Rituals." *Communication & Sport* 1 (4): 303–325.

Simmel, Georg. [1915] 1950. *The Sociology of Georg Simmel*. Translated by Kurt H. Wolff. Glencoe, IL: Free Press.

Skeggs, Bev. 2009. "The Moral Economy of Person Production: The Class Relations of Self-Performance on 'Reality' Television." *Sociological Review* 57 (4): 626–644.

Smith, Philip. 2008. *Punishment and Culture*. Chicago: University of Chicago Press.

Sonnevend, Julia. 2016. *Stories Without Borders: The Making of a Global Iconic Event*. New York: Oxford University Press.

Tincknell, Estella, and Parvati Raghuram. 2002. "Big Brother: Reconfiguring the 'Active' Audience of Cultural Studies?" *European Journal of Cultural Studies* 5 (2): 199–215.

Turner, Victor. 1974. *Dramas, Fields and Metaphors: Symbolic Action in Human Society*. Ithaca, NY: Cornell University Press.

Volcic Zala, and Mark Andrejevic. 2009. "That's Me: Nationalism and Identity on Balkan Reality TV." *Canadian Journal of Communication* 34 (1): 7–24.

Waisbord, Silvio. 2004. "McTV: Understanding the Global Popularity of Television Formats." *Television & New Media* 5 (4): 359–383.
Walla!News. 2011. "Big Brother: The Fiancé Is Going In, Lihi Is Freaking Out." January 27. https://e.walla.co.il/item/1785359. Accessed September 29, 2017. Hebrew.
Wong, James. 2001. "Here's Looking at You: Reality TV, Big Brother, and Foucault." *Canadian Journal of Communication* 26 (4): 489–501.
Yadgar, Yaacov. 2003. "A Disintegrating Ritual: The Reading of the Deri Verdict as a Media Event of Degradation." *Critical Studies in Media Communication* 20 (2): 204–223.
Ytreberg, Espen. 2009. "Extended Liveness and Eventfulness in Multi-Platform Reality Formats." *New Media & Society* 11 (4): 467–485.

CHAPTER 9

Absent Brother: Military Friendship and Commemoration

My final case study deals with an institution and form of sociability that are probably most readily associated with the nation-state and national solidarity: conscript military service and military friendships. Military cohesion and, more broadly, national integration are often viewed through the melting pot metaphor, which depicts the fusion of individuals or differentiated subgroups into a newly acquired collective identity (Hirschman 1983; Leander 2004). In this chapter, I call attention to the role of interpersonal and collective ties as equally important mechanisms of integration. Solidarity conveys more than simple reassurance in the existence of fellow soldiers or compatriots as a collective of individuals; it conveys reassurance in their existence as friends. Particularly in the case of universal military service, soldiers not only consider themselves representative of the wider civic community, but they also come to believe that their socialization as strangers-turned-friends ultimately stands for a similar relationship between compatriots in general. In turn, members of the wider civic community make sense of collective ties as akin to personal military friendship.

To demonstrate this claim, I describe the public staging of personal bonds between soldiers, drawing on my previous work on Israeli men's friendships (2005, 2006). I then go on to discuss the collective and cultural symbolic dimensions of military friendship drawing on a study of solidarity campaigns for Israeli soldiers missing in action (Kaplan 2008). I conclude by analyzing how the temporal dimensions of national solidarity evoke the figure of the brother and discuss its role in the meta-narrative of strangers-turned-friends.

© The Author(s) 2018
D. Kaplan, *The Nation and the Promise of Friendship*, Cultural Sociology, https://doi.org/10.1007/978-3-319-78402-1_9

THE INSTITUTIONALIZATION OF MILITARY FRIENDSHIPS

The birth of the mass army in Western Europe in the late eighteenth century was closely connected with the rise of nationalism (Posen 1993). Following Gellner's (1983) ideas about the crystallization of national identity through processes of socialization to a common culture, scholars singled out the introduction of mass conscription in the wake of the French Revolution as a key homogenizing force and catalyst for national solidarity. The mass army represented a breakthrough in the ability to instill motivation and camaraderie among soldiers by socializing recruits to a common language and forging strong mutual ties (Conversi 2007). It created conditions for new physical and emotional intimacy between soldiers (Martin 2011) and enabled them to experience a new kind of community held together by common danger and a common goal (Mosse 1993, 14–15). This signifies a gradual historical shift in the meaning of soldiering from that of paid work to its symbolic opposite: a collective civic act of solidarity.[1] The image of combat heroism was similarly transformed from a quality of the individual warrior to an asset of group activity, the so-called brothers-in-arms (Morgan 1994, 174). In turn, the experience of male bonding under fire projected to wider society an ideal of a fraternity of men united in the service of the higher cause of nationalism (Mosse 1982). Terms such as honor, bravery, and duty thus became heavily connected to both nation and manliness (Nagel 1998, 252). The gendered dimension of fraternity formed the basis for the androcentric, female-exclusionary dimensions of the modern civic social contract (Pateman 1989).

The institutionalization of military friendship as a model for national solidarity was reinforced by the establishment of commemoration rituals for fallen soldiers on an industrial scale. The rituals aimed to instill the memory of the fallen in all members of the community and connect them with values of fraternity and sacrifice. Official military cemeteries designed as shrines of egalitarian, collective worship reflected this national spirit. They were first established in the USA following the Civil War and spread throughout Europe in the aftermath of World War I (Grant 2005; Mosse 1990). Commemoration rituals elicited a key sentiment in the relationship between the nation and its soldiers: the need to repatriate the sacrificial dead, to provide an honorable sepulture for them in the nation's name, and to acknowledge that they died so that the nation might live.[2]

Tombs of the Unknown Soldiers, first erected in France and Britain following World War I (Inglis 1993), were considered by Anderson (1991, 9) as emblematic of the disembodied, abstract, "ghostly" imaginings of the national community. He argued that the empty tombs exemplify the kind of abstraction that enables the disentanglement of the trauma of actual, personal death from the productive consequences of the nation's sacrificial dead. James (2006), who shared Anderson's views of national attachments as a growing ability for abstraction, nonetheless conceded that there is still a universal experience of and need for embodiment that creates "bonds across settings of anonymity" and accounts for the fact that bodily symbols and signifiers, including those found in representations of the Unknown Soldiers, "draw on the power of symbolism to make sense through linkage and remembrance" (179).

In most instances, commemoration rituals therefore actually celebrate the familiarity of the dead and adhere to a symbolism of friendship (e.g., Kapferer 1988, 158–160; Mosse 1990, 215) rather than being saturated with ghostly imaginings. This is most noteworthy in the Israeli case, where the culture of commemoration is premised consistently on the notion that "we don't have anonymous soldiers" (Dekel 2003) and emphasis is placed on the imagery and rhetoric of friendship. Ever since the 1948 War of Independence, memorials have depicted fallen soldiers in situations of closeness and intimacy, stressing mainly the personal, individual pain rather than acts of heroism and national glory (Sivan 1991). Verses from King David's lament (e.g., "In life and death they were not divided" 2 Samuel 1:23) have become a common inscription in such memorials (Kaplan 2006, 144). The Israeli media deals with the death of soldiers by repeatedly broadcasting the deceased's close friends extolling the fallen soldier's virtues as a loving and caring friend.

The Public Staging of Personal Bonds Between Soldiers

Military conscription is perhaps the best example of a modern institution that not only makes explicit claims about simulating national solidarity but is also dedicated to turning strangers into a cohesive group of friends. Edward Shils and Morris Janowitz (1948) famously argued that intimate interpersonal ties between military comrades are the key factor in combat motivation and military effectiveness, above and beyond ideological identification with the national cause. Consequently, military studies began to employ concepts such as primary groups (Cooley 1962), interpersonal attraction (Hogg 1992), and buddy relations (Little 1964), suggesting that strong cohesive ties between fellow soldiers reinforce small-group solidarity, offer long-term emotional support, and become a source of social control in service of group goals (Manning 1991; Rempel and Fisher 1997; Siebold 1999).

This line of work called into question the relevance of broader organizational and ideological indoctrination on soldier's combat motivation. Malešević (2011) proposed a categorical distinction between the "genuine" feelings of solidarity forged between soldiers during face-to-face interactions under fire and the "ideologization" of macro-level solidarity attempted by organizational or state authorities (285–287). In contrast, my own work on homosocial emotions and interpersonal ties between Israeli combat soldiers suggested that micro-level cohesion is deeply connected to military organizational practice and norms and wider national ideology (Kaplan 2006; Kaplan and Rosenmann 2014). The Israeli military (Israeli Defense Forces, hereafter IDF) is noted for stressing interpersonal commitments and mutual support among unit members as part of its tactical doctrine in combat (Kellet 1982). To further this goal, combat soldiers are assigned to organic units throughout their term of service (Ben-Ari 1998).

The point is that military socialization produces a strong sense of continuity between personal, organizational, and collective attachments, which can be analyzed through the mechanisms of public intimacy. The military mobilizes new recruits uprooted from diverse localities into newly formed close-knit units where they are to interact with strangers and quickly transform into the most intimate of friends. As they go through military service, they publicly stage their personal ties in front of others, soldiers, and non-soldiers, while maintaining a sense of exclusivity. By enacting a male homosocial "joking relationship" (Lyman 1987), military buddies create a form of public intimacy based on a coded communication employed during their daily life within the military and in others settings (Kaplan 2005). This unique, shared language involves the use of personal, idiosyncratic expressions as well as wider military slang combining professional jargon and a macho discourse rich with "dirty talk" about sex. It serves to create a common denominator between the men and distinguishes them from their surroundings.

This coded communication originates in specific shared experiences but gains significance as a marker of the military bond when used outside of its original context, as recalled by Judd, one of the Israeli combat veterans that I interviewed:

> We had this special whistle that belonged only to the group, and behind it were two words...wanna fuck. It started as a song and later we turned it into a whistle, so that we could express it in public too. (Kaplan 2005, 578)

The unanimous exclamation by a group of men, "We wanna fuck, we wanna fuck!," is common among IDF soldiers and is often sung during social activities within the confines of the military base as an implicit outcry against the forced conditions of military service. The transformation of the dirty talk into a whistle enabled Judd's group to use it in completely different contexts, its original meaning no longer manifest. Shifting back and forth from private to public spaces, these coded expressions become the "stamps" that give their semipublic interactions the value of intimacy.

This type of communication rarely conveys explicit meaning. A telling example is the practice of using derogatory nicknames or greetings disguised in curses within the group. While these could easily be misinterpreted by an outsider as expressions of rejection or aggression, insiders consider them as expressions of affection and closeness. This was evident in the reflections of Haim, another veteran interviewee:

> I was on leave for a few days, I took my parents on a trip....On the way we passed through [a base where a friend was stationed]. Knowing he'd be there I entered the encampment with my parents, so they could meet him. So I called out to him, "Mussa, how's it going?" and he called me back "you son-of-a-bitch, on your mother's cunt, coming here on your leave, huh?...So my mother said to me "Why does he call you that way?!" and as we entered the tent and he saw my mother and my father he was totally floored. (Kaplan 2005, 580)

The curse form and other forms of coded communication are openended expressions that, in themselves, say very little about the emotional intentions of the speaker. It is left to the respondent to make sense of the expression—whether as an act of hostility disguised in joke form or as an act of affection disguised in curse form—and to resolve the ambivalent emotion in ways that may either extend animosity or further the attraction between the parties. Either way, because the content of such provocative speech or gesture is ambivalent and evades a clear-cut emotional reaction by the participants it teases them and entices them to engage with each other and deepen their mutual involvement.

No less significantly, this performance of public intimacy colored by ambivalent playfulness teases some of the bystanders and sends them a message that they are missing out on something. By sharing the same military-coded language, like-minded spectators—but not others—are invited to "join the club." As discussed in Chapter 3, "clubbability" is an elitist form of male socializing among equals who shared similar values, upbringing, and rank (Capdeville 2016, 77). Soldiers more likely to take part in the social performance are those serving in the same unit, perhaps also those serving in different units but familiar with the same military socialization, jargon, and manners.

By gradually expanding their social ties through practices of social club sociability, soldiers not only enact instances of strangers-turned-friends but also come to experience how their military friendships acquire new meaning as a collective bond. Particularly in countries with mass conscription, members of the same unit are likely to extrapolate from their own experiences of sociability to the larger national community. Thus, as they operate and travel across the country as a team and publicly stage their ties in front of other teams, they display their competence in friendship and gain confirmation about the competence of other members. Through this reassurance in shared codes of sociability, they may over time experience feelings of familiarity, exclusivity, and loyalty to soldiers at the wider military organizational level and to fellow citizens who underwent similar military service, all the while pushing non-serving citizens to the marginalized position of a national outgroup. In this way military male bonding often attains hegemonic status in society and operates as a form of private men's club network beyond the military setting, facilitating participation in the political and economic realm (Kaplan 2006).

From Public to Collective Intimacy: Expanding Circles of Solidarity with Missing Soldiers

While military bonding may impact wider society through concrete interactional mechanisms of public intimacy, much of its collective significance comes from meaning-making processes at the symbolic level. Commemoration rituals for the war dead illustrate how fellow citizens who are technically anonymous strangers transform at the collective level into fraternal friends. Soldiers known during their lifetimes to only a limited circle of family and personal friends attain upon their death public recognition by distant others through ritualized tributes of friendship. Missing soldiers trigger and sustain an even greater public display of familiarity and closeness. Whereas fallen soldiers are rescued from anonymity after their death, missing soldiers are situated at a unique juncture between the living and the dead. On the one hand, their unknown fate signifies heroic sacrifice similar to that of fallen soldiers; on the other hand, the prospect that they might be alive encourages both close affiliates and distant others to relate to them publicly in terms of an ongoing friendship. Solidarity campaigns for missing soldiers present a unique window into the role of friendship in national subjectivity and demonstrate how processes of public and collective intimacy relate to the symbolic cultural sphere.

Between 2004 and 2006 I conducted a semi-ethnographic study of public campaigns for Israel's missing soldiers. Israel's prolonged state of conflict with neighboring Arab countries, with Hezbollah, and with Palestinian militias has led to a series of military excursions in the borderlands, predominantly Lebanon, from which a number of soldiers have never returned dead or alive. The IDF distinguishes missing soldiers (the equivalent term "missing in action" or MIA is not used) from prisoners of war (POWs) and fallen soldiers with unknown burial sites. Focusing only on the first category, I investigated the public discourse surrounding missing soldiers that appeared in the print, electronic, and digital media, examined websites run by the soldiers' families, the military, governmental agencies, NGOs, and commercial initiatives, and conducted participant observations at selected commemoration sites for fallen soldiers.[3] The present analysis centers on two cases of missing soldiers, the case of Ron Arad, a pilot shot down over Lebanon in 1986 and declared missing ever since, and the case of Beni Avraham, Adi Avitan, and Omar Souad, who were abducted by Hezbollah at Har Dov on the Lebanese border in 2000. The bodies of the three soldiers were returned as part of a prisoner swap on 2004.

Feelings toward missing soldiers tap into the essence of military friendship. An important value in the IDF's code of ethics is fraternal friendship, defined as the soldiers' "constant devotion to each other, their willingness to provide valuable help, come to the rescue and even risk their lives for their fellow men" (Kasher 1996, 233). This includes an obligation not to leave them behind under any circumstances, even under fire (230). What happens, then, when this imperative cannot be met and the border crosser is left behind? How does it affect his immediate friends in the military unit? How does it affect the wider military community of comrades-in-arms? And how does it affect the wider civic or national community, ostensibly a community of strangers? Major Aviram, the pilot who flew with Arad and was rescued under fire, recalled:

> Every airman feels frustrated that Ron is still in captivity, but I feel the frustration a thousand times stronger. I was there. I was there and came back, and even though it was he who ejected both of us [from the plane] and saved us, he's the one who has eventually remained there. Although I couldn't have done anything to help him, I can't avoid a certain feeling of guilt, a sense of responsibility that lies on me like a heavy burden. (Air Force 1986)

Major Aviram felt in the most tangible way that his own survival depended on Arad's actions and sacrifice, and he experiences a sense of guilt for leaving his comrade behind. Such intimate feelings of identification and devotion to the missing soldier readily extend from their closest circle of personal friends and family to wider circles of affiliation and become a performance of collective intimacy at the national level.

The immediate circle of solidarity includes IDF soldiers who served in the same unit as the missing soldier but did not know him personally. On the website run by the families of the three soldiers kidnapped in Har Dov, a soldier from their unit recounted the atmosphere of commemoration created in the military barracks and its emotional impact. He also conveyed how it transformed into a local heritage:

> The first thing I recall from the day I arrived at the company is a huge number of posters with the names of the boys, their pictures, and a lot of objects made by soldiers in order to remember and pass on the events of the kidnapping, for soldiers who weren't there and didn't know them, like me. I remember suddenly experiencing a huge identification with the families, with the company, and with the boys....I and every member of the company will do everything to pass on the heritage, just as it was passed on to me a year and a half ago. (quoted in Kaplan 2008, 420–421)

In the civic sphere, various public agents propagate additional circles of solidarity with the missing soldiers. First among the prominent actors are the NGOs established expressly for the purpose of launching public campaigns for the soldiers. They fund street posters and newspaper and online ads and sponsor rallies and conferences, often assisted by local municipalities. A central foundation at the time of my research was Born to Freedom, which began as a lobby group representing the family of Ron Arad. It was headed by retired military personages and had become heavily funded by the government. After it declared a $10 million reward for any relevant information on Arad, the families of other missing soldiers appealed to the Supreme Court and the foundation was required to expand its advocacy efforts and extend the reward to include all IDF missing soldiers (Melman 2005). The campaign on behalf of Arad was nonetheless the most visible and included the distribution of bumper stickers that became extremely popular among Israeli drivers and a blue balloon that became the identifying mark of the campaign.[4] The foundation also produced public events such as an ultralight aircraft show, a yacht sale, and a parachuting display.

Another agent of solidarity is the educational system. The Ministry of Education prepared a detailed lesson plan guiding teachers how to address the case of missing soldiers in their classrooms and raise student awareness. The teaching kit included a proposal for a ceremony dedicated to the soldiers accompanied by songs and verses from the Jewish scriptures. It also provided guidelines for class discussions on what the students could do to help bring the soldiers home (Ministry of Education, n.d.). Both teachers and students seem to have been highly responsive to this education campaign, with the latter reported to have sent scores of letters to the then UN Secretary-General Kofi Annan and to have hung huge posters on school buildings. In one high school, students prepared a calendar counting off Arad's days in captivity, just like prisoners do (Levi 1994).

Commercial actors constitute a third and intriguing negotiator of civic solidarity. For instance, the Israeli Paz gas station chain joined together with the Born to Freedom foundation to distribute flyers in its stores and conducted a street poster campaign as part of the company's corporate social responsibility policy. Even more telling is a campaign for Arad funded by a popular fish restaurant. In the summer of 1994, the restaurant owners paid for a small aircraft to fly over the beaches of Tel Aviv towing a huge banner that read "Ron Arad we yearn for you—Ahmad and Salim" emblazoned with the image of two fish, the restaurant's logo (Levi 1994). Here, it seems, the restaurant's Arab owners, catering mainly to Jewish customers in metropolitan Tel Aviv, made a deliberate attempt to bolster their legitimacy by connecting to the heart of the Zionist-Jewish ethos: the missing soldiers.

Finally, expressions of solidarity with the missing soldiers extend beyond the circle of Israeli citizens to the wider Jewish world, where a broad range of Jewish organizations and denominations take part in public displays of solidarity. For example, in 1993, the United Synagogue of Conservative Judaism called on all of its North American congregations to participate in the effort to release Israeli missing soldiers by organizing letter-writing campaigns to the US president and members of Congress, posting information on synagogue bulletin boards, writing op-ed articles in local newspapers, and writing letters of solidarity to the soldiers' families (Kaplan 2008).

There are often contradictory interests between the military and government authorities officially responsible for negotiating a deal to return the soldiers or their remains and the grassroots campaigns by families and friends that demand to expand these efforts, but these points of contention are clouded by a generalized and depoliticized stance of solidarity. Given the centrality of military friendship as a national ethos and the public displays of solidarity that nurture support for the retrieval of the missing at all costs, the government, more often than not, chooses to essentially join the campaign rather than make difficult political decisions. A telling example of this depoliticized stance is a bill proposed by members of the Knesset (Israeli parliament) that would require the government to fund family members of missing soldiers who travel abroad to meet with world leaders. The legislators explain that these meetings "are a national undertaking, not a private whim [and]...indescribably more important than a meeting held by any statesman would be" (quoted in Kaplan 2008, 420). This official approval of family lobbying as a substitute for state diplomacy exemplifies the constant blurring of the boundaries between the private interests of the families, the civic sphere, and the government's security and foreign policy considerations.

Solidarity campaigns for missing soldiers can in this way be seen to extend the moral values of military friendship to a large number of fellow nationals who express feelings of familiarity with and loyalty to soldiers they have never met. This includes not only the military community but also Israeli schoolchildren, commercial entrepreneurs, and synagogue goers worldwide. An object of public veneration, the absent soldier operates as a totem for the national community, arousing feelings that personify the solidarity of the entire collective (Durkheim 2008). In this way, the public campaigns not only reiterate the symbolic relationship between the living and the dead but also recast the collective ties among the living as the potentially intimate bonds of friendship.

Together these examples demonstrate several aspects of the friendship-nation nexus. First, expanding circles of solidarity can be drawn within the national community, all relating to the same interpersonal experience of friendship, even if only on a symbolic level. Although most of the participants in these campaigns do not know the soldiers personally, some of them nonetheless experience concrete and often intense feelings of closeness toward them. Second, these public displays of solidarity demonstrate how the public staging of friendship ties in everyday life can extend, on special occasions, to the public staging of an imagined bond in collective life, in other words, showing how public intimacy culminates in collective intimacy.

In addition, this case study highlights how the collectively shared commitment to the safety of fraternal friends at all costs overshadows the conflict of interest between the different actors and neutralizes the political consequences of the governmental decisions made to rescue the soldiers or recover their bodies. In most cases, the Israeli government has historically opted to carry out disproportionate prisoner swaps in exchange for bodies of missing soldiers, which then may have encouraged the abduction of more soldiers. In one particular case, the abduction of two soldiers by Hezbollah in 2006 provoked the Israeli government to take military action and invade Lebanon in what has become known as the Second Lebanon War. This may well have been the first time in modern history that a country has declared war with the stated objective not of defending its citizens but of rescuing its missing soldiers, in other words, waging war in the name of military friendship.

THE LIVING AND THE DEAD:
BETWEEN SIMULTANEOUS AND MYTHIC TIME

Such linkage between friendship and national solidarity would not be possible were it not for an underlying cultural structure that gives meaning to people's emotional experience. Concrete instances of military friendship as well as public campaigns for missing soldiers become part of the discourse of national solidarity through the overarching meta-narrative of strangers-turned-friends, a symbolically potent carrier of feelings that invests a variety of social interactions and situations with sacred significance. The infatuation with missing soldiers taps into two underlying dimensions of the national solidarity discourse: the relationship between the living and the dead and cultural perceptions of time. The national discourse of solidarity juxtaposes the dead, the living, and the unborn in a single community of fate (Smith 1998, 140). Anthropologists have noted how in all kinds of communities death marks the onset of a complex, often heavily ritualized, ceremonial process by which the deceased becomes an "ancestor," in other words, a meaningful presence for the social identity of the survivor (Hertz 1990; Kaufman and Morgan 2005). Similarly, the national community reveres those who acted in the service of the nation and enacts rituals that aim to resurrect the sacrificial dead, as the future of the living is dependent on the symbolic presence of the dead (Handelman 2004, 145).

Fallen soldiers are likewise socially constructed as having symbolic immortality (Bilu and Witztum 2000, 4). In many Israeli war poems recited during commemoration rites, dead soldiers are brought back to life in order to address the living, often restating and reaffirming the collective commitment to sacrifice (Oppenheimer 2002). The imagery of the living dead serves to compensate for the guilt the living feel toward the dead; it operates as a literary solution to the acute paradox experienced by a society that sacrifices the lives of its sons in the name of collective ideals and at the same time assigns a central value to the sanctity of life (Hever 1986; Miron 1992, 95). Fraternal friendship plays an important role in deferring the finality of death. Emphasizing their personal bonds with the fallen soldier and celebrating the promise of eternal friendship help the living to partly conceal the sacrifice of the dead.

The relations among the living and between the living and the dead rest on two alternate perceptions of time: simultaneous time and mythic time (Anderson 1991; Gupta 2004; Singer 1996; Zerubavel 1981). Simultaneous time refers to the continuing reassurance of the existence of fellow compatriots and their ability to engage in collective action. This faculty of collective simultaneity is facilitated by changes in technology and mass communication in the modern and late modern era that have enabled people to imagine how they live their lives parallel to and in synchronicity with millions of distant others they have never met. Accordingly, the notion of "place" has become increasingly "phantasmagoric" and penetrated by distant relationships across space (Giddens

1990, 18–19). Simultaneous time becomes most tangible in ritualized social performances, when all members of the community focus their attention on concurrent events and experience feelings of collective intimacy.

Mythic time, on the other hand, refers to epic narratives in the community's heritage that are experienced as sacred, cyclic, and recurring and are often linked by a transcendent being whose point of view is "outside" the historical, linear sequencing of time (Eliade 1954; Freeman 1998).

In mythic understanding, solidarity is anchored in events and figures that are chronologically unrelated but that together carry significance for the members of the community. By freezing time beyond its contingency and drawing on myths of sacrifice, national rituals of commemoration connect the living with heroes of the past. In short, if identification with fellow citizens in everyday life reflects the simultaneous dimension of national solidarity, identification with fallen soldiers draws on the mythic dimension.

In this regard, solidarity with missing soldiers merges both temporal frameworks. On the one hand, missing soldiers arouse identification in much the same way that fallen soldiers do, namely, as emblems of sacrifice associated with "mythic" time. For instance, American public discourse on MIAs in Vietnam was fraught with mythic imagery of their ongoing torture in Vietnamese prisons (Keating 1994, 245), magnified by stories and movies that centered on MIAs as "icons of veterans' victimization" (Sturken 1997, 88). This ambience helped mobilize public support for their cause and framed attempts to put the issue to rest as acts of national betrayal (Doyle 1992; Franklin 1991). Similarly, Keren Tenenboim-Weinblatt (2008) analyzed techniques of non-closure practiced by Israeli media in its continual coverage of Arad's case and demonstrated how keeping the story unresolved, told, and retold served as a mythologizing strategy that helped sustain the perception that Arad is still alive and connect it with national myths of heroism and sacrifice.

On the other hand, identification with missing soldiers clearly reflects collective perceptions of simultaneity. The very possibility that the soldier is still alive implies that members of the community can imagine how he leads his life parallel to their own. The following account by Lieutenant Colonel H., Arad's former squadron commander, is a telling example of how a rhetoric of co-presence is employed to describe the soldier's absence:

Ron Arad lives in the squadron at every moment....His name is mentioned in the squadron almost every day and he is talked of as if he were here. In the squadron's new building, a building he's never seen, there's a locker waiting for him with his name on it. (Air Force 1986)

Another striking account is given by Lisa Katz, a US immigrant to Israel and occasional writer on Jewish affairs:

> I made aliyah [immigration] to Israel in August 1986; Ron Arad was captured by terrorists in October 1986. It is heart-wrenching to compare the life I have experienced in the years since I moved to Israel to that which Arad has experienced in captivity, assuming he is still alive. (quoted in Kaplan 2008, 423)

These and other examples—such as the aforementioned calendar prepared by high school students to keep track of Arad's days in captivity— demonstrate the perception that Arad is living his life, trapped in hell, parallel to the everyday life of the national community. In light of socio-technological changes in communication, distant others can more easily interact and connect through "mediated co-presence" (Auslander 2008, 61) and envision how their lives cross despite their physical distance. Through the faculty of simultaneity the soldiers, the epitome of absence, become the subject of collective imaginings of presence. The missing soldier is, in short, perceived to be alive and kicking like any other citizen, but he is also holier than others, taking his place in the national pantheon of military heroes. By merging simultaneous time and mythological time, he becomes the most intimately felt of all national heroes.

While these socio-technological advances can help us understand how people overcome distance and interact with absent others (known and unknown), and practices of commemoration can help us understand how people honor the dead, these practices alone cannot account for the deep meanings attached to these situations. In order to understand both individual and collective yearnings for connection and belonging, we must consider how social practice is linked to underlying cultural structures and embedded in a specific "horizon of affect and meaning" (Alexander and Smith 2001, 136). In the present case, the cultural process at work is the meta-narrative of strangers-turned-friends that confers upon a variety of social interactions—whether between personal colleagues or between distant strangers—an aura of friendship. As can be seen in the preceding quotes, Lieutenant Colonel H. had a personal relationship with Ron Arad, whereas Lisa Katz, the immigrant and writer, conveyed a sense of closeness toward a person she had never met. Yet both articulated their connection to Arad in terms of parallel life experiences and disclosed a similar affect consisting of familiarity, exclusivity, and loyalty. In expressing his devotion to the missing soldier, the lieutenant colonel was abiding to the concrete moral codes of military friendship (Kasher 1996, 233), while Katz was acting upon a vaguer national promise of friendship, her affinity to a national hero validating her sense of belonging to Israeli society. Both cases draw upon culturally shared meanings of emotional experience and demonstrate the continuity rather than disjunction between friendship and solidarity, between instances in personal life when strangers become friends and instances in collective life when strangers are celebrated as friends.

A Meta-Narrative of Strangers-Turned-Friends-Turned-Brothers

National commemoration of the war dead enacts and proclaims a meta-narrative of strangers-turned-friends, a narrative that, in more subtle ways, takes place in all nationally bounded social clubs. Throughout this book, I have discussed how this cultural structure encodes a shift from abstractness to concreteness, anonymity to familiarity, inclusivity to exclusivity, indifference to loyalty, and interest to passion. So far I have said very little about this last shift, nor have I discussed the role of passionate love in ties of friendship and particularly in military male bonding. Although soldiers routinely engage in performances of public intimacy, the emotional tone in these staged interactions is often muted, ambiguous, or displaced through the humorous coded communication and aggressive gestures described above. In contrast, during collective rituals of commemoration, public expressions of male intimacy take on an entirely different form and openly celebrate male love. At the same time, the commemorative performance transforms the personal friendship into a collective bond of brotherhood. This cultural dynamic merits a concluding comment.

In one of the grassroots commemorative booklets that emerged during the Israeli War of Independence, a yeshiva student lamented a friend who had died in battle:

> Whenever I talk of him, I do remember him still. My heart yearns for him, and my lonesome soul, orphaned from such a dear, old, and beloved friend, will not be consoled. Therefore, I allow myself to sincerely use the verse from David's lament for Jonathan "very pleasant have you been to me; your love to me was wonderful." (Sivan 1991, 166)

Why is it only now, after the friend's death, that the mourner "allow[s] himself" to "sincerely use the verse from David's lament"? The biblical lament, which is quoted extensively in the Israeli culture of commemoration, combines a battle scene with a declaration of a mysterious male love. By subscribing to the heroic script of combat fraternity in the face of death, men are "allowed" to experience a passionate love hitherto silent and unacknowledged.

In her seminal study of men's friendships in English novels, Eve Sedgwick (1985) introduced the phrase "male homosocial desire" to explore the continuum between the homosocial and the homoerotic, noting how in men's interactions emotional and sexual expression is often suppressed in the interest of maintaining power. The repressed erotic component of male desire accounts, she claimed, for "correspondences and similarities between the most sanctioned forms of male bonding and the most reprobate expressions of homosexuality" (22).

National discourse provides a framework for transforming this illegible emotion into a public performance. As I have discussed elsewhere (Kaplan 2006; Kaplan and Yanay 2006), acts of commemoration present a cultural setting in which desire between men is neither denied nor displaced but instead openly declared. Carrying homosocial desire to the collective sphere, the male relationship is removed of its physical–sexual connotations and, precisely for that reason, assumes homoerotic overtones. Only when the friend is dead can he be touched, stripped of his armor and uniform, and addressed by his physical qualities. The poem "HaReut" (fraternal friendship), the most popular Hebrew poem associated with military friendship written shortly after the 1948 War, depicts the fallen soldiers as "handsome of forelock and countenance" (Guri 2000, 147–148). Heroic death becomes the cultural marker that prevents the continuity between the homosocial and the homoerotic and at the same time stimulates and celebrates passionate male love. The act of declaring the friendship is an act of revelation. It creates a desire that never existed yet always was.

Underlying this declaration is a shift from the personal to the collective sphere, from an experience of simultaneity among the living to mythic relations with the dead, and from ties of friendship to bonds of brotherhood. This threefold shift is encapsulated in what may be termed "fraternization of friendship." Whereas commemoration of fallen soldiers represents only the end result of this fraternization, the public campaigns for missing soldiers reveal some of the underlying emotional processes at work.

First, there is an important difference in how friendship is construed in each of the corresponding temporal frameworks. Through the faculty of simultaneity, compatriots engage with distant others and become reassured of their mutual connection, enabling some strangers to become friends. Such relations between strangers have no place in the mythological framework. Although we do not personally know the mythic figures from our collective past, we do not consider them as ever having been strangers. Their starting point is as our "ancestral" heroes, ingrained in our familial heritage from time immemorial.

Second, and emerging from the previous point, just as the deceased becomes an ancestor in collective rituals of commemoration (Kaufman and Morgan 2005), so too the newly found friend becomes a timeless brother. While we may think of our collective past as preceding our common destiny, it is the experience of simultaneous co-presence and anticipated shared destiny with fellow compatriots that gives meaning to the cultural myth of a shared familial past. Thus, rather than turning strangers into friends, mythic time casts the friend as a rediscovered primordial brother, a discovery made possible by the liberating power of death.

Finally, while fallen soldiers receive public recognition and love only after their death in battle, missing soldiers win public declarations of passionate love prior to their confirmed death. This instance of "suspended death" condenses into one single moment the cultural transformation of strangers into friends and friends into brothers. It is in this moment that the full force of national solidarity as a "deep, horizontal comradeship" (Anderson 1991, 7) becomes apparent, as it dramatizes the ideological transformation of distant, absent others into co-present, beloved brothers.

NOTES

1. Soldiering in late Latin referred to paid work, stemming from the word *solidus*, meaning a Roman coin (Free Dictionary, n.d.). Solidarity stems from *solidum*, meaning the whole sum. It was applied in Roman law for a legal unit, such as a family, that accepted liability for the acts of each of its constituents (Brunkhorst 2005, 2).
2. Caroline Marvin and David Ingle (1999, 67) provided a piercing account of these sacrificial "totem" rituals in the nation-state. As elected members of the community cross the border in a violent act of sacrifice, the community reveres and worships those who do not return alive. The violent border crossing, repeated in a succession of military conflicts, serves to produce and reproduce national solidarity in a cyclic fashion.
3. The media sample included articles on missing soldiers in the three main daily newspapers (*Ha'aretz*, *Ma'ariv*, and *Yedioth Ahronoth*) and their respective online sites and talkback responses, in speeches, in op-ed articles by public figures, and in the television and radio coverage of events and ceremonies relating to the missing soldiers. For more details on the study see Kaplan (2008).
4. The use of banners echoes soldier campaigns elsewhere, such as the wearing of red ribbons by activists of the American MIA-POW movement (Santino 1992).

REFERENCES

Air Force. 1986. "Navigator Ron Arad Was Taken Captive." October 16, 1986. http://www.iaf.org.il/3937-5316-he/IAF.aspx. Accessed September 29, 2017. Hebrew.

Alexander, Jeffrey, and Philip Smith. 2001. "The Strong Program in Cultural Theory: Elements of a Structural Hermeneutics." In *Handbook of Sociological Theory*, edited by Jonathan H. Turner, 135–150. New York: Springer.

Anderson, Benedict. [1983] 1991. *Imagined Communities: Reflections on the Origins and Spread of Nationalism*. London: Verso.

Auslander, Philip. [1999] 2008. *Liveness: Performance in a Mediatized Culture*. London: Routledge.

Ben-Ari, Eyal. 1998. *Mastering Soldiers: Conflict, Emotions, and the Enemy in an Israeli Military Unit*. Oxford: Berghahn Books.

Bilu, Yoram, and Eliezer Witztum. 2000. "War-Related Loss and Suffering in Israeli Society: An Historical Perspective." *Israel Studies* 5 (2): 1–32. Hebrew.

Brunkhorst, Hauke. 2005. *Solidarity: From Civic Friendship to a Global Legal Community*. Translated by Jeffrey Flynn. London: Routledge.

Capdeville, Valérie. 2016. "'Clubbability': A Revolution in London Sociability?" *Lumen: Selected Proceedings from the Canadian Society for Eighteenth-Century Studies* 35: 63–80.
Conversi, Daniele. 2007. "Homogenisation, Nationalism and War: Should We Still Read Ernest Gellner?" *Nations and Nationalism* 13 (3): 371–394.
Cooley, Charles, H. [1909] 1962. *Social Organization*. New York: Schocken.
Dekel, Irit. 2003. "Militant Collectivism and Anonymity: The Case of the Israeli Unknown Soldier." Paper presented at the Annual Meeting of the American Sociological Association, Atlanta, August 16–19.
Doyle, Robert C. 1992. "Unresolved Mysteries: The Myth of the Missing Warrior and the Government Deceit Theme in the Popular Captivity Culture of the Vietnam War." *Journal of American Culture* 15 (29): 1–18.
Durkheim, Emile. [1915] 2008. *The Elementary Forms of the Religious Life*. Translated by Joseph W. Swain. Mineola, NY: Dover.
Eliade, Mircea. 1954. *The Myth of the Eternal Return*. Translated by Willard R. Trask. New York: Phanteon Books.
Franklin, Bruce H. 1991. *MIA, or, Mythmaking in America*. New York: Lawrence Hill.
Free Dictionary. n.d. "Soldier." http://www.thefreedictionary.com/soldier. Accessed September 29, 2017.
Freeman, Mark. 1998. "Mythical Time, Historical Time, and the Narrative Fabric of the Self." *Narrative Inquiry* 8 (1): 27–50.
Gellner, Ernst. 1983. *Nations and Nationalism*. Oxford: Blackwell.
Giddens, Anthony. 1990. *The Consequences of Modernity*. Stanford: Stanford University Press.
Grant, Susan-Mary. 2005. "Raising the Dead: War, Memory and American National Identity." *Nations and Nationalism* 11 (4): 509–529.
Gupta, Akhil. 2004. "Imagining Nations." In *A Companion to the Anthropology of Politics*, edited by David Nugent and Joan Vincent, 267–281. Boston: Blackwell.
Guri, Haim. [1950] 2000. *Until the Breaking of Day*. Tel Aviv: Ha-Kibbutz Ha-Meuchad. Hebrew.
Handelman, Don. 2004. *Nationalism and the Israeli State: Bureaucratic Logic in Public Events*. Oxford: Berg.
Hertz, Robert. [1907] 1990. *Death and the Right Hand*. Glencoe, IL: Free Press.
Hever, Hannan. 1986. "Alive is the Living and Dead is the Dead." *Siman Kri'a: A Literary Critique* 19. 188–195. Hebrew.
Hirschman, Charles. 1983. "America's Melting Pot Reconsidered." *Annual Review of Sociology* 9: 397–423.
Hogg, Michael A. 1992. *The Social Psychology of Group Cohesiveness: From Attraction to Social Identity*. New York: New York University Press.
Inglis, Ken S. 1993 "Entombing Unknown Soldiers: From London and Paris to Baghdad." *History and Memory* 5 (2): 7–31.

James, Paul. 2006. *Globalism, Nationalism, Tribalism: Bringing Theory Back In.* London: Sage.
Kapferer, Bruce. 1988. *Legends of People, Myths of State: Violence, Intolerance, and Political Culture in Sri Lanka and Australia.* Washington, DC: Smithsonian Institution.
Kaplan, Danny. 2005. "Public Intimacy: Dynamics of Seduction in Male Homosocial Interactions." *Symbolic Interaction* 28 (4): 571–595.
Kaplan, Danny. 2006. *The Men We Loved: Male Friendship and Nationalism in Israeli Culture.* New York: Berghahn Books.
Kaplan, Danny. 2008. "Commemorating a 'Suspended Death': Missing Soldiers and National Solidarity in Israel." *American Ethnologist* 35 (3): 413–427.
Kaplan, Danny, and Amir Rosenmann. 2014. "Toward an Empirical Model of Male Homosocial Relatedness: An Investigation of Friendship in Uniform and Beyond." *Psychology of Men and Masculinity* 15 (1): 12–21.
Kaplan, Danny, and Niza Yanay. 2006. "Fraternal Friendship and Commemorative Desire." *Social Analysis* 50 (1): 127–146.
Kasher, Asa. 1996. *Military Ethics.* Tel Aviv: Ministry of Defense. Hebrew.
Kaufman, Sharon, and Lynn Morgan. 2005. "The Anthropology of the Beginnings and Ends of Life." *Annual Review of Anthropology* 34: 327–341.
Keating, Susan K. 1994. *Prisoners of Hope: Exploiting the POW/MIA Myth in America.* New York: Random House.
Kellet, Anthony. 1982. *Combat Motivation: The Behavior of Soldiers in Battle.* Boston: Kluwer.
Leander, Anne. 2004. "Drafting Community: Understanding the Fate of Conscription." *Armed Forces & Society* 30 (4): 571–599.
Levi, Gideon. 1994. "The Ethos and Its Commercialization." *Ha'aretz*, Section B1, October 16. Hebrew.
Little, Roger W. 1964. "Buddy Relations and Combat Performance." In *The New Military: Changing Patterns of Organization*, edited by Morris Janowitz, 195–224. New York: Russell Sage.
Lyman, Peter. 1987. "The Fraternal Bond as a Joking Relationship: A Case Study of the Role of Sexist Jokes in Male Group Bonding." In *Changing Men: New Directions in Research on Men and Masculinity*, edited by Michael Kimmel, 148–163. Newbury Park: Sage.
Malešević, Siniša. 2011. "The Chimera of National Identity." *Nations and Nationalism* 17 (2): 272–290.
Manning, Frederick S. 1991. Morale, Cohesion, and Esprit de Corps. In *The Handbook of Military Psychology*, edited by Reuven Gal and David A. Mangelsdorff, 453–470. Chichester: Wiley.
Martin, Brian Joseph. 2011. *Napoleonic Friendship: Military Fraternity, Intimacy, and Sexuality in Nineteenth-Century France.* Lebanon, NH: University of New Hampshire Press.

Marvin, Carolyn, and David W. Ingle. 1999. *Blood Sacrifice and the Nation: Totem Rituals and the American Flag*. Cambridge: Cambridge University Press.

Melman, Yossi. 2005. "IDF Will Also Offer an Award for Information on the Missing Soldiers from Sultan Ya'acoub and Guy Hever." *Haaretz*, May 17. http://news.walla.co.il/item/716756. Accessed September 29, 2017. Hebrew.

Miron, Dan. 1992. *Facing the Silent Brother: Essays on the Poetry of the War of Independence*. Tel Aviv: Keter and Open University. Hebrew.

Morgan, David. 1994. "Theater of War: Combat, the Military and Masculinities." In *Theorizing Masculinities*, edited by Harry Brod and Michael Kaufman, 165–182. Thousand Oaks, CA: Sage.

Mosse, George L. 1982. "Friendship and Nationhood: About the Promise and Failure of German Nationalism." *Journal of Contemporary History* 17: 351–367.

Mosse, George L. 1990. *Fallen Soldiers: Reshaping the Memory of World Wars*. Oxford: Oxford University Press.

Mosse, George L. 1993. *Confronting the Nation: Jewish and Western Nationalism*. Hanover, NH: Brandeis University Press.

Nagel, Joan. 1998. "Masculinity and Nationalism: Gender and Sexuality in the Making of Nations." *Ethnic and Racial Studies* 21 (2): 242–269.

Oppenheimer, Yochai. 2002. "Transformations in the Schema of the Living Dead in the Poetry of Independence War." *Sedan: Studies in Hebrew Literature* 5: 416–442. Hebrew.

Pateman, Carole. 1989. *The Disorder of Women: Democracy, Feminism and Political Theory*. Stanford: Stanford University Press.

Posen, Barry R. 1993. "Nationalism, the Mass Army, and Military Power." *International Security* 18 (2): 80–124.

Rempel, Martin W., and Ronald J. Fisher. 1997. "Perceived Threat, Cohesion, and Group Problem Solving in Intergroup Conflict." *International Journal of Conflict Management* 8 (3): 216–234.

Santino, Jack. 1992. "Yellow Ribbons and Seasonal Flags: The Folk Assemblage of War." *Journal of American Folklore* 105 (1): 19–33.

Sedgwick, Eve Kosofsky. 1985. *Between Men: English Literature and Male Homosocial Desire*. New York: Columbia University Press.

Shils, Edward, and Morris Janowitz. 1948. "Cohesion and Disintegration in the Wehrmacht in World War II." *Public Opinion Quarterly* 12: 280–315.

Siebold, Guy L. 1999. "The Evolution of the Measurement of Cohesion." *Military Psychology* 11 (1): 5–26.

Singer, Brian C. J. 1996. "Cultural versus Contractual Nations: Rethinking Their Opposition." *History and Theory* 35 (3): 309.

Sivan, Emmanuel. 1991. *The 1948 Generation: Myth, Profile and Memory*. Tel Aviv: Maarachot, Ministry of Security. Hebrew.

Smith, Anthony D. 1998. *Nationalism and Modernity*. London: Routledge.
Sturken, Marita. 1997. *Tangled Memories: The Vietnam War, the AIDS Epidemic, and the Politics of Remembering*. Berkeley: University of California Press.
Tenenboim-Weinblatt, Keren. 2008. "Fighting for the Story's Life: Non-Closure in Journalistic Narrative." *Journalism* 9 (1): 31–51.
Zerubavel, Eviatar. 1981. *Hidden Rhythms: Schedules and Calendars in Social Life*. Chicago: University of Chicago Press.

PART III

Concluding Thoughts

CHAPTER 10

Toward a Research Program for Studying National Solidarity

THE NATION AND THE PROMISE OF FRIENDSHIP

The novelist E. M. Forster (1951) famously stated that if he needed to choose between betraying a friend and betraying his country, he hoped that he would have the courage to do the latter (68). While the potential moral contradiction between devotion to personal friendship and loyalty to a collective cause could not be stated any clearer, from a cultural sociological point of view this statement is not readily applicable to national attachment, as it ignores the deep cultural associations between friendship and national solidarity. This book argues that people's sense of national attachment depends not only on the collective identity they seem to share with others but also on a longing for connection with these multiple others, a longing that is cultivated (although often taken for granted) through recurrent participation in shared, nationally bounded social institutions, best considered as social clubs.

The overwhelming majority of research on national attachments centers on the study of identity rather than solidarity, privileging questions about the commonality of actors and overlooking the role of social ties and sociability between actors as an alternative and complementary category of analysis. Despite important contributions made by recent reappraisals of national identity discourse in foregrounding the study of institutional processes and everyday life (Brubaker and Cooper 2000; Edensor 2002; Eriksen 1993; Fox and Miller-Idriss 2008), sociological literature on

© The Author(s) 2018
D. Kaplan, *The Nation and the Promise of Friendship*, Cultural Sociology,
https://doi.org/10.1007/978-3-319-78402-1_10

nationalism has mostly remained silent on the role of interpersonal interactions and social networks (Eriksen 2004, 56). The limited theoretical work that explicitly addressed national solidarity highlighted primarily the analytic differences between small-scale, face-to-face relations and macro-solidarity understood as abstract relations between strangers (Calhoun 1991; Malešević 2011). Another body of work connects social networks and group interactions with rituals of solidarity (Collins 2004) or norms of civic engagement and democracy (Fine 2012; Putnam 2000) but makes no theoretical claims about national attachment.

Against this backdrop, I call for the systematic study of interactions between compatriots premised on a sense of continuity between personal and collective ties. This requires two things: first, the recognition that national attachment is comparable to the preferential and particularist attributes of friendship in projecting a sense of exclusivity, familiarity, and loyalty, and second, a research program for studying *how* national solidarity emerges from social ties and patterns of sociability.

Theories on the spread of nationalism have typically focused on one of the three processes: a political movement, a shift in institutional state structures, and a process of nation-building understood as the dissemination of a "national consciousness" among the local population (Wimmer and Feinstein 2010). My proposal centers primarily on the third process and partly on the second but does not assume an explicit consciousness-raising project nor does it concern state structures. Instead, it concentrates on the emergent properties of a particular community-building structure that has developed since the early modern era. Sociologists have offered various conceptualizations for the kind of modern social formation that has replaced the traditional clan, village, or medieval guild such as secondary groups (Cooley 1962), civic associations (Putnam 2000), or tiny publics (Fine 2012). At the risk of adding sweeping generalizations to the already reified distinction between modern and premodern formations, I would like to introduce into this discussion the concept of social club sociability. By this, I refer to any form of institutionally mediated social interaction that revolves around a common activity, interest, or purpose, establishes criteria for membership, prescribes certain rules of conduct, and, above all, occasions cooperation between strangers. Individuals in premodern societies participated in a limited number of differentiated institutions and relied primarily on familial ties of *filiation*. In contrast, the proliferation of social clubs in modern societies has provided the most extensive avenue for creating trust based on ties of *affiliation* (aligned by social, political, and professional practice), the precondition for building national communities.

Most of these social clubs were not, of course, intrinsically connected to the rise of nationalism or nation-states, and nor are they today. In order to understand the extent to which membership in a given social club corresponds to national groupings, we still need to address questions of group classification and boundary maintenance—issues that are widely researched in studies of nationalism (Erikson 1993). But to explain the mechanisms of national solidarity, we need to go beyond the questions of identity or boundary-work and examine the interactions taking place in these clubs and their symbolic meaning.

Given the historical observation that face-to-face social formations gradually transformed into attachments between distant others (Anderson 1991; James 1996), a phenomenological and cultural sociological approach is needed which asks how friendship can model for collective ties, such that a mass community is experienced as a close-knit bond, and, in turn, how the collective can model for friendship ties, such that interpersonal interactions become sanctified in the name of the nation. This recursive relation between concrete social ties and cultural collective meanings remains undertheorized.

The suggested research program translates into a particular research strategy for studying social club sociability both in everyday life and in public events through the mechanisms of public intimacy and the emergent feelings of collective intimacy. Others have addressed the term "intimacy" as a form of confiding communication that is extended to the national sphere (Herzfeld 2005), drawing on the growing legitimacy of authentic self-disclosure in public life (Ringmar 1998). I, however, employ intimacy as a form of exclusive relationship between actors which can carry interpersonal, public, and collective significance.

Thus, public intimacy refers to the staging of interpersonal ties in front of face-to-face as well as mediated audiences. Partly resonating with Simmel's (1949) discussion of informal sociability, it is a dramaturgical mechanism for establishing the exclusivity of interpersonal bonds and for seducing outsiders into becoming confidants and, ultimately, participants. By focusing on the ways in which institutions shape interactions between actors rather than on the identity of actors, the analytic construct of public intimacy provides more leeway for exploring how interpersonal bonds can extend to wider circles and give rise to feelings of collective intimacy. Having participated in similar social clubs throughout the course of their lives, compatriots acquire a sense of shared competence in making friends. What they develop is more than generalized trust in the ability of others to follow shared norms of civility, it is mutual feelings of familiarity, exclusivity, and loyalty. Consequently, when these anonymous strangers meet at public events and achieve collective effervescence and fusion (Alexander 2004; Collins 2004; Dayan and Katz 1992; Durkheim 2003), what is at stake is not only reassurance about the existence of like-minded citizens and confirmation of an imagined community (Anderson 1991); it is the fulfillment of the promise of friendship.

In and of itself, social club sociability cannot differentiate between national and civic solidarity, as there are not two different kinds of clubs when it comes to the basic process of forming friendships between strangers. While a strong we-feeling is more readily associated with the exclusionary ethos of nationalism than with the inclusive ideals of civil society, in terms of solidarity both are premised on the same purifying binary logic that distinguishes between friends and non-friends. It is only at the symbolic level and through the complex ways that national solidarity discourse is implicated in the temporal, epistemological, and semiotic aspects of the meta-narrative of strangers-turned-friends that we can connect social club sociability specifically to national attachment.

Viewed in this light, it is important to distinguish national attachment from ethnicity on the one hand and citizenship on the other. Although analytically and empirically one cannot readily separate national identity from ethnicity (Brubaker et al. 2004) or, as stated, national solidarity from civic solidarity, national attachment relies on a unique symbolic structure that has no parallels in the cases of ethnicity or citizenship. Simply put, while ethnicity invokes the notion of brotherhood and citizenship relates to a community of strangers, national attachment is the only category of belonging that encompasses and merges both terms through the lens of friendship, codifying a moral shift and a unidirectional movement from strangers to newly found friends to timeless brothers.

Throughout this book, I have described how this meta-narrative operates through a set of binary codes that transform mundane interactions in institutional life to sacred ties of collective life in such a way that abstract, anonymous, inclusive, indifferent, and interest-based relations between individual strangers become concrete, familiar, intimately exclusive, loyal, and passionate relations between fraternal friends. This deep-seated cultural structure conveys a quest for salvation (Alexander 2003). It reflects not only an understanding that compatriots share a common heritage and cooperate in a common public sphere but also that they share common lives, passions, and destiny.

Most intermediate social institutions in the modern era were male dominated, if not male exclusive, and many still are. In fact, the very term "club" continues to bear such gendered undertones, at least in the English language. While not all the case studies described in Part Two were explicitly structured along gender lines (*Big Brother* reality TV show can be seen to project a relatively gender-egalitarian ethos), they all employ the symbolism of brotherhood and fraternity in ways that link the social and cultural structures of national solidarity with male ascendancy.

For instance, mainstream Freemasonry and most military organizations continue to bar or restrict female participation while offering male members hands-on experience in managerial roles perceived as a model for good citizenship and civic engagement (e.g., Kaplan 2014; Sasson-Levy 2002). This serves to legitimize and reinforce male hegemonic arrangements in society at large, privileging male networking and men's participation in economic and political life. On a deeper symbolic level, these social clubs serve to uphold a fraternal social contract (Pateman 1989)—a political bond powered by passion rather than interest. On rare occasions, such as during commemoration rituals for the dead brothers, this social glue of homosocial desire is publicly celebrated as a declaration of love between men. Such passion rarely surfaces in everyday life, yet it drives the pursuit of sociability and friendship throughout men's routine activity in social clubs.

In advocating a research program for the study of national solidarity, I do not imply that a national community is necessarily a uniform, cohesive group of individuals forging long-lasting bonds. Similar to the way in which critics have underscored the incoherence and instability of national identity, a study of national solidarity must take into account both instances of integration and disintegration (Lainer-Vos 2012), consider how acts of inclusion for some are, by definition, acts of exclusion for others (Handler 1988; Nagel 1998), and, moreover, how the affect of political friendship is deeply entangled with that of hatred and enmity, as discussed by Niza Yanay (2013). But it is only by acknowledging the experiential relevance of friendship for people's sense of collective belonging that we can begin to examine and interrogate the social construction of national solidarity.

What is called for is a combined historical and ethnographically informed cultural analysis of a variety of social clubs set within national boundaries. By identifying and studying from bottom-up how mechanisms of public intimacy and feelings of collective intimacy shape distinct institutional manifestations of strangers-turned-friends, we can gain a better understanding of how national solidarity works at the micro-level, how it has remained the world's dominant social glue from early to late modernity, and why this societal glue may be weaker in societies characterized by limited institutional differentiation and therefore offer a more restricted choice of exclusive local clubs.

STRUCTURAL CONSIDERATIONS IN THE EMPIRICAL STUDY OF SOCIAL CLUBS

In closing, I would like to spell out the main structural issues to be considered when applying the proposed research program to specific social clubs. The three very different social clubs presented in Part Two were purposely chosen so as to demonstrate diverse institutionalized forms of sociability, which in turn entail various configurations in the relative position of participants and spectators in the social performance and different cultures of participation in civic and national life. The case studies were analyzed according to the three-layered theoretical model of national solidarity. While each study covered all three aspects of the model, it also served to highlight and showcase one specific element.

Institutional setting. Of the three cases, the study of Masonic lodges provided the clearest example of an institutional setting structured along the traditional lines of a social club, comprising concrete interpersonal ties of friendship between members and a network structure in which every member is, in principle, an equal actor who can assume various roles in the organization.

Public and collective intimacy. The *Big Brother* reality TV show demonstrated how concrete and mediated triads of public intimacy can turn the audience into confidants and confidants into accomplices. Social exchange about the show among viewers becomes a social performance in its own right, in which the contestants assume a totemic symbolic presence in the life of their audience. By concretizing the promise of social ties among all participants, the mass public event engenders feelings of collective intimacy.

Meta-narrative of strangers-turned-friends. The final case of military friendship highlighted how the national discourse of fraternal friendship infuses grassroots campaigns for missing soldiers in such a way that spectators in public displays of personal friendships become performers in collective displays of solidarity with the dead or the missing. This social performance provides perhaps the most explicit demonstration of the symbolic cultural codes that transform anonymous strangers at the interpersonal level into cherished friends at the collective level.

These case studies also differed in several important dimensions. First and foremost, in terms of organizational structure and modes of connectivity, social clubs straddle two forms of infrastructure: horizontal social networks and hierarchical social performances. Mid-range associational formations, groups, and communities that are based on either a thick or thin network of interpersonal ties exhibit a form of connectivity and communication that is horizontal, decentralized, dialogical, and interactive and that makes no a priori distinction between performers and spectators. In contrast, a public social performance that caters to a mass audience is based on a monological, centralized, and hierarchical form of connectivity consisting of performers and viewers, an infrastructure of attention that links individuals to a social and political center in synchronous time (following Frosh 2012). This distinction can be best illustrated by contrasting online social media such as Facebook and mass media outlets such as television. Given the horizontal structure of social network sites, all actors in the network can potentially shift from the position of passive spectator to full participant; in the case of viewers watching a live media event on television however, agency is seemingly restricted to those social actors actually performing on screen. In this regard, the international spread of Masonic lodges since the eighteenth century formed perhaps the first social network of global scope in modern times. Despite its obvious differences from online social networks, this "offline" precursor played a similar role in promoting a culture of civic participation.

Both the network and the social performance aspects are, nonetheless, central to social club sociability and vital for the enactment of national solidarity as a continuum between personal and collective ties.[1] A historical example of French cycling clubs can briefly illustrate how both these organizational structures are at play in nation-building processes.[2] Eugen Weber (1986) noted that from the mid-nineteenth-century cycling clubs in France began to stretch from the upper classes to wider social circles and were the first form of organized sport to suggest the pursuit of sport for pleasure among the general population. Clubs that combined cycling and touring played a role in the "democratization" of the French countryside, taking cyclists into remoter parts of the country equipped with pocket maps of the local landscape and monuments. The cycling culture was promoted by the sporting press and gave rise to dedicated cycling newspapers that covered track meetings and road races (203–209).

In 1903, as part of the growing competition of the sporting press, one newspaper came up with a grandiose publicity venture: a bicycle race around the whole of France to be named the Tour de France. The Tour became an immediate national success with the French public lining the roads to see the cyclists and following the race and its progress in the newspapers. The winners instantly became national heroes. The Tour de France brought civic festivity and spectacle into rural communities that seldom took part in high profile public events. Local fairs, concerts, and happenings accompanied the Tour and mobilized different sectors of society such as tourists, merchants, artisans, and laborers (Weber 1986, 210–212). All in all, the story of organized French cycling interweaves a concrete social club, a newspaper initiative, and a national media event. It would be interesting to investigate how mechanisms of public intimacy operate in each of these organizational contexts and how they serve to collapse the structural distinction between horizontal social networks and a hierarchical social performance and blur the lines between the amateur cyclist, professional competitor, and national hero.

A second dimension to be considered when studying social club sociability is whether the institution in question represents an explicit "model of" or only an implicit "model for" national solidarity. In this, I follow Don Handelman's (1990, 23–24) typology of public events in the nation-state. In line with the basic distinction between "knowing that" and "knowing how," public events and institutions may possess a certain "knowing how" and "modeling for" solidarity between compatriots even when they do not make explicit claims to be "models of" or to represent the nation. Thus, the case of military friendship and combat fraternity is state-related and makes explicit claims about the representation or simulation of national solidarity.[3] In contrast, institutions such as Freemasonry, reality TV, or Facebook have no intrinsic connection to national life. Similarly, there was no such connection in the emergence of the early modern newspaper reading community, most famously analyzed by Anderson (1991) as the epitome of the national imagination. In all of these cases, which characteristically involve mundane social activities, the implications of sociability for national solidarity may be less direct but no less revealing. Masonic organizational practices and triads of public intimacy in *Big Brother* offer a "pattern in miniature" (Handelman 1990, 23) that stands for the national community, not because they necessarily share with it a distinct set of features but because they encapsulate and embody similar patterns of relationships. In fact, such cases of "banal" social clubs may prove to be more illuminating for explaining the omnipresence and endurance of national solidarity.

Consideration of historical trajectories is a third important point of comparison. The three social clubs described in the book originated at different historical junctures in the development of national communities and exemplify different modes of participation in the public sphere. In the case of the Freemasons, contemporary lodge sociability consecrates and preserves an organizational model and values of civic friendship that took shape in eighteenth-century Europe and sanctioned an elitist version of liberal democracy coupled with enthusiastic patriotism, best encapsulated in the model of civic nationalism.

The institutionalization of military friendship and commemoration rituals for fallen soldiers and their use in nation-building in the course of the nineteenth and early twentieth centuries projected a more egalitarian ethos of civic participation and an impression of the national community as a horizontal comradeship and, at the same time, reinforced an image of vertical solidarity between the living and the dead.

The popularity of reality TV formats such as *Big Brother* at the turn of the twenty-first century points to the rise of a populist democratic ideology that favors authentic emotional expression over merit, civility, and rationality and establishes a culture of mass participation that conflates between witnessing and complicity and in so doing erases the distinctions between the personal, the political, and the national.

The growing contemporary use of interactive technology enhances the experience of collective intimacy and unearths how it is founded on interactions of spectators turned-participants. The groundbreaking success of online social clubs founded purely on mechanisms of public intimacy, such as Facebook, attests to the omnipresence of the meta-narrative of strangers-turned-friends, which can now be fulfilled by a mere click of a button, by simply sending a "friend request" to a stranger. Facebook epitomizes the missing link between personal friendship and collective solidarity as it capitalizes (figuratively and literally) on the same promise of friendship inherent in earlier "offline" versions. On the one hand, the implications of Facebook for civic and national life are not all that different from the ways in which nineteenth-century European cafés negotiated intimacy in public (Haine 1996) and literary salons mobilized local public opinion (Habermas 1991; Romani 2007). On the other hand, social media sites introduce or enhance patterns of sociability that were absent or highly limited in earlier institutions, among them bottom-up social norms generated by the end users, hyper-accessibility, an egalitarian and seemingly classless platform, and a restructuring of privacy norms (Livingstone 2008; Rosen 2007).

These are, however, only preliminary observations. A research program that explores and compares more systematically a range of social club platforms from the early modern era to the present time could indicate long-term transformations in collective patterns of sociability and identify additional cultural codes underlying national attachment.

A final dimension to be considered is the extent of the formalization of social clubs. Whereas traditional clubs have official criteria for membership and explicit rules of conduct, this research program can extend to social institutions whose access is less restricted and rules of participation more subtle and informal, such as coffee shops and most media outlets. For even a newspaper that is available to all and, in some cases, free of charge relies on a network of like-minded individuals as its organizing principle (Black 2012). Consequently, although social clubs vary greatly in the kinds of formal boundaries, selections, and exclusions they impose, the basic logic of clubbiness operates just like friendship: it entails both a sense of universal choice (I have many options from which to choose my friends) and a particularist practice (once chosen, my friends take precedence over others).

According to the civic-contractual model of nationalism, nation-states follow the same logic. In connecting citizenship with the symbolism of friendship and fraternity, national solidarity encapsulates the tension between universalist and particularist aspirations. Whereas the ethno-cultural model of the nation invokes only a particularist preference for a predetermined group of people that precedes the formation of political sovereignty, the civic-contractual model entails both a celebration of voluntary political ties and the veneration of a selected group of citizen-friends.

The logic of clubbiness goes hand in hand with the advent of modern liberal societies. As forcefully argued by Wimmer (2002): "The main promises of modernity—political participation, equal treatment before the law...and social justice and security—were fully realized only for those who came to be regarded as true members of the nation. The modern principles of inclusion are intimately tied to ethnic and national forms of exclusion" (1). Whether or not one considers civic nationalism a "political myth" (Yack 1996, 198), its logic has been practiced and propagated by multitudes of social club members over the past three centuries and has thus contributed to both the spread of participatory democracy and its implementation as an exclusionary national attachment.

The magic of social clubs lies in their ability to mediate the Great Divide between the structures of mass society and the cultural quest for community. While this divide has attracted generations of sociologists, a cultural sociological research program that is both empirically driven and theoretically grounded can help us understand how the interactional and symbolic aspects of social club sociability contribute to national solidarity so that the nation may come to be imagined as the ultimate social club of chosen friends.

Notes

1. The pioneering work of Elihu Katz and Paul Lazarsfeld (2017) already demonstrated the functional significance of a two-step flow of communication between a centralized form of communication and interpersonal networks. They explored how the influence of mass communication on the general public is mediated by individual actors acting as informal opinion leaders who intercept, interpret, and diffuse what they see and hear to the social networks in which they are embedded.
2. I thank Philip Smith for suggesting this example.
3. The prototypical example of this would be a state parliament, which is often conceived as a social club (Crewe 2010), but also non-state institutions that occasionally make explicit claims about friendship and sociability as a simulation or model for the political and national spheres, such as certain youth associations (Lainer-Vos 2014) or feminist organizations (Polletta 2002).

REFERENCES

Alexander, Jeffrey C. 2003. *The Meanings of Social Life: A Cultural Sociology.* New York: Oxford University Press.
Alexander, Jeffrey C. 2004. "Cultural Pragmatics: Social Performance Between Ritual and Strategy." *Sociological Theory* 22 (4): 527–573.
Anderson, Benedict. [1983] 1991. *Imagined Communities: Reflections on the Origins and Spread of Nationalism.* London: Verso.
Black, Barbara. 2012. *A Room of His Own: A Literary-Cultural Study of Victorian Clubland.* Athens, OH: Ohio University Press.
Brubaker, Rogers and Frederick Cooper. 2000. "Beyond 'Identity.'" *Theory and Society* 29 (1): 1–47.
Brubaker, Rogers, Mara Loveman, and Peter Stamatov. 2004. "Ethnicity as Cognition." Theory and Society 33 (1): 31–64.
Calhoun, Craig. 1991. "Nationalism, Political Community and the Representation of Society: Or, Why Feeling at Home is Not a Substitute for Public Space." *European Journal of Social Theory* 2: 217–231.
Collins, Randall. 2004. *Interaction Ritual Chains.* Princeton: Princeton University Press.
Cooley, Charles, H. [1909] 1962. *Social Organization.* New York: Schocken.
Crewe, Emma. 2010. "An Anthropology of the House of Lords: Socialisation, Relationships and Rituals." *The Journal of Legislative Studies* 16 (3): 313–324.
Dayan, Daniel, and Elihu Katz. 1992. *Media Events: The Live Broadcasting of History.* Cambridge, MA: Harvard University Press.
Durkheim, Emile. [1915] 2003. "The Elementary Forms of Religious Life," translated by Karen E. Fields. In *Emile Durkheim: Sociologist of Modernity*, edited by Mustafa Emirbayer, 109–121, 140–141. Malden, MA: Blackwell.
Edensor, Tim. 2002. *National Identity, Popular Culture and Everyday Life.* Oxford: Berg.
Eriksen, Thomas Hylland. 1993. *Ethnicity and Nationalism: Anthropological Perspectives.* London: Pluto.
Eriksen, Thomas Hylland. 2004. "Place, Kinship and the Case for Non-Ethnic Nations." *Nations and Nationalism* 10 (1–2): 49–62.
Fine, Gary Alan. 2012. *Tiny Publics: A Theory of Group Action and Culture.* New York: Russell Sage Foundation.
Forster, Edward Morgan. 1951. *Two Cheers for Democracy.* New York: Harcourt Brace.
Fox, Jon E., and Cynthia Miller-Idriss. 2008. "Everyday Nationhood." *Ethnicities* 8 (4): 536–563.
Frosh, Paul. 2012. "The Showing of Sharedness: Monstration, Media and Social Life." *Divinatio* 35: 123–138.
Habermas, Jürgen. [1962] 1991. *The Structural Transformation of the Public Sphere: An Inquiry into a Category of Bourgeois Society.* Cambridge, MA: MIT Press.

Haine, William Scott. 1996. *The World of the Paris Café: Sociability Among the French Working Class, 1789–1914*. Baltimore: John Hopkins University Press.
Handelman, Don. 1990. *Models and Mirrors: Toward an Anthropology of Public Events*. Cambridge: Cambridge University Press.
Handler, Richard. 1988. *Nationalism and the Politics of Culture in Quebec*. Madison, WI: University of Wisconsin Press.
Herzfeld, Michael. [1997] 2005. *Cultural Intimacy: Social Poetics in the Nation-State*. New York: Routledge.
James, Paul. 1996. *Nation Formation: Towards a Theory of Abstract Community*. London: Sage.
Kaplan, Danny. 2014. "Jewish-Arab Relations in Israeli Freemasonry: Between Civil Society and Nationalism." *Middle East Journal* 68 (3): 385–401.
Katz, Elihu, and Paul Lazarsfeld. [1955] 2017. *Personal Influence: The Part Played by People in the Flow of Mass Communications*. Abingdon: Routledge.
Lainer-Vos, Dan. 2012. "Manufacturing National Attachments: Gift-Giving, Market Exchange and the Construction of Irish and Zionist Diaspora Bonds." *Theory and Society* 41 (1): 73–106.
Lainer-Vos, Dan. 2014. "Israel in the Poconos: Simulating the Nation in a Zionist Summer Camp." *Theory and Society* 43 (1): 91–116.
Livingstone, Sonia. 2008. "Taking Risky Opportunities in Youthful Content Creation: Teenagers". Use of Social Networking Sites for Intimacy, Privacy and Self-Expression. *New Media & Society* 10 (3): 393–411.
Malešević, Siniša. 2011. "The Chimera of National Identity." *Nations and Nationalism* 17 (2): 272–290.
Nagel, Joan. 1998. "Masculinity and Nationalism: Gender and Sexuality in the Making of Nations." *Ethnic and Racial Studies* 21 (2): 242–269.
Pateman, Carole. 1989. *The Disorder of Women: Democracy, Feminism and Political Theory*. Stanford: Stanford University Press.
Polletta, Francesca. 2002. *Freedom Is an Endless Meeting: Democracy in American Social Movements*. Chicago: Chicago University Press.
Putnam, Robert. 2000. *Bowling Alone*. New York: Simon and Schuster.
Ringmar, Erik. 1998. "Nationalism: The Idiocy of Intimacy." *British Journal of Sociology* 49 (4): 534–549.
Romani, Gabriella. 2007. "A Room with a View: Interpreting the Ottocento Through the Literary Salon." *Italica* 84 (2–3): 233–246.
Rosen, Christine. 2007. "Virtual Friendship and the New Narcissism." *The New Atlantis* 17: 15–31.
Sasson-Levy, Orna. 2002. "Constructing Identities at the Margins: Masculinities and Citizenship in the Israeli Army." *The Sociological Quarterly* 43 (3): 357–383.
Simmel, Georg. 1949. "The Sociology of Sociability." Translated by Everett C. Hughes. *American Journal of Sociology* 55 (3): 254–261.

Weber, Eugen. 1986. *France, Fin de Siècle*. Cambridge, MA: Harvard University Press.
Wimmer, Andreas. 2002. *Nationalist Exclusion and Ethnic Conflict: Shadows of Modernity*. New York: Cambridge University Press.
Wimmer, Andreas, and Yuval Feinstein. 2010. "The Rise of the Nation-State Across the World, 1816–2001." *American Sociological Review* 75 (5): 764–790.
Yack, Bernard. 1996. "The Myth of the Civic Nation." *Critical Review* 10 (2): 193–211.
Yanay, Niza. 2013. *The Ideology of Hatred: The Psychic Power of Discourse*. New York: Fordham University Press.

Index

A
Adut, Ari, 84
Alexander, Jeffrey, 10, 46, 47, 55, 77, 78, 83, 88n4, 100, 101, 112, 117
Allen, Danielle, 36
American Revolution, 95, 104n1, 142, 146n8
Anderson, Benedict, 7–8, 24, 30, 44, 85–86, 96, 140, 156, 185, 214
Anderson, James, 124
Arendt, Hannah, 72
Aristotle, 36
associationalism, 44–46, 50, 113
audience participation, 150, 156–158, 163–165, 171–174
authenticity
  nationalism and, 49, 74, 152, 216
  of self, 49, 60, 73, 150, 160, 172, 209, 215
  of social performance, 82

B
Barbalet, Jack, 100
Barnes, Elizabeth, 86

Barth, Fredrik, 26
Bauman, Zygmunt, 94–95, 103
Bellah, Robert, 73
Bhabha, Homi, 43, 93
Big Brother show. *See* reality TV
Billig, Michael, 26, 57
Black, Barbara, 47, 49, 54
boyd, danah, 58
Brubaker, Rogers, 23, 25–27, 38n3, 110, 117

C
café sociability, 2, 35, 54–55, 76
  class relations and, 31, 35, 54
  public sphere and, 45, 215
Calhoun, Craig, 33, 74, 143
Capdeville, Valérie, 50, 53
case-study methodology
  data gathering and analysis, 13, 17n9, 121, 126, 145n2, 151–152, 176n3, 189, 200n3
  global context of organizational model, 13, 125, 152–153, 184–185, 213

local Israeli context of organizational model, 14, 126, 127, 151–153, 185, 186
Castoriadis, Cornelius, 16n5
choir, 2, 47
civic associations, 4, 44–47, 49, 63n3, 63n4, 71, 113, 144, 208
civic engagement, 2, 15n1, 46, 71, 128, 208, 211
civic nationalism, 14, 47, 97, 114–115, 116, 117, 123, 140–143, 144, 175, 215, 217
civic solidarity. *See* national solidarity
civil inattention, 31
civil society, 174
  democracy and, 36, 45–49, 63n4, 113, 116, 142
  discourse of, 101, 102, 117
  nation-state and, 55, 112, 210
  strangers and, 31, 32, 37, 101
club. *See* social club sociability
collective effervescence, 4, 10, 44, 62, 80, 81, 83, 86, 87, 113, 154, 171, 194, 210
collective intimacy, 10, 12, 17n9, 71–72, 80–87, 209–210, 212
  as alchemic transformation of strangers into friends, 3, 86, 104
  big brother show and, 153, 157, 166, 172, 174
  definition of, 3, 4
  freemasonry and, 123–124, 135–140
  simultaneity and, 3, 72, 80, 83, 155, 194
  solidarity with missing soldiers as, 188–193
  spectators-turned-participants and, 2, 4, 72, 77, 84, 215

Collins, Randall, 10, 16n7, 81, 113
commemoration rituals. *See* meta-narrative of strangers-turned-friends
community talk, 44, 50
complicity, 12, 14, 84–85, 150, 168, 173, 215
Cover, Rob, 156
cultural intimacy, 74, 84, 88n6, 153
cultural sociological perspectives, 32, 72, 100, 102, 173, 207, 209, 217
cultural pragmatics framework, 11, 77, 81
  strong program in, 3, 10, 98, 117
cycling club, 213–214

D
Davetian, Benet, 76
Dayan, Daniel, 83, 85, 154, 157, 176n5
democracy, 2, 44–48, 63, 113, 116, 142, 208, 215, 217
Dietz, Mary, 112
Dromi, Shai, 64n7
Duffett, Mark, 171
Durkheim, Emile, 4, 9, 34, 43, 44, 80, 83, 104n1, 113, 116, 154, 170
Dynel, Marta, 75

E
Edensor, Tim, 207
Egyptian democratic revolution, 61, 113, 142
Eliade, Mircea, 105n3
Eliasoph, Nina, 46, 71, 77
Ellison, Nicole, 58
empathy, 162–163
enemy, 32, 93–94, 102, 117, 174

Eriksen, Thomas Hylland, 26, 27
ethnicity. *See* national attachment
European Union, 88
Eyerman, Ron, 137

F
Fine, Gary Alan, 35, 37, 38n4, 71, 75, 113
Foucault, Michel, 173
Fox, Jon, 16n4, 26, 207
fraternal social contract, 50, 104n1, 184, 211
Freemasons, 2. *See also* social club sociability; secrecy
  civic nationalism and, 140–143, 144
  civic virtue and, 123, 132, 142, 143
  friendship and, 123, 129–132, 135, 137–139, 138, 143
  national movements and, 123, 142
  ritual activity and, 123, 125, 127, 128, 131–140, 141
  state loyalty and, 140
  White Table dinner and, 127, 128, 138, 139
  women and, 125–127, 135, 211
French Revolution, 10, 104, 146n8, 184
friendship, 5. *See also* meta-narrative of strangers-turned-friends
  and loyalty, 77, 79, 84, 87
  as social construction, 99–100
  civic, 36–37, 112, 215
  experienced as feelings of familiarity, exclusivity, and loyalty, 5, 12, 100, 101, 160, 188, 197, 208, 210
  fraternal, 1, 4, 14, 31, 35, 36, 97, 123–124, 129–130, 135–139, 189, 193, 196, 211, 213, 216
  male homosociality, 4, 75
  male homosociality and, 35, 36, 186, 198, 211
  solidarity as contradictory to, 4, 11, 24, 30–34, 207
  solidarity on a continuum with, 11, 34–38, 99, 100, 197, 208, 213
Frosh, Paul, 31, 155

G
Gellner, Ernest, 23, 51, 184
Gerth, Hans, 78
Giddens, Anthony, 73
Giorgi, Amedeo, 17n9
Goffman, Erving, 31, 48, 81
Gorski, Philip, 23, 29
Great Divide (between community and society), 43–44, 217
gymnastic movement, 55

H
Habermas, Jürgen, 45, 49
Haine, William Scott, 76
Handelman, Don, 214
Handler, Richard, 26
hatred, 98, 211
Heilman, Samuel, 137
Herzfeld, Michael, 84, 88n5, 88n6, 153
Hobsbawm, Eric, 23
Hoffmann, Stefan-Ludwig, 146n9
Honohan, Iseult, 37, 110, 118

I
Illouz, Eva, 73
interactive media practices, 47, 156, 157, 169, 172, 215

intimacy. *See* collective intimacy; cultural intimacy; public intimacy; trust
  as relationship vs as communication, 74, 75, 77
  identitarian focus, 12, 73
  pure relationship and, 73
  self-disclosure and, 160, 162, 164

J
Jacob, Margaret, 125
Jakobson, Roman, 59
James, Paul, 8, 16n6, 185
John, Nicholas, 62

K
Katz, Elihu, 83, 85, 154, 157, 217n1
Kaufman, Jason, 63n2
Kibbutz, 56
King, Anthony, 171
Kohn, Hans, 114, 142, 143
Kurakin, Dmitry, 104n3

L
Lainer-Vos, Dan, 24
Lévi-Strauss, Claude, 104n2
liberal ideology, 34, 73, 101, 143, 215, 217
Lichterman, Paul, 71

M
Malešević, Siniša, 25, 26, 30, 34, 186
Malinowski, Bronisław, 59
Mallory, Peter, 102
Marvin, Caroline, 200n2
media event, 3, 10, 12, 13, 15, 31, 61, 83, 176n4, 213, 214. *See also* reality TV
  meta-narrative of strangers-turned-friends, 1, 3–5, 12, 15, 80, 93, 110, 193, 210, 213, 215
  Big Brother show and, 174
  brother and, 5, 12, 15, 96, 97, 118, 183, 199
  commemoration and, 96, 97, 102, 184, 189, 190, 193–199
  cultural codes and, 3, 5, 12, 100–104, 105n3, 196
  demand for salvation and, 13, 101, 211
  enacted in collective intimacy, 86, 104
methodology. *See* case-study methodology
military friendship, 15, 183–193, 198, 213–215
  as social club, 188
military institution, 2, 51, 56, 141, 145n7, 183, 185, 186, 211
Miller, Vincent, 59
missing soldiers, 15, 97, 138, 188–193, 196–199
modernization and institutional differentiation, 2, 13, 30, 52, 72, 109, 212
Mosse, George, 95

N
national attachment
  ethnicity and, 6, 26–28, 110, 118, 210
  as umbrella team, 24–25
national imagination
  abstraction and, 7–9, 16n6, 30, 44, 185
  definition of, 7–8, 16n5
  paradox of collectivity of strangers imagined as friends, 1, 8, 14, 24, 32–34, 103, 190

nationalism
  ethno-cultural model of, 14, 97,
    114, 143, 144, 216
  ethno-symbolist approach, 25, 30
  methodological, 2, 115–116
  modernist approach, 7, 23, 25,
    29–30
  theories of, 5, 23–30, 33, 35, 43,
    73, 98, 208
  transformative events, 23, 26, 27.
    See also civic nationalism
national solidarity
  vs civic solidarity, 7, 13, 16n2, 37,
    44, 109–118, 118n3, 210
  discourse of, 93–98, 101–102, 110,
    117, 152, 193, 198, 210
  family versus friendship imagery in,
    12, 95–98
  interpersonal networks and, 27,
    32, 33, 38, 45, 56–57, 61–63,
    63n3, 77, 166, 208
  vs national identity, 5–7, 11, 16n4,
    23–30, 33–34, 74, 85, 86,
    109–110, 115, 154, 175–176,
    207–211
  political psychological approaches
    to, 15n1, 24
  universalist values of, 14, 114–115,
    116–117, 142, 216
Nelson, Dana, 104n1
newspapers, 54–55, 192, 214,
  215–216
  reading ceremony and, 8, 85–86,
    156, 214

O
Offe, Claus, 50

P
Palestinian national movement, 56

Panopticon, 173
Pateman, Carole, 104n1
patriotism, 14, 112, 113, 215
phatic exchange, 12, 59
Pike, Albert, 132, 145n4, 145n5
primary groups, 10, 44, 186
prison, 56, 173, 195
public intimacy, 12, 17n9, 71, 75–80,
  85, 86–87, 104, 209–210, 212,
  214
  Big brother show and, 14, 150, 157,
    160–167, 171–176, 212
  definition of, 3, 4
  freemasons and, 124, 133–135,
    140, 143
  military friendship and, 184–185,
    189, 193
  as seduction, 3, 12, 77, 124, 134,
    140, 150, 209
  vs Simmel's discussion of sociability,
    9, 75–77
  social media and, 51, 216
public-private divide, 73, 81, 84, 139,
  151, 155
  and intermediate institutions, 11,
    43–46, 50
public sphere, 33, 45–46, 48, 73, 74,
  80, 125, 139, 151, 211, 215
Putnam, Robert, 45, 47, 53, 71, 99,
  113

R
radio, 2, 156
Rai, Amit, 86
reality TV, 1, 2, 13, 149–176, 211,
  212, 214, 215
  as media event, 149–158, 165, 168,
    171–175
  national meaning of, 153–156, 176
  as social club, 155–157
Reed, Isaac, 84

relational sociology, 9
Rennie, Bryan, 105n3
Ringmar, Erik, 48, 74
Roche, Maurice, 101
Romani, Gabriella, 56

S
Salon, 45, 54, 216
Scannell, Paddy, 31, 173
Schaich, Michael, 55, 125
Schiller, Nina, 115
schooling, 2, 51, 52
Schwarz, Ori, 60, 61
Schwarzenbach, Sibyl, 36, 98
secondary group, 45, 50, 71, 208
secrecy, 3, 78, 84, 123, 133–134, 140, 143, 162–163
self-improvement
 Freemasonry and, 132, 143–144, 146n9, 176n5
 makeover TV and, 176n5
Sennett, Richard, 73, 103
Serazio, Michael, 171
Shils, Edward, 185
Shoham, Hizky, 82
Silver, Allan, 32
Simmel, Georg, 9, 11, 16n7, 17n8, 31, 64n9, 75, 76, 105n4, 133, 159, 209
Simonson, Peter, 44, 63n1
Smith, Anthony, 24, 30
Smith, Philip, 10, 117, 217n2
sociability. *See* café sociability; Simmel, Georg; social club sociability
social capital, 15n1, 44, 113
social club sociability, 2, 4, 13–15, 43–63, 72, 109, 143, 154–157, 188, 208–217
 class relations and, 53, 125, 127, 131, 135, 213
 definition of, 47, 208

elitism and, 56, 125, 131, 188, 215
English origins, 50–53, 54, 125
explicit national ideology and, 55, 57, 185, 209, 214
as expressive or non-instrumental, 2, 11, 47, 48, 51, 57, 59, 123, 155, 159
gendered male connotations, 50–54, 188, 210
social media, 2, 4, 12, 13, 57–63, 64n8, 74, 150, 156, 158, 168–169, 172, 213, 216
 convergence and, 59–61
 definition of social network sites and, 57–58
social performance, 3, 11, 12, 38, 61, 77–80, 81–87, 88n4, 136, 137, 171, 174, 195, 212, 213. *See also* media event
 focused attention and, 3, 80, 83, 113, 150, 171
 fusion and, 3, 4, 78, 82–83, 104, 149, 210
 vs network infrastructure, 61, 156–157, 172, 212–213, 217n1
solidarity. *See* friendship; national solidarity; trust
Strangership, 5, 11, 31–33, 93–95, 98, 102. *See also* meta-narrative of strangers-turned-friends, civil society
 as outsiders versus unknown, 103
 universal otherhood and, 105n4
Sztompka, Piotr, 99

T
Tavory, Iddo, 145n6
Tenenboim-Weinblatt, Keren, 195
Theiss-Morse, Elisabeth, 16n3, 45
therapeutic discourse, 73–74, 77, 160, 161–163, 172

Tocqueville, Alexis de, 44
Tomb for the Unknown Soldier, 8, 185
Tönnies, Ferdinand, 43
Torche, Florencia, 99–100
Totem, 150, 169–171, 173, 192, 200n2, 212
trust
  generalized, 5, 15n1, 50, 99–100, 210
  intimacy and, 49, 72, 99–100, 130
  solidarity and, 24, 27, 36, 44, 53, 136, 144, 209
  versus loyalty, 100

V
Valenzuela, Eduardo, 99–100
Viroli, Maurizio, 112

W
Wagner-Pacifici, Robin, 38n2
Warner, Michael, 33
Weber, Eugene, 54, 213–214
Weber, Max, 9, 43, 115
Weintraub, Jeff, 73
Wellman, Barry, 64
Wimmer, Andreas, 63n3, 115, 217
witnessing, 31, 174, 215
Wyrtzen, Jonathan, 82

Y
Yack, Bernard, 114
Yanay, Niza, 211
Ytreberg, Espen, 156

Z
Zionism, 56, 139, 141

The manufacturer's authorised representative in the EU is Springer Nature Customer Service Centre GmbH, Europaplatz 3, 69115 Heidelberg, Germany. If you have any concerns regarding our products, please contact ProductSafety@springernature.com

Printed and bound by CPI Group (UK) Ltd, Croydon, CR0 4YY
23/03/2026
02076672-0006